THE LITTLE BOOK OF KILDARE

CHRIS LAWLOR

The History Press Ireland

For my godchildren, Ann Marie Mooney and Niall Cummins, both from Kildare.

First published 2015

The History Press Ireland
50 City Quay
Dublin 2
Ireland
www.thehistorypress.ie

British Library Cataloguing in Publication Data.
A catalogue record for this book is available from the British Library.

ISBN 978 1 84588 862 6

Typesetting and origination by The History Press.
Printed and bound in Great Britain by TJ International Ltd.

CONTENTS

Introduction   5

1. Monastic Kildare   7

2. Kildare's Great Houses   20

3. Kildare Rebels   34

4. Success and Failure: Industrial Kildare   47

5. Kildare's Literary Ladies   60

6. A County in Chaos: Kildare in 1798   74

7. Kildare's Earls: A Noble Tradition   89

8. Troubled Times: Kildare 1914-24   102

9. Breeders and Bloodstock: Kildare and Horses   115

10. Kildare's Historic Towns   129

The towns of County Kildare.

INTRODUCTION

Kildare, a medium-sized Irish inland county, is unique, scenic and historic. Much of the east of the county is covered in glacial boulder clay soils, while the west is composed of peaty soils and contains part of the great Bog of Allen. The bogs were created by decaying ancient vegetation and they form a vital natural resource and a very important wildlife habitat. Kildare has a folk museum and bog interpretative centre at Lullymore.

Kildare's highest point is at Cupidstown Hill near Kilteel, but the county is generally flat. The most famous hill in the west of the county is the Hill of Allen, which commands a breathtaking view over the surrounding landscape. The plains of Kildare provide rich agricultural land, but the best-known plain in the county is the Curragh. This is a large undulating glacial outwash plain and, though dotted with freely wandering sheep, it is better known for its association with horse racing, an activity with which the county is synonymous. All parts of County Kildare provide attractive walking and cycling routes, and both are popular pastimes for many inhabitants and visitors.

While the natural beauty of Kildare attracts many visitors, the county's heritage is also a significant factor for many tourists. Historic sites such as Moone High Cross, Castletown House and Maynooth College abound throughout the county. This book takes a look at some aspects of Kildare's colourful history. It focuses both on what happened in the county and on the exploits of some of Kildare's sons and daughters, many of whom excelled and were influential in various fields of human endeavour.

Hard-nosed industrialists, sentimental poets, Unionists and Republicans all feature in these pages. The stories included in this book range from the lives of lords to the deaths of rebels. From saintly nuns to bloody battles, County Kildare has seen it all over the centuries. Kildare people have made history in many different fields and *The Little Book of Kildare* tries to capture some of that astonishing history. I am indebted to Mario Corrigan of the local studies section of Kildare County Library, Newbridge, for the illustrations used in the text. I hope you enjoy delving into the past of fascinating Kildare!

Chris Lawlor, 2015

1

MONASTIC
KILDARE

County Kildare has a long and proud monastic tradition, dating back to the fifth century, when St Palladius founded a church at Cillín Cormac near Kilcullen.

ST PALLADIUS

Very little is known about Palladius. He was born in Britain, probably around AD 400. The Palladii were among the noblest families of France and several of them held high rank about this time in the Gallic Church. Their move from Gaul to Britain probably occurred under Julius the Apostate, when there was a Palladius holding prominent rank in the army of Gaul, who, for his fearless profession of the Christian faith, was exiled to Britain. It is reasonable to assume that a descendent of this Palladius – and a member of such a privileged Gallic-British family – would attain the position of Deacon of Rome, would take much interest in the Church in Britain, and, would by his familiarity with the Celtic languages, be a natural choice to undertake the mission of becoming the first bishop of the Irish people.

Palladius became a deacon of the Church. He was already a deacon of St Germanus of Auxerre, but it is more probable that he attained the higher rank of Deacon of Rome. Palladius evidently had significant influence in Rome, as he would soon become a bishop. Prosper's *Chronicle* uses the word *diaconus* [which invariably refers to the deacons of Rome] to denote

Palladius, and the *Book of Armagh* expressly styles Palladius 'archdeacon of Pope Celestine, bishop of the city of Rome'.

The year AD 431 was a significant one for Palladius, as he was ordained as a bishop by Pope Celestine. Bishop Palladius was sent to the edge of the known world – the island of Ireland. According to Prosper's *Chronicle* in AD 431: 'In the consulship of Bassus and Antiocus [431] Palladius was consecrated by Pope Celestine and sent to the Irish believing in Christ, as their first bishop.'

The *Annals of Ulster* also state that: 'To the Irish believing in Christ, Palladius ordained by Pope Celestine, was sent as their first bishop.'

The wording of these sources is significant, as it confirms that there were some Irish Christians who pre-dated St Patrick. Despite the fact that the Romans had never conquered Ireland, there was a flourishing trade between some of the Roman provinces, such as Gaul, and Ireland. Contacts with Britain were even closer, and as early as the fourth century, Britain was a Christian country with an advanced ecclesiastical organisation. Commerce and Christianity probably passed back and forth between Ireland and the continent, and Christianity infiltrated and penetrated slowly. Moreover, the lives of some of the Irish saints, such as Ciarán of Saigir and Declan of Ardmore, indicate that they pre-dated St Patrick. Despite this, some pockets of Christianity were established in Ireland long before the 430s. In AD 431, Palladius and some clerical companions set out for Ireland, in search of one of these pockets of Christianity. They landed in County Wicklow, where Palladius and his followers established two churches, before crossing into County Kildare.

The third church that St Palladius founded was called *Cill Fine*. The name means 'the church of the septs' and this site has been identified as the old burial place of Cillín Cormac, located at Colbinstown, near Kilcullen. The site was significant, as it was a pre-existing cemetery and probably already used for religious ritual. Cillín Cormac was known to be the burial place of Cormac Mac Art, who is reputed to have been high king of Ireland from AD 254 to 277. Legend has it that Cormac died in battle and his body was placed on a cart drawn by two oxen. The king would be buried wherever the oxen stopped – and they stopped at Cillín Cormac. The myth goes that the king's men had taken his faithful hound away and placed him in a kennel in County Kildare. Different versions of the story place the kennel in Punchestown, on the Hill of Allen and at 'Cnoc a Dubh'. Anyhow, during the burial, the anxious hound broke free and with a gigantic leap he descended onto the king's headstone, leaving the imprint of his paw, which can be seen to this day.

Palladius chose this important pagan burial place as the site of his third church, and the symbolism is that of the Christian religion supplanting the older pagan traditions. The very name of the place indicates its Christianisation, as the pagan Cormac now rests in the Christian burial place, the *Cillín*, or little churchyard. Today, the site contains both pre-Christian and Christian headstones. Among the headstones of interest is an ogham (a type of ancient carved Irish writing) stone, another with a carving of a monk and the aforementioned 'dog's paw' stone marking the grave of Cormac Mac Art.

While Palladius was at work in County Kildare, St Patrick arrived on Irish shores in AD 432. Where Palladius's mission ran into problems, Patrick's met with success and he has become recognised as the man who converted Ireland to Christianity and as the patron saint of Ireland. The seventh-century 'Life of St Patrick' by Muircu Maccumachthenus in the *Book of Armagh* actually refers to the failure of Palladius' mission: 'Palladius was ordained and sent to convert this land lying under wintry cold, but God hindered him, for no man can receive anything from earth unless it be given to him from heaven; and those fierce and cruel men did not receive his doctrine readily.'

Palladius encountered opposition during his Irish mission, and was never as successful as Patrick. He and Patrick probably overlapped in their missionary work for a while, as (given the fragmented political structure of Celtic Ireland) there is every reason for believing that missionaries could have worked in different parts of the island without contact. According to tradition, Patrick also worked in County Kildare, converting people and performing baptisms such as those at Naas of Oilhill and Illann, the sons of Dubhlang, the King of Leinster. Ironically the success of Patrick as a missionary has meant that much of the groundwork done by Palladius has been forgotten, even in the Kildare region in which he operated. However, as a result of the introduction of Christianity, many monasteries flourished in Ireland, which by the end of the sixth century had entered the monastic golden age, and County Kildare was no exception.

ST BRIGID

One name stands above all others in relation to the establishment of a monastic tradition in Kildare, and unusually it is that of a woman – St Brigid, the patron saint of County Kildare and patroness of Ireland. Brigid built on the groundwork done by Palladius and Patrick and the Brigidine tradition in Kildare established the foundations of later devotion in the county. Not a lot of verifiable facts exist about Brigid's life and we are dependent on oral tradition and medieval hagiographies for the little information we have. According to folklore, she was born about eight years prior to Patrick's death in AD 453. Her father was a Celtic chieftain named Dubhtach, who hailed from what is today County Offaly, and her Christian mother, Broicseach, was his concubine, but Dubhtach sold the pregnant Broicseach to a druid from Faughart, County Louth, and this is where Brigid was born. The young Brigid was gentle and kind to all, and many tales are told of her loving and charitable acts for those less fortunate than herself. She was taught Christianity by her mother and eventually the child's holiness persuaded the druid and all his family to convert to Christianity as well. He granted Brigid and her mother their freedom and they returned to Dubhtach in Offaly, where her generous and charitable actions continued, causing the chief to observe that she would turn him into a pauper with her donations to the poor and needy! He tried to arrange a marriage for Brigid with his kinsman, but the young girl made her opposition to this plan very clear, choosing instead to become a nun and devote her life wholly to God.

At that time many converted Christian Celtic young men were flocking to the newly established monasteries to partake of the monastic life. Large numbers of women also joined convents and Brigid and seven other novices professed their vows at Croghan, County Offaly, *c*. AD 470, receiving the veil from St Mac Caille. The nuns founded two convents at Ushnagh (County Westmeath) and Elphin (County Roscommon), before going on to establish Brigid's famous house in County Kildare. Brigid's new convent was located in the shade of a huge oak tree, so it was known as *Cill Dara*, the church of the oak tree, and it is from this place that County Kildare got its name.

The new religious community would have lived in small huts, probably constructed from wattle and daub. Wattle was the name given to small saplings, usually of willow or hazel wood, interwoven horizontally around a series of vertical wooden stakes driven into postholes in the ground. Daub was a wet mud used as plaster, which covered the wattle, filled the cracks and kept out the draughts. When the mud dried, it hardened and created a weatherproof wall. The use of this construction method by early Irish monasteries and convents explains why so little remains of them. Typically, ruined ecclesiastical sites today contain stone buildings, but these were introduced at a later stage.

The community of nuns in Kildare included women from all backgrounds and, as their fame spread, a monastery was also founded there. This meant that a bishop was needed to rule over the establishments, and Brigid was instrumental in choosing Conleth, who hailed from Old Connell, beside the modern town of Newbridge, to 'govern the church with her in Episcopal dignity that nothing of the sacerdotal order might be wanting in her churches'. Stories of Brigid's enormous generosity such as her giving a leper the jewelled chain which she had received from the Queen of Leinster, her use of Conleth's fine new vestments to clothe the poor and her feeding the hungry with a special feast that had been prepared for a visiting bishop continued to emerge. Many other stories about Brigid attributed miraculous cures to her intercession. One such story concerns Brigid and the blind nun, Sister Dara.

According to this tale, Brigid was sitting with Dara on a splendid summer evening, describing to her the beauty of God's creation. Brigid was enraptured by the natural beauty around her, but her happiness was tinged with sadness due to the realisation that Dara could not see it. Wishing to share her joy on that beautiful evening, Brigid laid her hands on Dara and prayed to God to give Dara the gift of sight. Dara's blindness was cured and she could suddenly see. As Dara gazed around at the landscape with its trees, grass and flowers, she grew troubled and turned to Brigid. She thanked Brigid for what she had done, but then made a most unusual and unexpected request. She asked Brigid to pray again, this time that her blindness would be restored, saying, 'Please close my eyes again, for when I see the beauty of this world I forget the beauty of the next, and the image of God glows less brightly in my soul'. The surprised Brigid did as she requested, and Dara's world became dark again, leaving Brigid to realise that Dara believed that God had given her a gift more precious and more lasting than sight. The story illustrates not only the power attributed to Brigid, but also the spirit of asceticism and self-sacrifice among the early Irish converts to Christianity.

Miracle stories such as this enhanced the cult of St Brigid, which was very strong throughout all of Ireland in the Middle Ages. In Irish tradition, she was known as the 'Mary of the Gael'. She controlled about thirty convents during her lifetime, and, following her death, her feast day was marked all over medieval Europe. Many of the stories told about Brigid portray her as not only saintly, but also a superhuman being. She turns water into beer for an important visitor; she controls the behaviour of animals; she can even hang her gown on one of the sun's rays. These events suggest that Brigid was perceived in the light of an older pagan goddess – and the Celts did have such a goddess, also named Brigid (or Brigit), before the arrival of Christianity. Brigit has been loosely identified with the Roman Minerva (Greek Artemis) and her feast day, known as Imbolg, marked the beginning of spring. St Brigid's feast day falls on 1 February, which suggests that the Christian saint supplanted the pagan goddess in the belief systems of the Irish. In these circumstances, it is unsurprising that Brigid became not only the patron saint of County Kildare, but also the patroness of the whole of Ireland.

Brigid died around AD 523 and was buried in Kildare. Her tomb became a place of pilgrimage and attracted huge crowds annually on 1 February. She left a very impressive legacy to her adopted county, and she, more than anyone else, played a huge role in consolidating the Christian faith in both the county and the town of Kildare. Her foundation flourished, and the monastery in particular grew in size and importance as the centuries progressed. A famous scriptorium

Church and Tower at Castledermot in 1792 by Shuman.

was active in Kildare during the seventh century. The church, which contained the remains of both Brigid and Conleth, was described in glowing terms by the monk Cogitosis, and later, following the Norman invasion of 1169, when Giraldus Cambrensis (also known as Gerald of Wales) visited Ireland in 1185, he recorded the fact that he had seen a fantastic manuscript, the Book of Kildare, which he described as containing the gospel texts and many beautifully coloured illustrations and designs. The Book of Kildare seems to have been a rival to the famous Book of Kells, but sadly this Kildare treasure is no longer in existence, having been lost or destroyed at some time over the turbulent centuries. However, despite the loss of this written relic of Kildare's Christian past, the growth of the religious tradition during the centuries following the death of St Brigid ensured that the county contains many monastic archaeological sites. One of the finest of these is located in south Kildare, near its border with County Carlow, in the village of Castledermot.

CASTLEDERMOT

The Irish name for Castledermot is *Diseart Diarmada*, which literally means Dermot's desert. The idea of meeting God in a wilderness, a spiritual desert, is strongly embedded in the Christian biblical tradition, and in Irish monasticism it is particularly associated with the Céili Dé movement. As the larger monasteries grew wealthier and became embroiled in worldliness, a new dynamic began to emerge in monastic Ireland, one in which monks wished to return to the simpler way of life in the earliest monasteries. In AD 774, Máel Ruain of Tallaght instituted a new rule for his monks, stressing the importance of prayer over everything else. These monks made regular daily visits to the church for communal prayer, and recited all 150 psalms between these visits. They were encouraged to mortify themselves by praying the psalms while kneeling with arms outstretched, or even while standing in a river or stream. They partook of only one daily meal, abstaining from meat even on feast days and drank water rather than alcohol, which Máel Ruain viewed as the 'liquor that causes men to forget God'. Céili Dé monasteries began to appear in many parts of Ireland, and St Dermot founded one such establishment in Castledermot in approximately AD 812. Dermot would remain there until his death in around AD 825, but the monasteries faced a new threat from the ninth century onwards – Viking raiders. The first Viking attack was on Lambay Island, off the coast of County Dublin, in AD 795. Over the next two centuries or so, the Vikings raided and plundered throughout Ireland, settling down, building towns, intermarrying with local clans and vying for power with those clans until their power was finally broken by the Munster chieftain and Irish high king Brian Boru at the Battle of Clontarf in 1014. Monasteries, with their wealth, provided prime targets for Viking raids, and the ever-vigilant monks used round towers as watchtowers. These towers were also places of safety, and the monks and their treasures could retreat into them, pulling up the ladders behind them as they

Castledermot Abbey in 1793 by Sparrow.

entered the building through the inordinately high door. Inside the door a steep stairwell, where the defenders literally had the upper hand, made an uninviting prospect for any attacker who did manage to break through the stout door. The monastic site at Castledermot boasts a fine example of a round tower, on the north side of the church. However, the tower today is smaller than it was originally and it is probable that the tower was actually restored in the Middle Ages and that the top section is, in fact, medieval. It was constructed from rounded granite blocks bound with mortar, and the doorway, slightly above the ground level, has dressed blocks of granite for its lintel, jambs and sill. Castledermot also contains ruins dating from after the twelfth-century Norman invasion, including the tower of the 'Crouched Friary', which belonged to the Fratres Cruciferi who came to the walled Norman town of Castledermot in 1210 to work with the sick, and the shell of a Franciscan abbey dating from 1302.

The churchyard at Castledermot contains many interesting stones, some of which suggest Viking influence. The hogback recumbent stone is the only one of its type in Ireland. This elongated oval stone lies on four flat support stones and it has been suggested that it follows the shape of a Viking house of about the tenth century. The decorations on the ends of the stone are also attributable to this Viking period. The site also contains an upright granite high stone, on the east face of which is carved a rough cross, and it is holed through the centre. This is known as the swearing stone because bargains were sealed by shaking hands through the hole in the cross. This swearing stone was used to solemnise deals of all kinds, including marriage vows. Standing stones were perceived as pagan sites and part of the logic of this ceremony involved the Christianisation of the standing stone site, as bargains made on holy ground dared not be broken. In the case of Castledermot, the holed stone stands within the consecrated site. Such Viking holed stones are also associated with Killaloe and the island of Inishkeltra in County Clare, both of which were raided by the Norsemen. A similar holed stone exists in County Antrim, again near the scene of a Viking raid.

The Castledermot site also contains two fine granite high crosses; the high crosses of Celtic Ireland are famed for their fine stonemasonry work. It has been suggested that the round arms around the junction of the vertical and horizontal pieces on Celtic crosses are a throwback to ancient Celtic solar pagan rituals, with the arms representing the sun. However, the circular design may simply have been round buttresses to strengthen the stone crosses, many of which were tall and slim in their execution. Many, such as the crosses at Clonmacnoise, County Offaly and Monasterboice, County Louth, are intricately carved and show scenes from the Bible, which the monks used to illustrate Bible stories to an illiterate laity. In the case of Castledermot, the northern high cross has panels showing Isaac, the temptation of St Anthony, Adam and Eve, King David playing the harp, Daniel in the lions' den, the miracle of the loaves and fishes and the crucifixion of St Peter. The panels of the southern high cross are similar, and include sections depicting the arrest of Christ and his crucifixion.

MOONE

As impressive as the high crosses at Castledermot are, however, the most impressive high cross in Kildare, and one of the best-preserved examples in Ireland, is a few miles northward along the N9, in the village of Moone. This granite cross is 5.32 metres (nearly 18ft) tall and was known in the past as St Colmcille's Cross. St Colmcille was a father of the early Irish Church and is associated primarily with his last foundation on the Scottish island of Iona, but traditionally he also established many monasteries in Ireland, including the one at Moone. The image of the crucified Christ adorns one side of the head and animal carvings and geometric designs, including intricate interlacing, decorate the shaft. Below the slim shaft, the base of the cross widens out and is divided into panelled sections on all sides. The north face shows Saints Paul and Anthony, the temptation of St Anthony and a monster from the Book of the Apocalypse; the south side portrays the three children in the fiery furnace, the flight into Egypt and the miracle of the loaves and fishes; the east side contains panels showing Adam and Eve, the sacrifice of Isaac and Daniel in the lions' den, and the west side depicts the crucifixion and the twelve apostles. Though the scenes on the high cross of Moone are similar to those on the crosses at nearby Castledermot, and originate from the same school of sculpture, the carving at Moone is much more impressive and the detail is much finer. Stonemasons such as those who worked on the Moone high cross were skilled sculptors, and they decorated their crosses with circular and cruciform designs and patterns similar to those carved on rocks in pre-Christian Ireland, as far back as the Bronze Age.

While the Christian symbol of the cross was of primary significance on these crosses, many of the masons were not monks and it has been suggested that some of them adhered to a few aspects of the old pagan beliefs, resulting in the crosses displaying a combination of the old and the new religions, which can be seen in the different techniques of ornamentation that can be identified on the surviving high crosses. Generally, the intricate interlacing of the geometric designs is executed to a higher standard than the biblical scenes, but this may reflect the difficulties facing a sculptor carving, for example, Daniel in the lions' den, without ever having seen a lion or knowing what one looked like!

The remarkable state of preservation of Moone's high cross is due to the fact that it was dismantled and buried, section by section, when the religious houses of Ireland came under threat during the English Reformation of the sixteenth and seventeenth centuries, which of course also spread to conquered Ireland. Years later, in 1835 and 1850, sections of the cross were discovered in the abbey churchyard. They were in such good condition that it was immediately evident that they could not have fallen; they had been reverently and lovingly hidden away to protect them, so they escaped the rigours of the Penal Laws in Ireland. The Duke of Leinster commissioned three local stonemasons – David, Thomas and William O'Shaughnessy – to re-erect the cross and restore it to its former glory. However, the cross seemed ill proportioned for such a fine piece of workmanship, and the reason for this became evident later, when Michael O'Shaughnessy discovered another carefully buried part, which was actually the cross's central section. In 1893 it was inserted between the other sections of the cross, thereby making this the second highest monastic cross in Ireland. The ravages of the weather began to take their toll on the high cross, however, and it was dismantled once again in 1994. A Perspex roof was put in place to protect the cross and it was erected and displayed inside the newly roofed section of the ruins of Moone Abbey in 1996, a reminder to all of the village's long and proud monastic tradition, which is still carried on in the nearby Cistercian house, Bolton Abbey. That tradition at Moone is part of a wider Kildare ecclesiastical tradition, and this is evident in the present day by the existence, in the Irish Roman Catholic Church, of the diocese of Kildare and Leighlin and in the Church of Ireland, of the diocese of Meath and Kildare. The cathedral in Kildare town is, of course, named the Cathedral Church of St Brigid.

2

KILDARE'S
GREAT HOUSES

The eighteenth century was an era of building and improvement all across Ireland. The landed elite, who found themselves in possession of practically all of the land in the country in the wake of the Williamite Wars of the 1680s and '90s, were in a position of unprecedented power on the island. This encouraged them to accelerate their efforts to shape the landscape in their own Anglicising image, by building country seats, constructing big houses, erecting shooting lodges, founding new villages and improving existing ones. The fertile lowlands of County Kildare provided an excellent backdrop to many fine landlord houses.

Monasterevan Abbey in 1794 by Sparrow.

These large country houses became the most obvious symbol of the now universal paternalistic landlord-tenant relationship that concentrated wealth in the hands of the landlords during the eighteenth century. Landlords were linked to their tenants by economic rather than by social ties, and separated from them by language, ethnicity, religion and culture. Landlord mansions, or 'big houses', were home to the landed elite who controlled the country throughout the late seventeenth century.

The eighteenth century saw many fine houses erected in Kildare. At Kilcullen, Castle Martin was built for a Dublin banker named Harrison around 1720. It was surrounded by a 948-acre estate. In 1743, famed architects Richard Cassels and Francis Bindon also worked on Belan House on its 964-acre estate at Ballitore, home of the Earls of Aldborough. Burtown House between Athy and Moone, home to the Houghton family, dates from the same period. In the 1770s the Huguenot La Touche family of bankers, who had an estate of 11,282 acres, employed Whitmore Davis to design a new house at Harristown, adjacent to the village of Brannockstown.

There are many other such examples in the county, from Moore Abbey in Monasterevin, with its fine castellated entrance gate in the village, to Forenaughts House near Naas, the seat of the famous Wolfe family, who were connected to Theobald Wolfe Tone, the man known as the 'father of Irish republicanism'. However, two of the finest and most significant of Kildare's great houses are situated in the north of the county: Carton House at Maynooth and Castletown House at Celbridge.

CARTON HOUSE

Today Carton House is a luxury hotel but it was formerly the seat of the Dukes of Leinster. The Norman knight Maurice Fitzgerald, who had arrived in Ireland with Strongbow at the time of the Norman invasion of 1169, was granted the manor of Maynooth sometime before 1176, the year of his death.

In 1316 the Fitzgeralds were elevated to the status of Earls of Kildare, and went on to become the most influential family dynasty in Ireland, before their power was broken with the suppression of Silken Thomas's revolt in the 1530s. However, the family remained wealthy and in 1739 the 19th Lord Kildare decided to build a fine new residence. He commissioned the foremost architect of the day, Richard Cassels, to design and build Carton House. Lord Kildare died in 1745, but his widow continued the building project for their son James, the 20th earl, who married Lady Emily Lennox in 1747. Lady Emily was a sister of Lady Louisa Conolly of nearby Castletown House, and both were daughters of the 2nd Duke of Richmond. The building of the house was finished in 1747 and from then until his death in 1775, James (who was made first Duke of Leinster in 1766), did much to improve and embellish Carton House. He laid out a walled park, erected lodges, included new bridges in the grounds and planted numerous trees. The duke made efforts to attract the leading English landscape gardener Lancelot 'Capability' Brown to Carton. He invited Brown to come to Ireland, offering him £1,000 on his arrival 'in addition to the cost of all that he should do'. Brown famously refused the offer, informing the duke that he 'had not finished England' yet! Undeterred, the duke pressed ahead with enhancing Carton and its grounds. He was also active in parliament and his fifth son, Lord Edward Fitzgerald, a leader of the United Irishmen, was wounded while resisting arrest and died of his wound shortly after his capture following the 1798 uprising.

The entrance to Carton was off the old main road from Dublin to Galway, about a mile east of Maynooth. Behind the lodge gates stands a beautifully landscaped demesne, boasting an ornamental lake. This demesne was altered and enlarged to about 1,100 acres when the new Carton House was becoming a reality on the landscape. The Rye Water was widened, and later used to create the lake, and the surrounding parkland was modelled in a contrived natural style. In 1776 a visitor to Carton, the agriculturalist Arthur Young, wrote:

The park ranks among the finest in Ireland. It is a vast lawn, which waves over gentle hills, surrounded by plantations of great extent, and which break and divide in places, so as to give much variety. A large but gentle vale winds through the whole, in the bottom of which a small stream has been enlarged into a fine river, which throws cheerfulness on most of the scenes; over it is a handsome stone bridge.

The Shell Cottage is beside the lake, and from here Queen Victoria and Prince Albert were rowed to the main house when they visited Carton in 1849. Before she arrived, the queen had a dream that she was boating on a lake at Carton House. However no lake existed at that stage, so one was created especially for the royal visit.

Shell Cottage derives its name from a famous room in the building tastefully decorated with an incredible array of seashells. Past the cottage, the drive continues through the demesne and its finely laid-out parkland, crossing the White Bridge – designed by Thomas Ivory and built in the 1760s – before continuing up to the house. Another entrance to the house was provided in 1815, when the 3rd Duke of Leinster employed the famous Irish architect, Sir Richard Morrison, to work on extensive refurbishment, during which some major alterations were made to the house. Morrison moved the approach road and entrance to the house in order to provide the principal stately rooms with a southern aspect. Morrison also enlarged the house, as the duke had money to spend after he sold his Dublin residence, Leinster House, to the Royal Dublin Society. Later, the RDS moved to Ballsbridge and in turn sold on Leinster House, which is now home to the Irish parliament, the Dáil.

Carton House itself is built in the Palladian style. Andrea Palladio was a famous Venetian architect who modelled much of his work on the Italian classical past. Roman architectural design was exemplified in the writings of the classical author Vitruvius, whose principles of symmetry were clearly outlined in his great work, *De Architectura*. Palladian architecture was symmetrical, and the colonnades emanating from the central block of the main house to the two equidistant wings at Carton House are certainly pleasing to the eye of even the most fastidious and pedantic of symmetry lovers!

A fine, pillared portico protects the main doorway into Carton House, situated in the middle of the central block. It led into the main hall, which housed a picture of the original house and a landscape painted by F.W. Watts. This hall, now known as the Mallaghan Room, also contained the principal staircase and featured a Gobelins tapestry entitled 'The young gardeners', as well as a portrait of the 5th Duchess of Leinster. A beautifully inlaid hall table complemented the ornamentation in the hall. From here one could enter the Chinese dressing room, decorated with two Irish landscape paintings, and continue on to the Chinese bedroom, featuring Chinese wallpaper that was put up in 1759, and Chippendale carving. Queen Victoria used this room when she visited Carton. The garden face of the house contained the library, dominated by equine pictures, and which was decorated in 1815, but it also housed older books from the original Carton House as well as some rare maps. The inside of the library door is disguised to look like bookshelves. The Green Drawing Room, beside the library, has a fine fireplace with a chimney breast of Carrara marble and lapis lazuli. The paintings in this room date from the reign of King Charles II (1660-85). Huge mahogany doors lead into the Gold Saloon, one of the best-known rooms in Ireland. The room was built in 1739 as the dining room of the older house, but is now renowned for the fantastic stuccowork of the Francini brothers, Philip and Paul, who executed much of the stuccowork at Carton. These Italian master craftsmen were busily employed on many great projects in Ireland at this time, and were the *crème de la crème* of interior designers to the Irish Ascendancy. The stucco ceiling of the Gold Saloon is among the best examples of their art. The overriding theme of the stuccowork is the courtship of the gods, in keeping with the classical education received by members of the Ascendancy during the eighteenth century and the interest in Renaissance ideas in Ireland at this time. A Telford organ with a case designed by Lord Gerald Fitzgerald in 1857 dominated this room. The chimney here also features Carrara marble. The adjacent anteroom contained nine pictures depicting scenes from the life of King Charles I and two wall mirrors of Venetian glass.

Sir Richard Morrison built a new dining room in 1815. It also has fine plasterwork on the ceiling and housed pictures by the artist Sir William Beechey. A door leads from here into the gardens. These were landscaped on this side of the house during the 1815 renovations. Interesting features include a statue of Mercury executed in lead and a sundial that differs from Greenwich Mean Time by twenty minutes, signifying the fact that standardised time is a man-made phenomenon.

The Fitzgeralds retained possession of Carton House throughout the nineteenth century, but the first half of the twentieth witnessed the family's demise. The 7th Duke of Leinster, Lord Edward Fitzgerald, was born in 1892. He was the third son and lived a carefree lifestyle, accumulating gambling debts as he went. However, Sir Harry Mallaby-Deeley advanced Edward a loan of £60,000 on the understanding that if Edward did somehow succeed to the title of Duke of Leinster, Sir Harry would receive the income of the Fitzgerald's Irish estates. Lord Edward's rash acceptance of the loan bore fruit for Sir Harry, because the 5th Duke was killed in the First World War and the 6th died in 1922. From the time that

'Carton House, Maynooth', *The Graphic*, 24 October 1874.

Edward succeeded to the title in 1922, he had to pay Mallaby-Deeley approximately £80,000 per annum. The 7th Duke was declared bankrupt and, in 1949, Carton House was sold to the 2nd Lord Brocket, a Liverpudlian whose family fortune came from the brewing trade – a trade evidently with no shortage of customers! The 7th Duke eventually took his own life in 1976, by which time the Honourable David Nall-Cain (son of Lord Brocket) had opened a restored Carton House as a visitor attraction. In 1977 Nall-Cain sold Carton to the Mallaghan family.

Today, the house has become a hotel, and visitors who drive along the Main Street of Maynooth are faced with the gates of Carton directly ahead of them. Along with most of the town, the wide, tree-lined street with its uniform roofline was transformed to complement the new Ascendancy landmark, which rose on a greenfield site in the eighteenth century. As a luxury hotel, Carton House is enjoying a new lease of life and numbers many of the great and the good of Irish society among its guests, while also having played host to many international celebrities, following in the footsteps of earlier guests such as Queen Victoria, Princess Grace of Monaco and singer Marianne Faithfull. The fine golf course at Carton has been the venue for the Irish Open, most recently during the year of the 'Gathering' (a campaign to bring many of the Irish Diaspora back for a visit and to boost tourist numbers nationally) in 2013. The Irish rugby team also uses the venue as their base, and many of the original fixtures and fittings are still on display. The history and atmosphere of Carton House make this place well worth a visit!

CASTLETOWN HOUSE

Castletown House, the entrance to which is decorated with handsome sphinxes and is situated at the end of the main street of Celbridge, will forever be associated with William 'Speaker' Conolly. He was a most unusual man, and his rise to prominence in Irish society during the early eighteenth century was a remarkable phenomenon. His father was an innkeeper in Ballyshannon, County Donegal. The inn provided a good, middle-class living and the modestly rich family could afford to send William to Dublin to study law. For some twenty years after he qualified, William Conolly practised law on Ireland's Northwest circuit. He was a shrewd man, whose acumen and ability allowed him to rent lands wisely and to purchase estates in the wake of the failure of the Jacobite forces during the Williamite Wars of the 1680s and 1690s. With his wealth, power and influence rising, Conolly's cause was further advanced when he married Katherine Conyngham, daughter of General Sir Albert Conyngham. He purchased Rodanstown House near Kilcock, County Kildare, which acted as his country residence until, in his later years, he decided to pump some of his copious wealth into the construction of his magnificent mansion, Castletown House.

No expense was to be spared on the new building project, which was designed by Alessandro Galilei (1691-1737) and finished by Sir Edward Lovett Pearce. Conolly commissioned Galilei, best known for his work on the Basilica of St John Lateran in Rome, to design a totally new type of house for Ireland. The exterior design of Castletown began a trend in Irish architecture, setting a pattern that would be repeated again and again in other aristocratic country seats such as Carton House and Russborough House in County Wicklow. Castletown was the first and probably the finest Palladian-style mansion in Ireland. The central block is linked to the two smaller wings by curved colonnades, which sweep forward from the main house like two embracing arms. The best materials were to be used in its construction, and imported if necessary. In a letter dating from 1722, Bishop Berkeley, who was advising Conolly on the building of the house, was informed:

> You will do well to recommend to him the making use of all the marbles he can get of the production of Ireland for his chimneys, for since this house will be the finest Ireland ever saw, and by

your description fit for a prince, I would have it as it were the epitome of the kingdom, and all the natural rarities she affords should have a place there.

The letter also suggested the use of other Irish building and decorating materials including oak, Irish silver for the grates and locks, 'black palmers stone' and Irish furniture of the highest quality. The result was spectacular, and the new mansion on its greenfield site was unquestionably 'fit for a prince' and 'the finest Ireland ever saw'. Mr Conolly of Castletown – as Speaker was proud to be known – was undoubtedly the richest commoner, and probably the richest man, in Ireland. Jonathan Swift commented on this fact during the 'Wood's Halfpence' episode of the 1720s. This happened because there was a shortage of coin in Ireland in 1722 and much of it was old and worn. Ireland had no mint, so a patent was granted to a Wolverhampton man, William Wood, to supply just over £100,000 in halfpennies and farthings for Ireland. However, this evoked massive protests in Ireland, where there was an almost complete refusal to use the coins. Swift's anonymous *Drapier's Letters* in 1724-5 inflamed anti-English feeling further. Swift wryly claimed that Speaker Conolly would need 240 horses to deliver his half-yearly rent to Castletown, and two or three huge cellars underneath the house to store the coin! In the event, Woods' patent was revoked in 1725 and he was compensated for the loss. The episode demonstrated just how tense Anglo-Irish relations were at the time. This tension was reflected in the fact that Conolly repeatedly refused to accept an English title because of his fierce adherence to what he saw as his Irish identity. Despite his lowly birth and the absence of a title, Conolly was elected Speaker of the Irish House of Commons in 1715 (hence his sobriquet), a post that he held almost up to his death in 1729. Speaker's widow remained at Castletown and is kindly remembered in Irish history. She built a charity school in the village of Celbridge, but is best known for commissioning the erection of 'Conolly's Folly', a large

Conolly's Folly.

140ft-high ornamental obelisk with an elaborately arched base near Castletown House. This was done in March 1740 as a response to the very severe winter, during which local tenant farmers were severely affected by the cold weather. Land was life to these people and, cropless and penniless, they were saved by the income generated by the employment provided by the folly's construction.

Following Katharine's death in 1752, her estate passed into the hands of a nephew, William Conolly. However, he died two years later and the house was passed on to his son, Thomas Conolly, when he came of age in 1759. A year previously, Thomas had married Lady Louisa Lennox, daughter of the second Duke of Richmond, whose sister Emily was living at nearby Carton House. Lady Louisa's sisters regarded Tom Conolly, as he was known, as 'silly' and 'tiresome', but Louisa herself had a huge impact on decorating and improving Castletown House and the interior of the building owes much to her ideas and her work. Two styles, Italianate and Irish, were already evident in Castletown. The entrance hall encapsulated both, with its noble Italianate proportions, pillars, pediments and balcony and its simpler narrow oak doors and wainscoting. During Lady Louisa's tenure as mistress of Castletown (1759-1821) she left her own stamp on the house, having several rooms refurbished and redecorated. She created the Print Room (the only one of its type to survive in Ireland) with her own hands. A popular hobby for eighteenth-century ladies was the collecting of prints, which were then pasted on to walls. Joshua Reynolds' portrait of Louisa's sister Sarah is included in the prints on display. Louisa also had the house's main staircase, which for some reason had never been put in, installed in a separate hall adjacent to the entrance hall, and commissioned the Francini brothers to execute marvellous stucco work in the Baroque style as decoration, while managing to insert family portraits into the plasterwork. However, she trumped even this when she had the Long Gallery decorated in the fashionable Pompeian manner in 1775. Charles Ruben Reilly and Thomas Ryder carried out the work. Three Murano chandeliers were imported from Venice and frescoes, marble statues and busts on classical themes taken from mythology, philosophy and literature adorn the informal space. The whole room also features elaborate plasterwork on the walls and ceiling.

There are many other rooms of note in Castletown House. On the ground floor these include the Brown Study, which has oak doors and walls panelled with wood. It was decorated in the 1720s and includes a fitted desk, but was originally a bedroom. A tapestry in this room shows a Volunteer meeting of 1782. Tom Conolly was involved in the Volunteers, an organisation originally established to defend Ireland from the threat of invasion by the French during the American Revolution, but which later became concerned with political reform in Ireland. The ground floor contains two 'withdrawing' or drawing rooms. The Green Drawing Room, originally panelled in oak but now covered in silk, was the principal reception room, which could be accessed from both the entrance hall and the garden. It was much altered during Lady Louisa Conolly's tenure in the 1760s.

The Red Drawing Room was another important reception room. It was also extensively redecorated by Lady Louisa in the 1760s. Both drawing rooms have chimney pieces of fine Carrara marble. Also on the ground floor is the State bedroom, which was used by Speaker Conolly. It was later converted into a library. However, the books were lost by the 1960s and the library collection is no longer extant, so visitors today will find the room furnished as a bedroom of the period of its original use. The bedrooms on the first floor were used by both the Conolly family and visitors to Castletown. Lady Louisa's bedroom, dressing room and the adjoining boudoir were the personal space of the mistress of the house. The boudoir was in effect a private sitting room for the woman who was responsible for much of what one sees today at Castletown.

The Blue Bedroom is a typical example of the room of a wealthy early Victorian. It boasts two adjoining dressing rooms. The pastel room, with its excellent collection of portraits (from which it gets its name) was fitted out as an anteroom for the Long Gallery, but it became a schoolroom during the nineteenth century. All of the rooms contain portraits and paintings, many of which are by well-known artists and reflect Irish affairs and the lives of Ireland's landed elite during the eighteenth and nineteenth centuries.

Historically, Castletown is one of the best documented of Ireland's 'big houses'. Many papers pertaining to the house and estate survive, as does much correspondence by members of the Conolly family. The Castletown documents provide a unique glimpse of a life and a lifestyle that has long since gone. Documents such as the bill for the brass staircase made by Mr King from Dublin in 1760, an account book stating that Mr Nicholls of Celbridge received £3 per annum for polishing these stairs and the later bill of £16 3s 4d from a stonemason in Maynooth for the sphinxes on the entrance gates all add to the minutiae of Castletown's historical record.

Castletown House remained in the possession of Speaker Conolly's descendants until 1965, when Major Wilson, who was a property developer, bought it. However, many people were horrified at the prospect of losing the house, which was rightly viewed as a national treasure. In 1967 the Hon. Desmond Guinness, founder of the Irish Georgian Society, stepped in and purchased the house and 120 acres of the demesne lands for the sum of £93,000. The Irish Georgian Society, which was founded in 1958, was concerned with the preservation of Ireland's Georgian heritage, and it built up a fine collection of photographs and data relating to Irish architecture, sculpture, silver, plasterwork and furniture. Once the society had secured the house, it began a mammoth programme of restoration, beginning with the repair of Conolly's Folly. Mrs Zalles of Washington purchased this landmark piece of estate furniture from Carton estate and donated it to Castletown, so that it now belonged to the estate that commissioned its building. Castletown House itself was also open to the public in 1967. The Irish Georgian Society, aided by donations from philanthropic individuals, began to execute refurbishments at Castletown, which became the society's headquarters. The house had fallen into a state of disrepair over the years. Windows needed to be painted, leaking copper roofs over the colonnades needed to be repaired, and wet rot in the house itself had to be treated.

However, little by little, these and other restoration jobs were tackled.

In 1979, a charitable trust called the Castletown Foundation was established and the ownership, maintenance and restoration of the house passed to the new body. Fifteen years later, in 1994, the house passed into the care of the Irish state and it is now managed by the Office of Public Works. This change of ownership accelerated the restoration programme, and increased funding was available for repair works. The long-term goal of these was to preserve one of Ireland's most significant houses for future generations. Refurbishments to the house, the acquisition of more parkland surrounding it and improvements to enhance visitors' experiences at Castletown have all added to the house's charm. The fact that Castletown received a certificate of excellence from the TripAdvisor website in 2014 bears ample testimony to the fact that this is indeed a special place, where visitors will be rewarded with an enriching historical experience.

KILDARE REBELS

Despite, or perhaps because of, the fact that most of the flat and fertile land of County Kildare was under English control from the twelfth century onwards, the county has produced more than its fair share of rebels over the centuries. Two of the best known were Silken Thomas, who rebelled against King Henry VIII in the 1530s and John Devoy, who was involved in subversive Fenian republican activities throughout the late nineteenth and early twentieth centuries.

THE REVOLT OF SILKEN THOMAS

Following the Battle of Bosworth in 1485 in England, King Henry VII became the first Tudor monarch. Both he and his son, Henry VIII, left the running of their Irish lands to the Earls of Kildare, the Fitzgeralds, the most powerful Anglo-Norman dynasty on the island of Ireland. The younger Henry even appointed Gearóid Óg Fitzgerald as his viceroy in Ireland in 1513. Henry's reign was characterised by political intrigue, and his Irish viceroy had powerful enemies such as the Butlers of Ormond (a rival Anglo-Norman dynasty based in Kilkenny). Gearóid Óg was summoned to London to answer trumped-up charges against him on three occasions. Twice he managed to clear his name, and might have done so the third time but for events at home. In 1533 Gearóid left for London, leaving his eldest son, Thomas, Earl of Offaly, in charge while he was away. The choice proved foolish, as Thomas was young, rash and inexperienced in diplomacy. His nickname, 'Silken Thomas', insinuated that his chief interest lay in foppery and fine clothes. He certainly did not possess the prudence or tact necessary to fulfil the role of viceroy in perilous times. When a false rumour (possibly started by the Butlers of Ormond) that his father had been executed in London reached Thomas, the young man rushed into rebellion.

However, the popular conception that the revolt of Silken Thomas was a knee-jerk reaction to the rumour about his father's death may not give us the full picture. The 1530s witnessed the Henrician Reformation in England, and the Earls of Kildare had genuine grievances. English men were being appointed to key positions in both Church and state in Ireland, undermining the power of the viceroy and of the Kildares. An English cleric, John Alen, was appointed as Archbishop of Dublin and in May 1534 Sir William Skeffington arrived in Ireland as Henry's deputy. This effectively rendered the Earls of Kildare redundant in that position and removed the king's protection from Thomas and his followers. Intriguingly, the earliest mention of Silken Thomas's revolt is found in a letter from Robert Cowley to Thomas Cromwell dated June 1534. Cowley informed Cromwell that Thomas and his followers 'boast that they be of the pope's sect and they will serve against the king' who they maintain 'is accursed and as many as take his part will be accursed'. This letter is dated a week before Thomas could possibly have known that Gearóid was arrested in London. Hence, it is possible that there was more to Thomas's decision to rebel than the rumour about his father.

Having despatched Skeffington to Ireland, the king also summoned Thomas to the royal court in London. This summons was to be given to Thomas at a meeting of the Council of Ireland in Dublin. Thomas arrived for this meeting with an escort of 1,000 armed men. Apparently 140 horsemen acted as bodyguards as he rode through the city of Dublin to the council meeting at St Mary's Abbey. At the meeting,

Thomas renounced his allegiance to the king and threw down the sword of state, confirming him to be the king's sworn enemy. He and his retinue of armed retainers left Dublin and headed back to their stronghold at Maynooth Castle.

Whether the causes of the revolt lay in the immediate short term or the longer term, the fact remained that Silken Thomas was now in open rebellion against King Henry VIII. Thomas had the advantage of possession of the king's ordnance in Ireland, but there was a shortage of ammunition for these guns, a fact that was to bedevil the rebels' efforts throughout their military campaign. However, some Gaelic clans, who saw a chance to throw off the English yoke, rallied to the Fitzgerald cause. Thomas and his followers, known as the Geraldines, laid waste to the lands around Dublin and besieged the city with a view to capturing Dublin Castle. Thomas was heard to boast that he would receive help from Catholic Spain, so the rebellion could now be seen as a part of the larger religious wars that engulfed Europe in the wake of the Protestant Reformation. Thomas and his followers openly castigated the king for his role in the English Reformation. An act of attainder was passed against Thomas, which specifically condemned him for slandering Henry with 'the most shameful and detestable infamies'. The rebellion caused initial panic in London, and in August 1534 the king sent two envoys to negotiate peace terms with the rebels. Thomas would have none of it, however, so Henry mustered a large army, which he sent to Ireland under the command of Skeffington.

In the meantime, Thomas had requested military aid from the Emperor Charles V. A large army was being prepared in Spain, and Thomas hoped that it would sail for Ireland and tip the balance of war in his favour. Charles V had an agent (possibly Gonzalo Fernandez) working in Ireland at this time. The imperial agent managed to enlist support from both Anglo-Norman lords (such as the Earl of Desmond) and Gaelic Irish clans (such as the O'Briens). At least one contemporary document referred to a Spanish plan to capture Irish coastal cities, and knowledge of such a plan would explain Thomas's bragging about the anticipated help from Catholic Spain for his cause. At home, his forces laid waste large areas in the east of Ireland, and much of the province of Leinster was under his control. Crucially though, the rebels lacked the firepower necessary to capture strongly fortified and stoutly defended targets. The rebels failed to take both Drogheda in the north and Waterford in the south. Thomas's forces were divided, as campaigns on his northern and southern flanks took men away from the main prize, Dublin. The rebels continued to pillage and plunder the hinterland of the capital throughout August, razing settlements to the ground and eliminating pockets of resistance, but the city itself stood firm against them.

The failure of the rebels to take Dublin allowed the English army to land safely in Ireland, and Thomas and his men now faced a serious threat. The rebels murdered Archbishop Alen at Clontarf when he attempted to escape from Ireland, which brought the anger of the Church upon them. Thomas's military inexperience matched his diplomatic naivety, and doubts arose among his men regarding his leadership of the campaign, leading to the desertion of some of his followers. Skeffington's army advanced from Dublin, and he eventually captured Thomas's headquarters at Maynooth Castle. He showed no mercy to the defenders. Skeffington informed Henry:

> We attacked the great castle, which within awhile yielded, wherein was the dean of Kildare ... with divers other gunners and archers to the number of thirty-seven, which were all taken prisoners and their lives preserved by appointment, until they should be presented to me, your deputy and then to be ordered as I and your council thought good. And considering the high enterprise and presumption attempted by them against Your Grace's Crown and Majesty ... we all thought expedient and requisite that they should be put to execution for the dread and example of others.

The tide of war had turned against the rebels, and though Thomas held out for a while longer, the fall of Maynooth Castle meant that the revolt was doomed unless foreign aid arrived. Thomas continued to hope for Spanish intervention. However, the huge Spanish army assembled by Emperor Charles V did not sail for Ireland. It actually embarked for Tunis in North Africa, capturing the city from the Muslims in July 1535. The non-arrival of the Spaniards was the death knell to Thomas and the Catholic cause in Ireland. His military situation becoming ever more desperate, Thomas eventually surrendered to the new Lord Deputy, Leonard Grey, on the promise that his life would be spared and the possibility that he would be granted a pardon. In England, Gearóid Óg was a broken man and, crushed by the outcome of events, he died in the Tower of London.

The defeated Thomas was also brought to London. He was now only too aware that his Catholic cause was a mere pawn in a much larger European power struggle, and that his rashness had caused him to be used in a way that played into the hands of the Butlers of Ormond in a national struggle for supremacy among the leading Anglo-Norman houses of Ireland. He had gone into the rebellion convinced that he could not trust King Henry VIII but, ironically, his only hope of survival was now to throw himself on the king's mercy.

In the event, no mercy was shown. The Tudor administration took the opportunity to break the power of the Kildares once and for all. Gearóid Óg was already dead, and Thomas was hanged in London along with five of his uncles. The only survivor of the House of Kildare was Gerald, the 12-year-old half-brother of Thomas, and the authorities moved swiftly to get their man. However, some of the most powerful Anglo-Norman lords and Irish chiefs, including Manus O'Donnell, joined forces in an alliance known as the Geraldine League. Following many adventures, the young Gerald was eventually smuggled out of the country and taken under the protection of the Emperor Charles V. Thanks to the rebellion of Silken

Thomas, his family would never again play a leading part in the government of Ireland.

Silken Thomas's rebellion had failed and, with hindsight, unsurprisingly so. However, Thomas evidently thought that he had a chance of success, principally because he expected to receive help from Spain. Had this happened, it could have altered the whole course of events, but as it was, Thomas's rebellion met the same fate as previous uprisings against English rule in other parts of Ireland. Thomas's revolt had hoped to establish an independent Irish lordship, free from the yoke of English domination. However, Thomas's rebellion was different in one crucial respect – it was the first Irish rebellion to include a sectarian element.

The fledgling English Reformation had stirred up resistance in Ireland. By appealing to the Catholic faith, in addition to the overwhelming suspicion of English rule and English law among the Irish, Thomas had unfortunately introduced a new and bitter element into Anglo-Irish political relationships.

No records exist to indicate what form Thomas's new order would have taken had his attempts to throw off English rule succeeded. However, his rebellion and the response to it among the native Irish point to the fact that there was a large proportion of the Irish populace, both Gaelic and Anglo-Norman, who would rally to the cause of the Catholic faith. The old religion could be invoked to undermine loyalties to the English Crown. As the Reformation progressed, Irish society polarised along Catholic and Protestant lines, and the viceroys of succeeding Tudor monarchs had to tread very carefully in Ireland when it came to introducing religious changes. Nonetheless, in the wake of Silken Thomas's futile revolt, religious schism was a fact of life in Ireland throughout the remainder of the sixteenth century, and resistance to the Crown almost always included a sectarian element from the 1530s onwards. There was Spanish and papal support for the unsuccessful Desmond and Baltinglass rebellions (in around 1580). This resistance culminated during the final decade of the century with the Nine Years War of 1594-1603, when Irish rebels under Hugh O'Neill again received aid from Catholic Spain. Ultimately, though, it was all to no avail and the rebels were defeated. The Catholic cause would lie dormant until the 1641 Rebellion, when it was unleashed with savage fury once more. Truly Silken Thomas's rebellion and his adherence to the Catholic faith had been the start of a new and bitter era in the tangled relationships between Ireland and England.

JOHN DEVOY, FENIAN

The Great Famine struck Ireland in the mid-nineteenth century and it had many consequences. One of these was bitterness among the Irish people, especially the landless, the small farmers and the cottagers. At home, the system of paternalistic landlordism had failed them utterly, while the growing Irish Diaspora of famine and post-famine emigrants carried with

'Cottagers at Kildare', *Illustrated London News*, 9 April 1870.

them resentment against English rule in Ireland, particularly in the USA. In these circumstances it was unsurprising that a new revolutionary organisation emerged: the Irish Republican Brotherhood, founded in 1858.

Often referred to as the Fenians (named after the Fianna, a mythical band of Celtic warriors in ancient Ireland), the IRB was widespread throughout the country. It was also well organised at grassroots level, with local members formed into units called 'circles'. Each circle was headed by a local leader called a 'centre' and there was a hierarchy of leadership right up to the supreme council at national level. There was also an Irish-American branch of the Fenian organisation, the avowed aim of which was to rid Ireland of English rule. The Fenians were a secret military organisation and they staged an abortive rising in 1867. Police barracks were attacked and there were skirmishes with the authorities in Louth, Dublin and in parts of Munster. However, a combination of factors led to the rising turning into a fiasco. Unusually inclement weather affected the turnout of men; the activities of British spies within the organisation meant that the authorities knew of Fenian plans in advance, and arms and ammunition expected from America failed to arrive. Ill prepared and ill equipped, the Fenian rising never had a chance of success, but a new breed of Irish Republican leader had emerged. The new Fenian leaders included Charles Kickham, Jeremiah O'Donovan Rossa, John O'Leary and John Devoy.

Born close to Johnstown, near Naas, County Kildare in 1842, John Devoy devoted his adult life to the Irish Republican movement, both within his native Ireland and later in the USA. When John was still a child, the Great Famine swept through the country and the Devoy family moved to Dublin where John was educated by the Irish Christian Brothers in a number of schools in the city. Having left school, the young man entered further education at the newly established Catholic University of Ireland and used his spare time to attend Irish language classes in the city. At these classes, Devoy was first introduced to the republican movement, as the Fenians were actively recruiting members from nationalistically minded young men. The exact details of his swearing in to the Irish Republican Brotherhood are unknown, but it is that probable that Devoy joined the organisation in or around 1861. His republican career had begun.

Devoy joined the National Petition Movement to 'take England at her word' with respect to the attestation of the right of national self-determination voiced by Lord John Russell in relation to Italy, which the Fenians wanted to be applied to Ireland. This resulted in a petition of half a million signatures, presented at parliament by The O'Donoghue. Devoy was also charged with meeting the Young Ireland leader, John Mitchel, in France. While in France, Devoy joined the Foreign Legion, primarily to gain military experience, because he was under the impression that a rising against British rule was imminent in Ireland. Following a year's service with the legion in North Africa on the Algerian front, he returned to Ireland, and was told by the Fenian leader James Stephens to organise the Fenian movement in his native County Kildare, concentrating his efforts in and around the town of Naas. Devoy proved to be an excellent choice for this role and came to the attention of the supreme council. Following the arrest of numerous IRB leaders in a clampdown by the authorities, Stephens appointed Devoy as Chief Organiser of the IRB in the British Army in 1865. The Fenians saw infiltration of the enemy forces as key to their success and, by 1866, Devoy and his followers had 'turned' over 15,000 Irishmen in British regiments by enlisting them into the Fenian organisation.

Devoy had got the attention of the authorities, and he was arrested in 1866, but not before he had arranged the audacious escape of fellow Fenian leader James Stephens from a heavily guarded wing of Dublin's Richmond Prison in 1865. Devoy worked with prison guard John Breslin, who was also an IRB man, to rescue the incarcerated Stephens. Breslin made an impression of the key to Stephens' cell in a bar of soap, and Devoy made a duplicate key, which Breslin managed to smuggle in to Stephens on 24 November. On the night of the escape, Devoy waited at the back of the prison to meet the fugitive Fenian leader. He then delivered the IRB head to a safe house, before leaving him to continue with plans for the uprising that he felt was now imminent.

The early part of 1866 was promising for Devoy and the IRB. Devoy estimated that the number of Fenians in the British Army in Ireland had reached an all-time high of about 80,000 men. He argued that the time to strike had come and pressed Stephens to instigate an immediate insurrection. Stephens however delayed – possibly because he lost his nerve – and the order to rise was not given. This caused a rift to develop between Stephens and Devoy, who later observed 'the signal never came and all my and other men's risks and sacrifices were thrown away through incompetent and nerveless leadership'. The British authorities learned of the planned insurrection and the possible mutiny within the army from informers, and Devoy was arrested in February 1866 at the Pilsworth public house in James's Street, Dublin, where he had been participating in a meeting of the IRB leadership. Devoy was imprisoned in Mountjoy Gaol and tried on a charge of treason. In court the odds were stacked against Devoy, who was described in a statement (by Michael J. Kehoe) as 'the guilty my lord type of Irishman in front of British courts', and he was indeed found guilty and sentenced to fifteen years' penal servitude in Britain.

Devoy was a troublesome prisoner. He arrived at Portland Prison, where he organised and ordered a number of strikes by the prisoners, causing him to be transferred to Millbank Prison. However, he also caused unrest there and was subsequently moved to Chatham, before fortunately securing his release under the British Government's General Amnesty of 1870, after only five years of his fifteen-year sentence had been served. However, under the terms of his release, he was required to leave Ireland and not return until the term of his penal servitude had been completed. American pressure had been a key element in securing the General Amnesty, with Fenians on that side of the Atlantic instigating the US intervention. Devoy now decided that his best option was to travel to the United States and to join with allies in New York.

Devoy quickly established himself in his new home, where he arrived in mid-1871, and found employment as a journalist with *The New York Herald*. He also joined the American branch of the Fenians, Clan na Gael, whose objective was to achieve the 'complete and absolute independence of Ireland from Great Britain, and the complete severance of all political connections between the two countries by unceasing preparation for armed insurrection in Ireland'. Devoy's subversive activities in Ireland and his background as a Fenian prisoner opened doors in the Clan and, late in 1871, Devoy was installed as head of the New York chapter. He immediately set about using this position to attain a republic in his native land by a campaign of educating the American people about the Irish cause and engendering a sympathetic response towards Ireland's plight in the USA.

Devoy's organisational skills were useful in his new role and he was very successful, raising vast amounts of money for the Republican cause. However by 1879, Devoy felt out of touch with developments in Ireland and with the Irish people. He returned to Ireland on a fact-finding mission, during which he reacquainted himself with the changed political and social realities. At home he found the Fenian movement in disarray, but a new Land War loomed as tenant farmers resisted landlordism and, in parliament, a new Irish Home Rule party was on the rise. During this visit Devoy liaised with Fenian leaders such as Charles Kickham, Land Leaguers such as Michael Davitt and Home Rulers such as Charles Stewart Parnell. These meetings bore fruit, and Devoy agreed that Clan na Gael would lend its support to an informal agreement known as the 'New Departure', which was effectively a coalition of those pressing for land reform, Home Rule politicians and Fenians against British rule in Ireland, with land reform taking precedence in the list of nationalist aims.

However, the late nineteenth century witnessed the decline of the Fenian movement as new organisations such as the Land League and the National League took on the mantle of the Irish cause. Despite this, for the next thirty-five years, Devoy never wavered and continued his efforts on behalf of Irish Republicanism, engaging in various campaigns including fundraising tours across the country, such as the tour in 1914 to save St Enda's school (run by Padraig Pearse, later one of the principal leaders of the 1916 Easter Rising) from closure and the tour to provide financial support for the publication of the Clan na Gael newspaper the *Gaelic American*. Devoy edited the paper and frequently used his own articles as propaganda in order to recruit new Clan na Gael members, to continue to present the cause of Irish Republicanism to an American readership and, during the First World War, to do all in his power to persuade the USA not to enter the conflict, protesting vociferously when Woodrow Wilson eventually decided to support the Allies. During these years, Devoy had become the principal advocate of the Irish cause in the USA. In the words of Judge Harvey of Australia: 'he, the editor of *The Gaelic American*, has been for many years Clan Na Gael's leading spirit in America'.

The year 1914 saw Devoy still plotting against the Crown. That August he had a meeting with Roger Casement to plan the smuggling of an arms shipment, for use in a proposed future rebellion, into Ireland. They hoped to bring these arms in from Germany and liaised with America's principal German diplomat, Count Von Bernstroff. Devoy sought to convince the count that an Irish rebellion was a real possibility, and that any arms sent from Germany would be put to good use against the Crown forces stationed there. The idea of an Irish rebellion tying up British soldiers in Ireland rather than on the Western Front was attractive, and Von Bernstroff promised to relay Devoy's message to Berlin. Devoy also sent an envoy to Berlin to follow up on the count's report to the Kaiser. When the envoy returned, he presented Devoy with a document signed by the Kaiser himself recognising the Republic of Ireland, and a promise of German arms to be sent to Ireland when they were needed. Though now in his seventies, Devoy funded Roger Casement's visit to Germany to acquire these arms. They were despatched aboard the *Aud*, but the British captured the vessel before the arms could be landed.

Devoy was one of the very few men to be kept abreast of plans about the 1916 rising, a fact that in itself points to his reputation and significance in Republican circles. Though elderly, he planned to travel to Dublin for the event, but could not do so as his travel documents did not clear in time. Following the abortive rising, the aged Devoy remained in the USA throughout the period of the Anglo-Irish War and the Irish Civil War. He kept abreast of events, however, and considered Eamon de Valera to be 'an arrogant opportunist and a dangerous demagogue'. His distrust of de Valera meant that he supported the pro-treaty side in the Civil War, but his support made little material difference as a new generation of Irish Republican leaders had now emerged.

John Devoy died on 29 September 1928, in Atlantic City, New Jersey. He was brought back to Ireland for burial and, fittingly, he is buried in Glasnevin Cemetery in Dublin, where he lies alongside other nationalist leaders. He was almost unique among Irish republican leaders, as his longevity meant that he was one of the very few men involved in the Fenian rising that lived to see the Irish Free State in operation. He played a pivotal role in almost all the nationalist and republican events in the late nineteenth and early twentieth centuries. Today he is remembered by Irish Americans as well as at home. One American commentator put it very well when he wrote: 'Devoy was a rebel with a cause ... Certainly, few if any figures in the history of America and Ireland more fully embody the ties between our two people ... than John Devoy'. The unapologetic rebel from Kildare left a rich legacy and a long shadow.

SUCCESS AND FAILURE: INDUSTRIAL KILDARE

County Kildare's proximity to Dublin places it well within the commuter belt of Ireland's primate city. The capital is no more than an hour away from any part of the county and considerably less in the case of north Kildare. The fact that Kildare is adjacent to Dublin with its port, airport and excellent transport links has helped to attract industries to the county, and today Kildare is perceived as a wealthy county that is doing well from its industries. Older agriculturally based industries are well represented and there are numerous food processing companies including bakeries and meat factories, such as Kildare Chilling Company in Kildare town. The Glanbia Corporation (global leaders in the production of cheese, whey proteins and sports nutrition products) have a plant at Ballitore. Craft industries are also to the fore in Kildare; the best-known example is probably the world-renowned Newbridge Silverware Company, which also has a visitor centre in its hometown. However, the industry that has come to symbolise (but not define) modern Kildare is the computer industry. Many leading software and hardware companies have been attracted to the county, but the showcase example has to be the Intel plant at Leixlip. Intel Ireland has been located in the County Kildare town since 1989, when the company spent over $7 billion dollars turning a 360-acre stud farm into an ultra-modern computer facility. The geologically stable, level site, with adjacent motorway access and close to Dublin port and airport, was chosen with a view to future expansion of the plant. Intel Ireland, which produces microprocessors and silicon chips, is the largest manufacturing plant outside America and is Intel's European centre. It is a major employer in the area and has attracted many spin-off industries, as well as working closely with Ireland's universities, including the nearby campus of the National University of Ireland, Maynooth. Intel has been at the cutting edge of the computer industry over the years. It produced Intel Core 2 products and, at the time of writing, the plant is working on the Galileo development board – but this is an industry that changes so fast that products become obsolete very quickly. Whatever changes occur in years to come, Intel and Kildare are well placed to meet new challenges and are set to retain their place as global leaders in the future. However, the story of industrialisation in Kildare goes back a long way, and the county has a long history of start-up ventures. The rest of this chapter examines two such stories: one that began in the mid-eighteenth century and one in the mid-nineteenth. These two industries – Guinness stout and Thornton lace – met with very different fates over time.

GUINNESS STOUT

Arthur Guinness is possibly the best-known Irishman of all time. His name and his product have become synonymous with Ireland, which, rightly or wrongly, has a worldwide reputation as a country that likes its alcohol. This fact horrifies some Irish people and actually delights others, but this is not the place to delve into the correctness or otherwise of the perception of Ireland as a drinking nation. However, the perception that Guinness originated in Dublin can be shattered at the outset! Arthur Guinness was a Kildare man through and through.

Paradoxically for such a talismanic figure, little is known about Arthur's early life. He was born in 1725 in the Celbridge area of north Kildare. His father, Richard Guinness, was employed as a land steward by Archbishop Arthur Price of Cashel, and his job

'Leixlip River', *Illustrated London News*, 1884.

entailed, among other things, the supervision of brewing beer for the estate employees. Archbishop Price was Arthur Guinness's godfather and, when he died, he left a bequest of £100 to his 27-year-old godson in his will. Arthur evidently used the money wisely, and four years later he was the owner of a brewery in Leixlip. Thus the first Guinness's brewery was based in Kildare. However, in 1759, when Arthur was 34, he passed this on to his younger brother and went to Dublin to establish himself in the brewing trade there. He set up his brewery at St James's Gate – an address that has become iconic to many people – and began brewing beer. He had rented the premises on a 9,000-year lease, and it contained a copper, a mill, a kieve, two malthouses, twelve stables and a hayloft. On 1 December of that year, 'swearing day', Arthur Guinness first signed his name in the Dublin Brewers' and Maltmasters' minute book. Guinness was in business, but there was one cloud on the horizon. An adequate water supply was essential for the brewing trade. Dublin got its water supply from the Rivers Poddle and Dodder, and the city cistern was located at St James's Gate. Arthur's lease included a clause that stated he would receive his water supply free of tax. However, as the industry expanded, Dublin Corporation had to revisit this clause, and they tried to revoke Guinness's free water supply. Arthur stuck to his guns and on one occasion even used a pickaxe to threaten workmen who were sent to cut off the water, telling them in no uncertain terms (and in very colourful language) not to do so or they would have to answer to him. The workmen retreated, and the ensuing wrangle between Guinness and the Corporation lasted for many years, but eventually common sense reigned and an agreement acceptable to both sides was entered into.

As a brewer, Arthur Guinness participated a great deal in Dublin society and the city's public life. He accepted positions as governor of the Meath Hospital and secretary of the Friendly Brothers of St Patrick. He rose in his own trade too and by 1767 he was master of the Corporation of Brewers, later becoming the official brewer to Dublin Castle, the centre of British administration in Ireland and the hub of the civil service. When Arthur began production at St James's Gate, brewing was one of the handful of Irish industries that was doing relatively well. At this stage Arthur was brewing traditional Dublin brown ale and stout was unheard of. Irish brewers were under threat from English imports, however, and in the 1770s a new drink began appearing in Dublin hostelries. The new drink was made from roasted barley, making it almost black in colour, and was originally known as 'entire' because the entire amount was served from one barrel. However, its popularity with the porters of Billingsgate and Covent Garden markets soon earned it the nickname of 'porter'. Arthur rightly perceived the new product as a threat to home-produced ales, so he decided to brew his own brand of porter. He was the most successful Dublin brewer of the new drink, and eventually opted to solely concentrate on its production, ending his brewing of brown ale altogether in 1799. His choice turned out to be a wise one.

Surprisingly, beer was uncommon in rural Ireland at this time and the preference of the rural populace – the bulk of Ireland's population – was for gin, whiskey and the ever-present poteen (a spirit distilled illegally, usually from potatoes). Arthur's market expanded as the new porter slowly made its way into rural areas and proved popular with Irish rural people. By the final decade of the eighteenth century, Guinness had also been introduced to London hostelries and the boot was now on the other foot as it was exported from Ireland in large quantities. Guinness was becoming part of London life and an issue of the *Gentlemen's Magazine* in 1794 claimed optimistically that drinking Guinness would bring 'health, peace and prosperity'! Guinness was rapidly becoming recognised as a drink of choice among the upper as well as the labouring classes.

The success of Arthur's brewing venture meant that he had become a wealthy man. He married Olivia Whitmore, who was related to Ireland's most famous parliamentarian of the day, Henry Grattan. Their eldest son, Hosea, entered the Church of Ireland, taking holy orders and becoming curate at St Werburgh's church. Now in his seventies, and living in a fine house on Dublin's fashionable Gardiner Street, Arthur continued to turn up at the brewery every day, as well as riding out to visit his flour mills at Kilmainham, where Dublin's new gaol rose menacingly into the sky. This building would soon be filled with rebels captured at the time of the failed 1798 rising, but the conflict did not seem to affect the Guinness business. By the time of his death in 1803, Arthur Guinness, from County Kildare, had established what was to become a huge business empire. His body was returned to Kildare for interment, and his almost forgotten tomb may be visited today in the quiet country cemetery at Oughterard.

With Arthur's passing, the mantle of leadership fell to his son, another Arthur. He took over during a period of rapid expansion during the Napoleonic Wars, but the business was hit by the post-war slump after 1815. By the 1820s, Guinness sales were back down to a level not seen since the turn of the century. Arthur's response was inspired – he decided that quality was vital to improving sales – and in 1822 the company introduced a set of rules for the brewing of 'extra superior porter'. This was a brave decision, taken at a time when many other brewers were trying to cut costs by watering down their beers, but it paid off handsomely. Sales of the extra superior porter improved and those who had watered down their products went out of business one by one. With the demise of many other Dublin and provincial brewers, by the 1830s Guinness had unquestionably become the brewer with the largest brewery in Ireland. As the nineteenth century progressed, the Guinness business expanded, availing of the transport revolution and the advent of steamships to export the product to England and further afield throughout the British Empire, which then covered about a quarter of the globe. As Guinness gained in popularity in England, some interesting references to the beer emerged. It appeared in an illustration by Phiz in *The Pickwick Papers* by Charles Dickens, and Benjamin Disraeli, the British prime minister, recorded the fact that he had Guinness and oysters at London's Carlton hotel. The novelist Robert Louis Stevenson wrote that he would put himself 'outside a pint of Guinness' when he was in Samoa, to which he had brought his own supply of stout. The word 'stout' began to appear in the nineteenth century. It was first used as an adjective and Guinness was described as 'stout porter' to distinguish it from other, thinner porters. However, 'stout' was eventually used in its own right as a noun to describe Guinness. The name stuck, and probably owed its use to Arthur's decision to concentrate on the quality of the product during the recession of the 1820s. Following Arthur's death in 1855, the business continued to expand and it prospered throughout the twentieth century. The company continued to brew Guinness in the time-honoured fashion, using malt, yeast, hops and water. In 1997 Guinness merged with Grand Metropolitan to form the super company Diageo, which trades on the London stock exchange, but the production of Guinness remained at St James's Gate.

The Guinness Storehouse had been opened to the public and today it is a major tourist attraction in Dublin: Queen Elizabeth II and Prince Philip even visited it during their state visit in 2011. The famous beverage was celebrated on 'Arthur's Day', a commercial promotion of the product first held in 2009 to commemorate the 250th anniversary of the founding of Guinness's brewery, and involving live music and entertainment at many venues throughout Ireland and across the world. Little did those involved in the celebrations realise that the first brewery started by Arthur Guinness was founded earlier in the 1750s at Leixlip, County Kildare! As revellers worldwide enjoy a Guinness, the remains of Arthur, the man who began it all, repose in the quiet solitude of Oughterard cemetery.

THORNTON LACE

It is not widely known, but Thornton, a tiny rural townland in the parish of Kilcullen, County Kildare, holds an esteemed position in the world of lace making. There was a period during the mid-nineteenth century when Thornton lace was a much sought-after commodity and it was to be found in the homes of the rich and famous, not only in Ireland, but also in Britain, Continental Europe and even further afield. In common with much of County Kildare and with Ireland as a whole, the Kilcullen area experienced a population boom during the 1830s. However, that boom involved many of the rural poor and accelerated the creation of a large underclass of landless farm labourers and cottiers. A decade later, it was this underclass who were most devastated by the Great Famine. The famine impacted heavily on the Kilcullen area during the years 1845-50 and losses through death and emigration here were comparable to many of the worst-affected parts of the West of Ireland.

The role of the landlord class during the Famine has been much debated and Elizabeth Smith of Baltiboys House, who kept a diary throughout the Famine, was particularly scathing in her comments about the landlords of Kildare and neighbouring Wicklow at that time. Many landlords in the region did not enhance their reputation during the Famine but there were exceptions; the Smiths themselves, for example, did try to alleviate the horrendous poverty surrounding them. Another such example of attempted famine relief was the project instigated by Mrs W.C. Roberts of Thornton, and it was from this project that Thornton lace was born.

However, the story of Thornton lace really began much earlier and on the mainland of Europe. In the late 1820s, Mademoiselle Riego de la Blanchardiere discovered that a certain type of Spanish needlepoint could very effectively be adapted to Irish materials. In 1836 she published a book of patterns – a *magnum opus* that had taken her five years to compile. This book led to the establishment of many 'Crochet Centres' in Ireland, the first one being at the Ursuline Convent in Blackrock, County Cork. The sisters saw this new industry as a means of providing gainful employment for the girls in their care, so Irish crochet was often referred to as 'Nuns' Work' and that was certainly the case until the Great Famine struck the country in 1845. Crochet is often regarded as allied to, rather than as 'real', lace. It reputedly originated in the Orient and spread westwards through Europe: it was certainly popular in many convents in France long before the 1789 French Revolution. Its introduction to the Ursulines of Blackrock was probably through a French connection, as nuns from the Continent often made the journey to Ireland, but the real expansion of the craft occurred during the Famine and in the immediate post-Famine period.

Many areas of County Kildare experienced serious potato loss. On 1 December 1845, Archbishop Murray of Dublin was informed of the situation in Castledermot, where 'the affected potatoes become quickly decomposed' and 'the infected portion will be quickly exhausted, only two thirds, apparently sound, remain for food and for seed'. The parish priest, Fr Dunne, feared the onset of a 'calamity on the poor', because 'good seed potatoes will be beyond their reach'. Dunne was in no doubt about the gravity of the situation and hoped 'that here, as elsewhere, efforts will not be wanting ... in the impending calamity, to meet the necessities of our fellow-creatures, not only for the current, but for the succeeding year'. The conditions of the poor in County Kildare gave much cause for concern, and local gentry and clergy were called upon to help to alleviate the plight of the labourers. On 25 March 1846, a meeting was held in Naas to decide what public works should be proposed to lessen the effects of the twin food and financial crises in the Naas poor law union, which included Kilcullen.

In 1847, at the height of the famine, Mrs W.C. Roberts of Thornton, near Kilcullen, provided the initiative and drive to start up crochet in this area as a means of creating some employment for the famine-smitten poor of the district. The crochet industry in Cork gave employment to many girls, whom the mayor described as being 'in a state of the most helpless and hopeless idleness, a burden upon their humble parents and of little use to the community'. Mrs Roberts may have visited Cork in 1846 or 1847 and in a letter of hers that survives, she refers to the first crochet classes held at Thornton. The classes were started at a time when the polka [wool] knitting done in the district could no longer be marketed. Finding a piece of crochet that her sister-in-law had brought from Dover, she set five women to copy it. The piece was 'poorly designed, not unlike crabs and spiders in succession', but she lent the women 'bits of handsome old lace to study as well and of their own ingenuity they brought it [crochet] to its present perfection'. The knitting carried out in the other polka enterprise must, she observed, have given the workers some training in accuracy and speed. So began a cottage industry that was to thrive over the next decade or so.

In the middle of the nineteenth century, simple crochet was not only saleable, but also easy to make and launder as well as being cheap to produce. It needed no equipment except thread and a home-made hook and the rise of the middle classes in Europe in the second half of the nineteenth century, prior to the Franco-Prussian War of 1870, created a demand for a cheap form of lace. The Thornton lace industry flourished quickly and at its height in the early 1850s it employed about 700 workers. Although Thornton was a remote rural area, Kilcullen was the nearest urban centre of any size and a large proportion of the females employed by Mrs Roberts came from the town and its immediate hinterland. The industry was so successful that it generated payments of between £100 and £300 every month between the years 1852 and 1859 inclusive. As the workforce expanded, the level of skill improved and it was during the 1850s that specialised pieces of Thornton lace became prized possessions in many upper-class homes within the British Isles and far beyond their shores.

However, factors that would eventually cause the demise of the Thornton lace industry were now at work. As crochet centres spread throughout all of Ireland, the Thornton industry faced stiff competition. It has been suggested that the Thornton industry lost out 'for the want of strictness in compelling the workers to do perfect work'. The poor working conditions and uneducated workforce were probably factors in the refusal of some of the girls to take instruction from their teachers. 'They were supported in this independence by people who bought up their uncultivated work'. Poverty meant that the girls were more interested in producing quantity than quality and many of them sold their work as quickly as they could, as this speed of production generated a steady, if small, income from the lower middle-class market.

Coupled with the independent spirit of many workers was a suspicion of the intentions of their teachers and patrons, such as Mrs W.C. Roberts, if they belonged to the established Church of Ireland, which was not the Church of most of the girls employed; they were predominantly Roman Catholic. The girls were often ignorant of changing fashions abroad and, although Mrs Roberts kept up sales for as long as possible, the difficulty of getting good designs made by workers who wanted to follow their own ideas finally killed off the industry. By the 1860s, crochet had degenerated back into a cottage craft and the output was bought by unscrupulous commercial agents who were no longer motivated by any spirit of Famine relief in Ireland. Mrs Roberts now reported sadly that the total earnings of her school of Thornton lace were reduced to £2 10s per month.

Moreover, the post-Famine years saw the large-scale production of machine embroidery and lace, so handmade

'Interior of a mud cabin at Kildare', *Illustrated London News*, 9 April 1870.

crochet became an uncertain occupation. There was still a demand for really fine crochet work, but the Thornton standards had slipped and there was more competition around, notably from the newly established Clones lace industry. The demise of Thornton lace was, in fact, inextricably linked with the rise of Clones lace, and therein lies a tale of the pupil surpassing the master!

Shortly after the establishment of the Thornton lace industry in 1847, Mrs Cassandra Hand, wife of Revd Thomas Hand of Clones, County Monaghan, asked Mrs W.C. Roberts to send a teacher of crochet making to Clones in an effort to provide Famine relief similar to the Thornton model. In fact, in the years following 1847, Mrs Roberts' school of Thornton lace sent no less than twenty-eight teachers of crochet to various distressed districts of Ireland. Cassandra Hand had been in contact with Mrs J. Maclean from Tynan in County Armagh, who, in turn, had visited Colonel and Mrs Tottenham of New Ross in County Wexford. Both the Tottenhams and the Macleans had received crochet teachers from Mrs Roberts in Thornton. The diffusion of crochet teachers from Thornton to Clones thus went via Wexford and Armagh.

Mrs Cassandra Hand was a remarkable woman. She threw herself into the new venture with great energy and she had considerable business acumen. A cottage industry took root in Clones and it thrived. Within a few years, 1,500 people were employed in making Clones lace. Of course, Clones was a much larger urban centre than rural Thornton, or even Kilcullen, but it was not the larger size of the Clones workforce (at one stage Mrs Hand was very worried that her creation was getting too large) that signalled the death knell for the Thornton product. It was, rather, the superior quality of the Clones material that ensured its survival in a post-Famine world of increased competition and new methods of mass production. In an ironic twist, the crochet teacher sent by Mrs Roberts to Mrs Hand was actually too good, and her higher standards established the fineness of Clones lace as a byword for quality. By the 1860s, Clones had totally outstripped the now almost defunct Thornton as a lace-making centre. The lessons learned in Thornton bore fruit in Clones and the high standards established in the Monaghan town, where careless and inferior work was immediately rejected in no uncertain terms by Mrs Hand, meant that just as Mrs Roberts' teachers had spread from her centre in Thornton, Mrs Hand and her successors sent teachers into neighbouring counties to teach the Clones type of crochet. Lace from these northern counties became famous in its own right, but none more so than the original Clones lace, and formed a specialised part of a wider northern textile industry, which eventually became best-known for the production of linen. However, the seed that spawned this northern lace industry originated right the townland of Thornton, on the eastern border of County Kildare. In yet another twist to the tale, Thornton lace became very collectable as the years rolled on. The short duration of the Thornton industry meant that surviving samples of Thornton lace work are quite rare and they now command an extremely high price at sales and auctions. Thornton lace is well known and widely respected in the world of lace collectors, and much of the earlier work in particular is among the best examples of its kind anywhere. Today, the industry is almost forgotten, but while Mrs W.C. Roberts' 'white stuff' may not ultimately have been as commercially successful as Arthur Guinness's 'black stuff', the name 'Thornton lace' is instantly recognised and revered by the curators of lace collections in museums all over the world.

KILDARE'S LITERARY LADIES

Over the years, Kildare has produced more than its fair share of female writers. This chapter briefly examines the lives and careers of four of these ladies.

MARY LEADBEATER

Mary Leadbeater was born Mary Shackleton in the village of Ballitore, home to a large Quaker community, in 1758. The Shackleton family were well established in Ballitore in the eighteenth century. Mary, a diarist, was herself a member of the Society of Friends, and her religious beliefs coloured every aspect of her life and her writing, which faithfully recorded village life over a long period of time.

She was a granddaughter of Abraham Shackleton, an English immigrant who had founded a boys' school when he arrived in Ballitore. His school quickly gained a good reputation, and Abraham did not confine his education to Quaker boys, taking in students of all faiths. The list of old boys included men of very disparate backgrounds and beliefs, including the politician and rhetorician Edmund Burke, the revolutionary James Napper Tandy and the Roman Catholic cleric Cardinal Paul Cullen. Abraham's son succeeded him as the local schoolmaster and Mary was born in the master's residence of the school. She lived at the school until 1791, when she married William Leadbeater and moved into his house in the main square of the village.

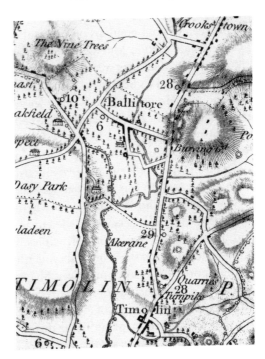

Ballitore in
Alexander Taylor's
map of 1783.

Mary was an avid reader and a well-educated woman,
and her diary provides a window on rural life in Kildare during
the late eighteenth and early nineteenth centuries. It revealed
a multitude of characters in its pages, painting a picture of
pleasant rural life, though her recording of tragic events such
as child mortality occasionally revealed the dark side of life in
Ballitore. Indeed, Mary's own daughter died in an accident in
her house.

During the 1790s, Ireland was becoming very politicised
due to the influence of the French Revolution. The Society of
United Irishmen espoused French Republican ideals, and in
Kildare the organisation comprised a majority of Catholics
who had suffered various forms of discrimination at the hands
of the Anglican-controlled state. Mary's writings show that she
was attracted by the ideals of liberty, equality and fraternity,
but she was a woman of her times and women were not

usually seen to hold opinions on political matters. In addition to her female status, Mary Leadbeater was also a Quaker. Like Catholics, Quakers were not members of the established Church, and had to be careful in relation to what they both said and did. However, Mary's diary was a private document and was not meant for publication. She could safely record her thoughts and opinions on its pages, such as her opinions on the repressive actions of the government. In 1795 she recorded a sickening spectacle that she witnessed while journeying through Naas: 'On top of the jail at Naas is fixed the head of Connor the schoolmaster, who was hanged for being a Defender'. The Defenders were a violent agrarian secret society and, though Mary's religious principles meant that she was opposed to violence, she displayed sympathy for the grievances of the oppressed local population. She concluded the entry about the schoolmaster Connor by reflecting that he 'showed on his trial a spirit worthy of a better cause'.

Mary kept abreast of political developments and often quoted William Godwin's *Political Justice* in her own writings. She certainly saw the general air of political change in the wake of the failed French landing at Bantry Bay. In December 1796 she wrote 'Robinson, the minister of Bomba Hall ... expressed very liberal sentiments, and rather more in the new way that one should expect from his cloth. Republicanism, both in Church and State affairs, seemed now to be very prevalent; and serious divisions arose in our society'. Mary's own gradual awakening to the aspirations of the United Irishmen was reflected in her friendship with the Delany brothers, Malachi and Peter. Malachi in particular was one of the principal agents of radicalisation and a leading member of the United Irishmen in the Ballitore region.

Mary's diary also acts as a unique primary source for historians of the 1798 rebellion, in which Ballitore was heavily involved. During the period immediately before the insurrection, she noted 'William Cooke, of Ballylea, about three miles hence, was attacked by a number of men, who set fire to his house, and demanded his arms. The house was burned, the family went to Baltinglass, and we all saw with dread the approaching flames of discord'. Her premonition regarding 'the approaching flames of discord' was to prove, unfortunately, all too true. She also recorded that there was 'too much exultation in the military'. Once again, this observant woman hit the nail on the head. The populace could only be pushed so far before a reaction occurred. When the rebellion broke out in May 1798, Mary wrote: 'All was uncertainty, except that something serious had happened, as the mail-coach had been stopped ... sad havoc ensued; many on both sides fell, particularly among the undisciplined multitude. The courthouse at Narraghmore was attacked, and many met their death there'. She went on to record the event at local level in grim detail. When the Irish national broadcaster RTÉ made a major television documentary about the rebellion, readings from Mary's diary featured prominently.

The diary is best known for its account of the rebellion, but it is also an important socioeconomic record of life in rural Ireland over many decades, spanning the period from 1766 to 1824. Two years before she died, Mary complied her writings into a unique record of village life through a turbulent era. She died in Ballitore in 1826 and, though she published other material during her lifetime, the work that has made her famous was only published posthumously in two volumes entitled *The Leadbeater Papers* in 1862. Volume one contains her diary, entitled *The Annals of Ballitore*, a work now familiar to all serious students of Kildare's rich history.

EMILY LAWLESS

Emily Lawless came from a very different background to Mary Leadbeater. She was born into a gilded lifestyle, the fourth child of Edward and Elizabeth Lawless of Lyons House, County Kildare. Her father was the 3rd Baron Cloncurry and the young Emily was brought up in England, often visiting her mother's relatives in the west of Ireland. The novelist Margaret Oliphant encouraged Emily to become a writer and her first work, *A Chelsea Householder*, was published in London in 1882. This early work, in three volumes, was a romantic fiction about a female artist and was followed up in 1885 by the publication of another novel entitled *A Millionaire's Cousin*. In that year she turned her attention to Irish subject matter and published *Ireland: A History* as part of the Unwin 'Story of Nations' series. However, though she was to deal with Irish-subject material in many of her books, she was an unlikely Irish writer. Her Loyalist background was out of keeping with many other Irish writers of the time. The late nineteenth century was the apex of the Irish literary renaissance and the Anglo-Irish literary revival was in full swing. There is no doubt that many works dating from this time presented an idealised and romantic portrayal of Ireland and all things Irish. Lawless's next novel, *Hurrish*, published in 1886, underlined many of the differences between her and the mainstream writers of the Celtic Revival era.

Hurrish is set in County Clare, amid the bleak Burren landscape of Ireland during the Land War, and features a murder in the locality. The chief suspect is the title character, Hurrish O'Brien, but the local magistrate (who is also a landlord) does not believe Hurrish to be the perpetrator and will not allow his arrest. This action increases the landlord's popularity with the local peasantry, who are portrayed as putting class loyalties before the desire to see justice done. The attitude of the local people in the novel was at odds with the romantic ideal of the Irish peasant so prevalent in the literature of the day. The book was very influential, but received mixed reviews. It was well received abroad, however, with *The New York Times* claiming that no other work 'will carry more weight or reach a larger circle', and the *Scotsman* contending that it painted a realistic picture of Irish life. In England the prime minister, William Ewart Gladstone, thanked Lawless for the novel, which he said demonstrated 'not as an abstract proposition, but as a living reality, the estrangement of the people of Ireland from the law'. However, Nationalist Ireland was hostile to the novel as in the book, the author had made it clear that she was not a supporter of the Home Rule movement and regarded the whole idea as folly. A review in the *Nation* maintained that her portrayal of the Irish peasantry was outrageous and insisted that she had exaggerated peasant violence out of all proportion. The *Nation* did not mince its words, stating that the author looked down on the Irish lower classes from 'the pinnacle of her three-generation nobility', and contemptuously dismissed *Hurrish* as 'slanderous and lying from cover to cover'.

Emily Lawless's novel had created a storm that reflected her place as an outsider within the milieu of the Anglo-Irish literary revival. Though she corresponded regularly with some of the principal figures of the movement, including Lady Augusta Gregory and William Butler Yeats, Lawless was never at home in their world and did not share many of their opinions. She once stayed for a weekend at Coole Park with Lady Gregory. Yeats was also present and he and Lawless argued incessantly. Yeats insisted that a writer's first duty was to his or her art. Lawless disagreed, pointing to the necessity of some writers to earn money to support themselves and their families. Gregory was quick to defend Yeats and his idealism, suggesting that Lawless's mercenary attitude might be expected due to her British and commercial background. It is true that the British Loyalist Lawless thought Yeats was disloyal, but Gregory's comments were little short of ethnic profiling! Yeats would later say of Emily Lawless that she was 'in imperfect sympathy with the Celtic nature, and has accepted the commonplace conception of Irish character as something charming, irresponsible, poetic, dreamy, untrustworthy, voluble, and rather despicable, and the commonplace conception of English character as something prosaic, hard, trustworthy, silent altogether worshipful and the result is a twofold slander'. Given Yeats's own background and his struggle, especially in his earlier work, to create a romantic

Irish identity, his view of Lawless is perhaps more than a little ironic. The two writers evidently experienced a personality clash as well as a cultural one, and perhaps what Yeats really meant was that Lawless did not conform to his idea or ideal of Irishness, embodied in his view of the Celtic nature.

Lawless, who sometimes wrote under the pseudonym Edith Lytton, was undaunted by the controversy over *Hurrish* and in 1890 published another work set in Ireland, this time a historical novel entitled *With Essex in Ireland*. This novel and its sequel *Maelcho*, which appeared in 1894, both attracted negative responses from Irish Nationalists. The books were set during the Desmond rebellions, ending with the unsuccessful Spanish landing at Smerwick Harbour, but Nationalists maintained that the characterisation of the Irish, and especially of Maelcho himself, was little short of ignorant savages, while the English were portrayed in a superior light. Some readers have taken the characterisation in the novels to symbolise Lawless's belief that the Irish nation was not capable of governing itself, and perceive the works as an anti-Home Rule vehicle. Despite this, ironically Yeats included *With Essex in Ireland* in his list of 'thirty best books', because, he stated, 'it helps one ... to imagine Elizabethan Ireland, and certainly does contain one memorable scene in which the multitudes slain in the Irish war rise up complaining'.

Lawless published many other books, including *Grania* (1892), which was about a girl from the island of Inishmaan who eventually commits suicide. Again, many people frowned upon the storyline and the inclusion of the taboo subject of suicide, but this was a work ahead of its time. Its depiction of the Irish peasant class was a forerunner to similar later works such as John Millington Synge's *Riders to the Sea* and even the short stories of Liam O'Flaherty. Lawless's prodigious literary output continued into the early twentieth century. Though she remained a controversial figure, she later received a D.Litt. from Trinity College, Dublin, and the enigmatic and perhaps misunderstood Kildare author died on 19 October 1913.

B.M. CROKER

Though not a native of Kildare, the novelist B.M. Croker has strong associations with the village of Rathangan in the west of the county. Birtha Mary Sheppard was born in 1849 in County Roscommon, and her father was Revd William Sheppard, the rector of Kilgefin. Very little is known about her early life, but by 1870 or so she was resident in Rathangan and riding with the Kildare Hunt. She married an officer in the British Army, Lieutenant John Croker (1844-1911), in 1871. The marriage took place in the Church of Ireland church in Rathangan, and the couple lived in Oakley House in the village for a number of years in the 1870s, from 1871 until 1876, when their names were crossed out in the Valuation records of the time. Birtha did not write anything during her time in Rathangan; perhaps she was busily looking after a young child, as her only daughter Gertrude was born there in 1872. Before long Birtha's husband John was posted to India and she soon found herself in Madras, where John was first stationed. The couple moved about the subcontinent during their time there, later going to Bengal and being posted to a hill station in Wellington. In all, Birtha spent fourteen years living in India and it was there in 1882 that she began writing.

Birtha was 33 years old when her first work, *Proper Pride*, was published in 1882. Sales of the novel increased significantly when William Ewart Gladstone was seen perusing it during a lengthy debate in parliament. Birtha promptly followed up her first novel with *Pretty Miss Neville* in 1883. In all she continued writing for thirty-seven years, finishing in 1919, and her literary canon ran to over fifty books. Many of her works were set in the British colonial world, mostly against the backdrop of Indian military life, but some were also set in Egypt and other parts of the African continent. She wrote popular fiction and her works usually contained a heroine who had to undergo many setbacks before she could finally be united with her one true love.

It is, however, perhaps harsh to stereotype her books as light romantic fiction as her work, which contains many deep and very well-written passages, has been compared to more serious Victorian contemporaries such as Thomas Hardy. Her portrayal of life in India under the British Raj and the cultural context of her work have also been the subjects of posthumous academic studies.

Following John Croker's retirement from the army, the family returned to Ireland and lived for a time in a cottage in County Wicklow. Birtha also set some of her stories such as *Beyond the Pale* (1890) and *Lismoyle* (1914) in Ireland. Before she left for India, Birtha had ridden with the Kildare Hunt and foxhunting in Ireland formed the backdrop to part of the plot in her 1891 work *Interference*. The story of greatest significance in the context of Kildare, however, is the 1918 novel *Bridget*, in which the author evidently drew heavily on her life experiences in Rathangan. The military camp on the Curragh, the Bog of Allen, the Grand Canal and the Canal Stores all feature in the book. The action is set in a place called Rathkill, a fictitious name incorporating both Rathangan and Kildare. However, other smaller landmarks mentioned in the text pinpoint the location of the imaginary Rathkill squarely in the Rathangan area – the two locks on the canal, the glebe, the Leinster Arms Hotel, the Bullring and place names Bracknagh, Rathilla and the Derries are all mentioned.

B.M. Croker also had another string to her bow, however. In addition to romantic tales, she was also a renowned writer of supernatural fiction, and many of her works incorporated a Gothic element of which she was very fond and at which she was very adept. During the late nineteenth and early twentieth centuries, ghost stories and stories of the occult and the macabre were extremely popular and were ravenously devoured by the reading public of the day. Here again, Birtha drew on her early life experiences in Kildare. Despite the reforms of the Roman Catholic devotional revolution and the Synod of Maynooth, there was another world of hidden

Kildare Hounds at Canny Court, ILSDN.

belief out of sight of the new Catholic chapels. This was the world of fairy legend, and belief in fairies persisted in Kildare throughout the nineteenth century. According to these legends, fairies inhabited an 'otherworld', and contact between this and the real world formed the basis of many stories. Fairies, it was believed, existed under the earth, in air and in water and lived parallel lives to humans. They could steal children away, leaving changelings in their place; they could bring disease on crops, animals, farm produce (such as milk and butter) and humans – but they could also reward kindness. Fairies were strongly identified with place, and hills and ancient earthen mounds where they supposedly abided were perceived as places of sanctity. In Kildare, Gormanstown Hill near Kilcullen was such a place. In 1863, Fr John Francis Shearman (who was the parish priest of Moone for a time) recorded a fairy legend concerning the fairies of Gormanstown to which some 'persons now living' attested. According to the legend, the fairies were luring cattle from a neighbouring area to Gormanstown Hill at milking times, thus causing economic distress to their owners. Local people consulted a fairyman, who told them to implore another fairy host to protect them and to stop the harmful activities of the Gormanstown host. This was done, and in the words of Fr Shearman:

> When milking time came, the cattle as usual fled frantic and excited from their pastures. They galloped as usual through the town to the ford [on the River Griese]. Here they were stopped and could go no further. They bellowed and pawed the ground. A whirlwind raised a cloud of dust around them and enveloped the entire herd. This was looked on as a most extraordinary appearance, and no one doubted that a fierce combat was being waged in the whirlwind above the flock by the rival fairies. When all was calm, and the dust and storm laid, the cattle were driven home from the side of the ford, and the ground where they stood was sprinkled with drops of blood, which was believed to have fallen from the wounds of the ethereal combatants.

This narrative is revealing of the nature of folk beliefs in nineteenth-century Kildare. Many high-altitude sites were believed to be fairy forts or fairy raths, and the association of fairies with hills and ancient mounds places beliefs in Kildare in line with those of other parts of Ireland. The failure of cows to give milk – the principal source of income for many agricultural families and a commodity also associated with female fertility and child-bearing – was another common theme of fairy legends in many parts of Ireland. However, the most significant part of Shearman's account concerns the consultation of a fairyman. Nineteenth-century antiquaries noted the existence of 'fairy doctors', whom country people consulted for the relief of illness and injury in humans and animals. The existence of such a figure suggests that belief in fairy forces was strong within the local community, rivalling the ever-growing power of the priests. Despite the devotional revolution and the omniscient presence of the Church and its clergy, the gap between the official beliefs and the actual beliefs of many local people ensured that folk belief flourished in Kildare in the 1860s.

In addition to fairies, other spirits also figured prominently in the folk beliefs of nineteenth-century Kildare. Ghosts formed an almost tangible part of these beliefs. Perhaps the most feared supernatural manifestation was the banshee. Literally meaning the 'fairy woman', this female spirit was a harbinger of death. Described as a wizened old woman combing her hair, this spirit was witnessed by a number of people in Kildare in the second half of the nineteenth century. Hauntings and the superstitions associated with them were part of the everyday life of many Kildare people in the nineteenth century, and Birtha drew on these experiences in writing her supernatural tales which, like her romantic stories, sold very well and brought her great financial success. In 1897, Birtha moved to Folkestone and she died there in 1920. Some of her supernatural short stories are still published today in anthologies of the genre.

TERESA BRAYTON

Many Irish people know, have sung or have listened to the sentimental emigrant song 'The Old Bog Road'. Over the years numerous Irish artists including Josef Locke, Johnny McEvoy, Finbar Furey, Daniel O'Donnell and Louise Morrissey have recorded it. However, one wonders how many of those listening know that a Kildare woman, Teresa Brayton, wrote the song. Born Teresa Boylan at Kilbrook, Kilcock in 1868, she was a renowned writer, poet and Irish nationalist. Little is known about Teresa's youth, but it is recorded that she was educated at Newtown school, close to Enfield. When her schooldays were at an end, she became a teaching assistant, helping her sister Elizabeth, who was a fully-fledged teacher at the time. The young woman became interested in the Irish nationalist cause and submitted some poems to the nationalistic newspaper the *Nation*, which were published under the initials T.B. However, Teresa's opportunities were limited in Ireland so, like so many of her contemporaries, she decided to emigrate and sailed to America in 1895, eventually settling in

Boston. Also like many of her emigrant contemporaries, she got married in her new land, in her case to a French-Canadian called Richard Brayton. However, tragedy struck and Teresa was widowed shortly afterwards. She threw herself with renewed vigour into her nationalist writing, and was published extensively in many Irish-American periodicals. In 1913 she published her first volume of poetry entitled *Songs of the Dawn*, which included the now famous emigrant lament 'The Old Bog Road', which was later set to music by Madeline O'Farrelly of Rochfortbridge, County Westmeath.

Apart from the emigrant experience of Ireland's Diaspora, of which she was a part, Teresa Brayton's works also concentrated on themes such as nationalism, Celtic myths, spirituality and, like B.M. Croker, the supernatural. Her poems included such titles as 'In Bethlehem', 'Rosary Time in Ireland', 'The Land Where Fairies Play', 'A Druid Speaks' and 'The Green and the White and the Gold'.

Brayton also grew up in a place where superstitions about fairies and the otherworld abounded, and her fascination with the Celtic past was in keeping both with the literary trend in Ireland during the Anglo-Irish Renaissance of the late nineteenth and early twentieth centuries and the wider contemporary international craving for stories of ghosts and the occult.

Her nationalistic ideals put her in touch with many of the leaders of the Easter Rising of 1916, some of whom she met during their visits to America, and she wholeheartedly supported their cause and the Irish electorate's swing towards Sinn Féin in the wake of their military failure. Countess Con Markievicz sent her a letter enclosing part of the flagpole from which the tricolour floated over the GPO, which can be seen today in the Teresa Brayton Memorial Library, Kilcock. She continued writing, publishing *The Flame of Ireland* in 1926. Unlike emigrants who were less wealthy, Teresa frequently returned to Ireland, and maintained a keen interest in political matters throughout the period of the Irish Revolution and the birth of the new state. In 1932 she returned permanently to Ireland, first settling in Dublin before later moving back to her native area in 1940. Shortly after her return to Ireland she gave an interview to the *Irish Press* in which she stated: 'I feel that it is the crowning glory of my return to Ireland that Mr De Valera's party has come to power'. The author was evidently both deeply involved and hugely admired in Irish political circles. She died in 1943 and Eamon De Valera, who was still Taoiseach of Ireland, was present at her funeral in Cloncurry cemetery. In 1959, when he was President of Ireland, De Valera returned to the spot to unveil a monument – a Celtic cross – over her grave. Today, visitors to Teresa Brayton's area of north Kildare may not know that they are passing by the old bog road, but most of them will have heard the song, and many of them will know the words. Historians may argue that there was more to the Kildare author than just one ballad, but perhaps her greatest memorial is the enduring popularity of the song and its sentiments.

A COUNTY IN CHAOS:
KILDARE IN 1798

In many places, 1798 is remembered as the year of the great Irish rebellion, and it all started in County Kildare. Contrary to popular belief, the revolt was not confined to parts of Ulster, Wexford and Mayo, though certainly these areas saw some of the heaviest fighting. However, many areas of the country were also affected, and the conflict was prolonged in Kildare; Timahoe camp (in the west of the county) for example, held out against the authorities long after the Wexford rebels had been crushed. The whole rebellion came as a shock to the British authorities, who knew of the activities of the United Irishmen and thought that they had averted the threat of a revolution, because many United Irish leaders were arrested before the rebellion. However, in many places, including Kildare, it was local rebels – with local figures to lead them – who were involved in the rising.

The existence of the United Irishmen was central to events in 1798. The following extract from their 'catechism' makes their aims abundantly clear.

Question:	What have you got in your hand?
Answer:	A green bough.
Question:	Where did it first grow?
Answer:	In America.
Question:	Where did it bud?
Answer:	In France.
Question:	Where are you going to plant it?
Answer:	In the crown of Great Britain.

Here, then, was an organisation that posed a threat to the British authorities, and all who were loyal to the British Crown. It made reference to both the American War of Independence and the French Revolution, both of which were anathema to Great Britain and its monarchy. The American War of Independence threatened the very concepts of empire and British superiority in an age of imperialism. The loss of the American colonies was the first real blow suffered by the British Empire, and it cut deeply. The colonies were gone, but at least they were 3,000 miles away. Now Ireland, the island on Britain's doorstep, was showing separatist tendencies and British Loyalists (in Ireland as well as in Britain) were horrified. The French Revolution did not affect Britain as directly as the American Revolution, in that the Empire lost no land as a result of it. However, in its own way, it had an even more profound effect on British Loyalists, because it threatened the very concept of monarchy. Europe's *Ancien Regime* and the idea of the divine right of monarchs were swept aside. After all, who were Irish Loyalists loyal to, if not the monarch? Coupled with this, in the British case, the monarch was the head of the Anglican Church (in both England and Ireland). In Ireland, where the overwhelming majority of the population was Catholic, religious fears grew and added to the Loyalist anxiety about Republicanism in the form of the United Irishmen rearing its ugly head.

The eighteenth century was generally peaceful in Ireland, but by the 1790s the situation had changed. Agrarian unrest, Republican ideas and continuing religious problems contributed to the melting pot that was Ireland in the 1790s. In October 1791, the society of United Irishmen was founded in Belfast and before its inaugural meeting on 18 October, thirty-six members – including Theobald Wolfe Tone – had already been secured; an additional six were elected on that occasion. Its objectives were to achieve a cordial union among all the people in Ireland, to bring about a radical reform of parliamentary representation, and to secure the inclusion in that reform of Irishmen of every religious persuasion. However, as the 1790s wore on, the organisation became much more radical, seeking to break the link with Britain altogether. By 1796 Wolfe Tone was aboard a French ship, but inclement weather prevented a French landing at Bantry, County Cork in 1796. The frustrated Tone had prepared an 'Address to the People of Ireland' for the occasion, part of which stated: 'The alternative which is now submitted to your choice, with regard to England, is, in one word, union or separation! You must determine, and that instantly, between slavery and independence; there is no third way.'

Predictably, in such a political climate, Loyalists were uneasy. The Orange Order was founded in 1795, to counter the threat posed by a Catholic agrarian movement called the Defenders. The order, however, also opposed the United Irishmen. The possibility of a French invasion and the Republican threat was enough to ensure that Loyalists' attitudes hardened and, after 1796, there was a hard-line Loyalist backlash against the Whigs (more liberal Loyalists). This led to a reign of terror being unleashed throughout much of Ulster and Leinster – and that terror lingered longer in Kildare than elsewhere. Suspects were rounded up all over the county and tortured. In Prosperous, Captain Richard Swayne favoured the use of the pitch cap. This consisted of a bowl of boiling pitch or tar placed on the prisoner's head. When the tar solidified, the bowl or 'cap' was forcibly removed, often taking the scalp and sometimes even parts of the brain with it. Some suspects died; some went mad; nearly all gave information.

Despite, or perhaps because of such atrocities, the society of United Irishmen was growing rapidly. In County Kildare, as elsewhere, the society flourished, and the county provided one of the leading figures within the organisation. Lord Edward Fitzgerald of Carton House, Maynooth was a son of the Duke of Leinster, born into a life of luxury. He joined the British Army in 1779 and fought in the American War of Independence. He later went to Canada and crossed that vast country, being made a Huron chief on the journey. When he returned to Europe, he became an ardent supporter of the

French Revolution, travelling to Paris to see the revolution in action. On his return to Ireland, he joined the United Irishmen and began actively to plot a rebellion, becoming one of the principal leaders of the movement in Leinster. The United Irishmen was a secret society, and many of their records do not survive. However, we do have figures for the numbers of United Irishmen in most areas of Leinster for the spring of 1798. Kildare had the second largest membership: 11,919. Only County Wicklow returned a higher number.

On the other side of the coin, County Kildare had a large Loyalist population. However, the local Loyalists were divided. The basic division was between the hard-line Loyalists (Tories or Conservatives) on the one hand and the easier-going liberals (Whigs) on the other. Whigishness was a talking point among Loyalists, but it became a threat when faced with the growth of the United Irish organisation, and there was talk of a French invasion. One dominant Loyalist in County Kildare, however, was not a Whig – far from it, in fact. The Earl of Aldborough had a mansion called Belan, near Athy in County Kildare, and his parliamentary seat was also in Kildare.

On 9 June 1797, Aldborough's younger brother, Benjamin O'Neale Stratford, wrote from Wicklow to Dublin Castle. His letter stated 'I hear that the contagion of the County Kildare is likely to creep into this part'. Another letter to the castle from John Ravell Walsh, written in the same week informed the authorities that attacks on ultra-Loyalist figures had already begun in Kildare. However, if United Irishmen were to be convicted successfully, solid evidence was needed. Hard-line Loyalist fears regarding the leniency of the magistrates did not take into account the fact that those self-same magistrates could not act harshly if they lacked such evidence. Even if suspects were arrested, they might walk free if the courts could not convict them. This led to a type of revolving-door system in the prisons, which did little to ease Loyalist fears or anger. Evidence of this system in operation is contained in a letter written by Judge Robert Day from Naas on 16 August 1797:

Sixteen prisoners have been this evening discharged, each of whom I have no doubt would be acquitted, and who now, instead of the triumph and audacity inspired by impunity, carry home with them impressions of the moderation and mercy of that Government which they are taught to abhor ... Thus Connolly has committed twelve or fourteen as implicated in the same offence, and though the information be very loosely drawn, and the committal such as they might well be bailed upon ... I have been forced to grope my way here for want of evidence, and much time has been wasted in dispatching expenses through this county for the justices.

Loyalists were anxious, and the Orange Order, recently formed in the north of the country, was one way for Loyalists to express their feelings, and the movement spread rapidly. Orangeism was widespread in Kildare. Evidence of the activities of the Orangemen was contained in a letter that was found in the drawing room of John Harte on 27 March 1798.

We are very glad too, or that you got yourself made a United Man, for you will know all their secrets, you are the only man in that county that we can depend upon to give us all intelligence ... We understand the barony you live in is very strong and in general the whole county. You had better make out a list how many United men in the country, as you said you could do it and send it to us in Naas ... and we will all know better what to do, may our orange cockade be strengthened, now over from our society at present.
I.H., I.C., C.W., D.J. 4 friends,
Burn this letter as soon as you read it.

The spread of the Orange Order into County Kildare also saw the spread of sectarian tensions throughout the area. Kildare was polarising along sectarian lines as the new year of 1798 dawned. Among the final batch of letters received in Dublin Castle in 1797 was one from Mr R. Nevill of

Furness, Naas, to Edward Cooke, the under-secretary, dated 10 December 1797. Nevill was worried about the increasing number of robberies, especially those involving the theft of arms in the region.

> There having been six robberies committed since last Sunday, vid. the widow Finnamore near Kilteel, where two blunderbusses were fired into the house and one man severely wounded. Peter Burchill's of Kilteel, where one blunderbuss was fired and both houses robbed of arms. Roberts and Byrne of Rathmore of arms and money, and Hill of Cromwellstown of money; also Adam Abraham and Slater at Beggar's Inn; we think it would be not only useful but necessary to have an officer and twenty men stationed at the village of Rathmore.

The response of the government to continuing and increasing United Irish activity in the country was to clamp down hard on the suspected Republicans, which in practice meant on the Catholic populace. The military's reign of terror spread from Ulster into Leinster. County Kildare merited special attention; the activities of Captain Swayne in Prosperous and Colonel Campbell in Ballitore were notorious.

A unique record of events in the village of Ballitore has survived, because a local woman kept a detailed diary. Towards the end of 1797, Mary Leadbeater wrote:

> Soldiers now constituted part of the inhabitants of Ballitore; the Cork militia were stationed here. William Cooke, of Ballylea, about three miles hence, was attacked by a number of men, who set fire to his house, and demanded his arms. The house was burned, the family went to Baltinglass, and we all saw with dread the approaching flames of discord.

Leadbeater's diary contained more instances of violence in and around Ballitore as the spring of 1798 wore on. Early in 1798, she wrote:

Amongst other precautions, the names of the inhabitants were posted on the doors of each house, and the authorities had liberty to enter at any hour, night or day, to see whether they were within or not. This appeared a necessary precaution, yet it exposed the quiet of families to be sadly broken in upon. Houses were now searched for fire-arms, proving the wisdom of our friends in banishing all such weapons from theirs. Notices were put up demanding the arms taken by the 'United men' to be restored, on pain of allowing the military to live at free quarters; for many nightly incursions had been made by these robbers to plunder houses of whatever arms they contained. A detachment of the King's County militia was at this time sent here from Athy, where Sandford Palmer, an old Ballitore Boy, was stationed as their captain.

The government's reign of terror was now spreading into the Ballitore region, where the enforced billeting of soldiers in people's houses (free quarters) was put into operation, as Mary Leadbeater testified:

The threat respecting free quarters was now put into execution; foraging parties went into the country, shops and private houses were searched for whisky, which was ordered to be spilled; and seditious papers were sought for … Robert Bayley was pursued because he attempted to take away one of his own horses; his horse was captured, and himself made a prisoner. Ephraim Boake's house was plundered, and he very narrowly escaped personal injury.

The diary also recorded the continuing and increasing violence fuelled by the free quarters tactic:

Great waste was committed, and unchecked robbery. One hundred cars loaded with hay, potatoes, oats etc. led by the poor owners, and guarded by soldiers, were in one day marched into Ballitore. Colonel Keatinge urged his yeomen to take with a sparing hand; to remember that this was the "scarce season," when the new food was not yet come in and the old was nearly exhausted, and not to bring famine upon the country. But he spoke to deaf ears, for pity seemed banished from the martial bosom ... Public Notice was given that the nightly patrol should be withdrawn, to give opportunity for returning the arms of which the "United men" had possessed themselves, and that if not returned within a stated time, the whole neighbourhood should be burnt.

Blacksmiths came in for particular persecution as suspected pike-makers; Owen Finn of Narraghmore, for example, was executed in 1798. The military clampdown was enforced with rigour. In Ballitore, the clampdown was quite effective and the once tiny number of captured United Irish arms was increasing in May 1798. Squire Keatinge, having raised a regiment, now became a colonel. However, Keatinge was noted for his liberal views, and Keatinge's corps was constantly under suspicion for United Irish activities. In May 1798, the squire bowed to Loyalist pressures and decided to leave the area. With Keatinge gone, whatever protection he had given to his men had also disappeared. The way lay open for a full-scale Loyalist backlash in the area, and the military presence was stepped up to enforce such measures as were deemed necessary to root the United Irishmen out of the local yeomanry. Once again, the observant Mary Leadbeater noted the increasing number of soldiers in her diary.

The Ancient Britons, dressed in blue with much silver lace – a very pretty dress – came from Athy, seized the smiths' tools to prevent them from making pikes, and made prisoners of the smiths themselves ... Several of these were whipped publicly to extort confessions about the pikes. The torture was excessive, and the victims were long in recovering; and in almost every case it was applied fruitlessly. Guards were placed at every entrance into the village, to prevent people from entering or leaving it. The village once so peaceful exhibited a scene of tumult and dismay, and the air rang with the shrieks of the sufferers and the lamentations of those who beheld them suffer. These violent measures caused a great many pikes to be brought in: the street was lined with those who came to deliver up the instruments of death.

The terror tactics were now in full swing, and this deterioration in the situation led directly to the arrest and imprisonment of some members of the Narraghmore corps of yeomen who were later executed.

A party of military from Naas entered Ballitore and took prisoners, twelve of our neighbours, whom they removed to Naas gaol. Most of the villagers stood outside their doors to see them depart ... followed by their weeping wives and children. One child, with his cries of, 'O father, father!' excited great compassion. Six yeomen were taken prisoners to Dunlavin. I was walking in our garden when they passed on a car, with their coats turned inside out, and one of their guards, a mere boy, cried out to me in a tone of insulting jocularity. These unfortunate yeomen were shot! There was too much exultation in the military.

The arrest of the six yeomen was part of a wider tapestry of events that was unfolding across Kildare. The populace could only be pushed so far. If the reign of terror continued unabated, something had to snap. This is exactly what happened in late May, and it was no accident that Kildare was the first area in Leinster to experience rebellion at that time.

As the situation was deteriorating across Kildare, the United Irishmen suffered a hammer blow when many of their leaders were arrested in Dublin, where they had gathered to attend a meeting to plan a rebellion in Leinster. Among the few to escape was Lord Edward Fitzgerald, who promptly went into hiding. However, the Castle authorities were closing in, and Fitzgerald was captured at a house in Dublin's Thomas Street. He killed one of his captors and wounded another, but he was also wounded in the affray. He was imprisoned, but his presence in jail was an embarrassment to the authorities, who feared that no Irish jury would convict him because of his social standing. However, a decision was taken not to operate on him to remove the bullet and his wound turned septic. Racked with poison, he became delirious and died a slow and agonizing death, raving about the battles that he imagined were taking place as the rebellion went on outside the prison walls.

Surprisingly, however, and against the odds, the rebellion did go ahead. Although the situation in Kildare had worsened in May 1798, the outbreak of hostilities was unexpected. The authorities seemed to think that the reign of terror was working, and General Ralph Dundas, stationed in Kildare, wrote a reassuring letter to the Castle on 16 May. Dundas was confident that the situation in Kildare was now under control as he wrote: 'Be assured that the head of the Hydra is off, and the County of Kildare will, for a long while, enjoy profound peace and quiet'. One week after this letter was written, the revolt

Stopping of the mail coach at Kildare.

broke out. On 23 May 1798, an express galloped into Dundas's headquarters in Kilcullen with alarming news: a rising was expected at any moment in Dublin and the adjacent counties. The prearranged signal for such a rising was very simple – the mail-coaches from Dublin to the provinces were to be stopped. That night the Munster mail-coach was approaching Naas. A party of rebels attacked it and the passengers were brutally murdered. The coach was set alight, and this was the torch that started the rising in Kildare.

The burning of the Munster mail coach meant that much of Kildare was in full revolt from 24 May onwards. Many parts of the county were thrown into confusion and turmoil.

Battles and Engagements in County Kildare

Prosperous	24 May
Clane	24 May
Old Kilcullen	24 May
Naas	24 May
Monasterevan	24 May
Narraghmore and Red Gap Hill	25 May
Rathangan	25 May

At Prosperous, the rebels scored a small but significant victory. Captain Swayne was killed and many other Loyalists were piked to death by the jubilant insurgents. However, they failed to follow up on their success, and the village was soon recaptured.

The battle for Naas was a particularly vicious affair where the rebels, led by Michael Reynolds of Johnstown, took very heavy casualties. The rebels attacked the town from the Dublin Road. They advanced up the main street but were caught in a deadly bottleneck, as the military had installed artillery at the top of the town. They were well prepared and had taken measures to improve the artillery's field of fire. The use of grapeshot made the rebels disperse, and cavalry pursued the fleeing rebels. About 300 rebels were killed, and more than 800 pikes and approximately twenty-five

Surprise attack on the barrack at Prosperous.

guns were recovered from the town and surrounding fields. The following day (25 May), three rebel sympathisers were hanged on the main street of Naas. The rebel leader Michael Reynolds escaped and was later prominent in the second Battle of Hacketstown. The Battle of Naas was the first instance of a large town coming under rebel attack, and it set a pattern that was to be followed in many other urban spaces during the course of the rebellion. The rebels did not lack courage, but they were tactically inept. They had few guns and no artillery, depending on the pike as their principal weapon. They had no way of dislodging defenders from well-fortified positions, and were powerless against sniping from securely defended town houses.

Although the battle in Naas and the rebels' attempts to capture the jail had ended in failure, rumours abounded. Mary Leadbeater's diary provided a vivid description of the situation in Ballitore, further along the main road to the southeast, that morning.

The morning of the 24th of the Fifth-month [May] orders came for the soldiers quartered here to march to Naas. A report was circulated that Naas gaol had been broken open – that Dublin was in arms, and so forth. All was uncertainty, except that something serious had happened, as the mail-coach had been stopped. The insurrection was to begin in Dublin, and the mail-coach not being suffered to leave the city was the signal for general revolt. This purpose being defeated by the vigilance of government; the mail-coach had got to Naas before it was stopped, yet its detention there persuaded the people that the day was their own. They threw off the appearance of loyalty, and rose in avowed rebellion. In the morning the Suffolk fencibles first marched out, nine men remaining to guard their baggage at the mill, which was their barrack. The Tyrone militia followed taking their baggage with them. All was hurry and confusion in the village. Several who had kept out of sight now appeared dressed in green, that colour so dear to United Irishmen, and proportionally abhorred by the loyal. The Suffolks went by the high road, the Tyrones through Narraghmore. As they marched out, a young woman privately and with tears told their lieutenant her apprehensions that their enemies lay in ambush in Narraghmore wood. He was therefore prepared to meet them, and sad havoc ensued; many on both sides fell, particularly among the undisciplined multitude. The courthouse at Narraghmore was attacked, and many met their death there. We heard the report of firearms, and every hour the alarm increased.

The Battle of Narraghmore was bloody and violence also surfaced in Ballymore-Eustace, which was the scene of a skirmish on the morning of 24 May. The element of surprise meant that the rebel attack there was almost successful, and Lieutenant Beavor's 9th Dragoons suffered seven fatalities, along with a lieutenant of the Tyrone militia, before the attack was repulsed. When the rebels eventually retreated, in the aftermath of the battle, members of the Ancient Briton regiment executed twelve rebels, captured during the engagement, in reprisal for the surprise attack. Rebels also attacked the Kilcullen area, meeting with initial success before hundreds of them made a valiant but futile last stand. In the west of the county, there was action in

BULLETIN.

DUBLIN CASTLE, MAY 24th, 1798.

Extract of a Letter from Lord Viscount Gosford, Colonel of the Armagh Militia, and Major Wardle, of the Ancient British Light Dragoons, to Lieutenant General Lake, dated Naas, Thursday, Morning, 8 o'clock.

"This morning, about half past two o'clock, a dragoon, from an out-post, came in and informed Major Wardle, of the Ancient British, that a very considerable armed body were approaching rapidly upon the town. The whole garrison were instantly under arms, and took up their positions according to a plan previously formed in case of such an event happening. They made the attack upon our troops, posted near the gaol, with great violence, but were repulsed. They then made a general attack in almost every direction, as they had got possesson of almost every avenue into the town. They continued to engage the troops for near three quarters of an hour, when they gave way, and fled on all sides. They cavelry immediately took advantage of their confusor, charged in almost every direction, and killed a great number of them. A great quantity of arms and pikes were taken, and within this half hour many hundred more were brought in, found in pits near the town, together with three men with green cockades, all of whom were hanged in the public street. We took another prisoner, whom we have spared, in consequence of his having given us information that will enable us to pursue these Rebels ; and from this man we learn that they were above a thousand strong. They were commanded, as this man informs us, by Michael Reynolds, who was well mounted, and dressed in yeoman uniform, but unfortunately made his escape—his horse we have got.

"When we are able to collect further particulars, you shall be made acquainted with them. About 30 Rebels were killed in the streets ; in the fields, we imagine, above a hundred ; their bodies have not yet been brought together.

"It is impossible to say too much of the cavalry and infantry ; their conduct was exemplary throughout."

1798 Bulletin detailing the attack on Naas.

and around Rathangan. Again the rebels, under the command of Edward Molloy and John Doorly, were initially successful, capturing the settlement and establishing a headquarters in the canal stores near the bridge. They also drained part of the canal to hinder any counter attack by government troops. They defeated the first squadron of dragoons sent against them, but later succumbed to Crown forces during another attack. Colonel Longfield of the Cork Militia, who took part in the second attack, wrote to Dundas informing him that 'there are fifty or sixty dead. I took no prisoners'.

Despite heartening initial successes for the rebels in many Kildare villages, all of the major Kildare towns, including the strategically important centre of Naas, had withstood the rebel attacks. The truth began to dawn on the rebels during that furious final week of May. Many of them realised that the cause was hopeless, and a large number of them were tempted by the offer of an amnesty from Dundas. Rebels from all over Kildare gathered at the ancient circular enclosure known as Gibbet Rath to lay down their arms, knowing that Dundas had shown clemency to surrendering rebels at Dún Áillinne, near Kilcullen, the previous day. However, the military that arrived at Gibbet Rath was not led by Dundas, but the hard-line General Duff, and hundreds of rebels were slaughtered, effectively ending meaningful resistance in Kildare. Though there was some lingering rebel activity in the county, notably at Timahoe Bog, the rebellion in Kildare was crushed. The ferocity of the fighting and the atrocities committed by both sides during the brief but bloody conflict in Kildare tainted relations between landlord and tenants, Catholics and Protestants and ordinary people and the ruling landed Ascendancy class for decades, if not centuries, afterwards.

KILDARE'S EARLS:
A NOBLE TRADITION

When the Anglo-Normans arrived in Ireland in 1169, much of the land they conquered was given to powerful knights. The Normans successfully conquered most of eastern Ireland (roughly corresponding to today's province of Leinster) relatively quickly and consolidated their position by building castles, tower houses and walled towns. As time went on, the position of many of the new landowners was formalised by their being granted English titles. Thus, the Irish peerage was born. Some of the bigger landowners became earls, and the earldom of Kildare was created in 1316. It was granted to the Fitzgerald family, who owned nearly all of County Kildare. Over the centuries, through inter-marriage and other forms of land settlements, earls of other places also acquired some lands in County Kildare. This chapter focuses on two earls – both with Kildare connections – who lived centuries apart and who had very different lives. They are Gerald Fitzgerald (Gearóid Mór), the 8th earl of Kildare (1456-1513), known as 'the Great Earl' and Richard Southwell Bourke, the 6th Earl of Mayo (1822-1872) known as the 'Pickled Earl'.

THE GREAT EARL

During the Middle Ages and the early modern period, Ireland was divided into a patchwork of different sections. English law only applied in the Pale, a small area around the city of Dublin. The rest of the island was ruled either by Gaelic

Irish chiefs or Anglo-Norman lords. The most powerful of the latter was the House of Kildare, of which Gearóid Mór was a member. Gearóid's father, Thomas Fitzgerald, the 7th earl, did much to establish the Kildare supremacy in Ireland. He supported the House of York in England's War of the Roses and saw off the threat from the rival Butlers of Ormond in addition to recapturing former Kildare lands that had been overrun by Gaelic clans. When Thomas died in 1478, he left the earldom of Kildare in a very healthy state, and provided a springboard for his son Gearóid to become the dominant figure in Irish political life. Like his father, Gearóid supported the Yorkist cause in England. However, on 22 August 1485, Henry Tudor of Lancaster defeated King Richard III of York at Bosworth Field, and Richard's death in battle effectively ended the Yorkist cause. King Henry VII married Elizabeth of York and so began the House of Tudor. On the face of it, the defeat of the House of York augured badly for Gearóid. His father had been Governor of Ireland for eleven years, and he had carried on as Lord Deputy – but under the auspices of the House of York. Now that the House of Lancaster had triumphed, it seemed that the new king might move against him. However, Henry VII was kept busy with English affairs, and the protracted conflict that had just ended had lightened his coffers and weakened his military capacity. In this situation there was no immediate threat to the powerful Gearóid, as it was unlikely that Henry would challenge him or start another Irish war in the circumstances. Therefore, Gearóid Mór remained in place as Governor of Ireland.

Gearóid's power was based on a number of factors. Firstly, the Fitzgeralds were enormously wealthy; their lands encompassed Kildare and many parts of neighbouring counties. Their position adjacent to Dublin made the Fitzgeralds natural mediators between the Pale and the rest of Ireland, and their prestige was enhanced by the fact that they were descended from one of the first Norman settlers in Ireland, and further increased by the fact that both Gearóid and his father before him held the position of Governor of Ireland. More important in Gearóid's case, however, was his *manraed* or network of connections, since he had allies throughout Ireland. His sister was the wife of Conn O'Neill, the leading Gaelic chief in Ulster. His daughters married powerful Gaelic and Anglo-Norman figures such as McCarthy Reagh, Mac Liam Uachter and Piers Butler. One also wed the Englishman Fleming, a great landowner in the Pale. These connections enabled him to defend the English Pale while also providing London with a cheap but effective method of governing its Irish province. This depended on Gearóid's loyalty, but he was ready enough to submit to the English monarch, at least nominally, thus leaving him free to administer the law unhindered after his own fashion. One observer described Gearóid as 'a mighty made man full of honour and courage, soon hot and soon cold, somewhat headlong and unruly towards the nobles whom he fancied not'. In effect, the Great Earl was left alone to do as he pleased.

Gearóid's power was clearly demonstrated in 1487 when he supported Lambert Simnel, a pretender to Henry's throne, who came to Ireland to enlist support, claiming to be the Yorkist Earl of Warwick. Many Irish lords were very keen to support a candidate from the House of York, and Gearóid himself actually crowned Simnel as 'Edward VI' in Dublin's Christ Church Cathedral, with a crown hastily purloined from a convenient statue of the Blessed Virgin Mary. With support from many Irish leaders and help from abroad (including aid from the Duchess of Burgundy, the real Earl of Warwick's aunt), Simnel raised an army and crossed to England, but his defeat at the Battle of Stoke ended his hopes of becoming king. Once again Henry might have been expected to move against Gearóid after this direct challenge to his authority, but he was unwilling to tackle the power of the Great Earl head on. He feared that a move against Kildare would inflame anger, resentment and resistance throughout Ireland, so he contented himself with a mild rebuke of Gearóid, who went to England, swore allegiance to Henry and was allowed to remain in power. Tellingly though, some years later, when another pretender, Perkin Warbeck, claimed to be one of the princes of the House of York murdered in the Tower of London, Gearóid took no part in the rebellion – whatever his real sympathies may have been. When Gearóid returned to Ireland after the Simnel support trial, the long-running rivalry between the Great Earl and Sir James Butler resurfaced. A meeting of the two leaders was arranged in St Patrick's Cathedral. On arrival, Butler suspected that he was to be the victim of foul play and locked himself in the Chapter House, out of reach of his foe. A hole was cut in the door and the two leaders shook hands through it, with Gearóid promising not to injure Sir James. Butler emerged and the two embraced, but the feud between the two families simmered on.

Plotting and accusations against Gearóid continued, and in 1492 he lost his position as Henry's Lord Deputy. Sir Edward Poynings, an Englishman, was appointed to the position two years later. Poynings was Henry's agent in an attempt to increase royal power and to curb the power of the Kildares and other Irish leaders. In 1494, he summoned a parliament to meet at Drogheda and the famous act known as Poynings' Law was passed. Poynings' Law had two main provisions. Firstly, no parliament could be held in Ireland and secondly, no bill could be introduced for debate in the Irish parliament, unless it had prior approval from the English king and his Privy Council. At the time Henry simply wanted to make sure that Kildare could never use the Irish parliament to pass laws simply for his own convenience, but the act had far-reaching consequences and in later times it was used as a means to control the Irish parliament in England's interests. Another provision of the act aimed directly at Gearóid was the banning of war cries such as '*Crom abú*' or '*Butler abú*' – which were the usual battle cries used in the long-running Fitzgerald-Butler conflict.

The Drogheda parliament also accused Gearóid of plotting against Poynings and the king. Kildare was summoned to England to answer these charges and incarcerated in the Tower of London. However, at his trial in 1496, his acute mind and ready wit proved more than a match for Henry's advocates, and he convinced the king that the ruling factions in Ireland were 'false knaves'. One of his accusers observed bitterly, 'All Ireland cannot rule this man.' The admiring Henry quickly replied, 'Then let this man rule all Ireland.' The king matched his words by his actions by allowing the Great Earl to marry his cousin, Elizabeth St John, and reinstating him as Lord Deputy and Governor of Ireland. Gearóid returned home in triumph, leaving his son Gerald in London as a hostage. The king's trust in him was such that in 1503 he was allowed to take Gerald back to Kildare.

Gearóid's grip on power was tightened and the royal favour he enjoyed increased his standing in Ireland, even among the English of the Pale. Henry's royal favour also meant that Gearóid was now the keeper of the royal artillery – the first to be used in Ireland. This increased his military capacity further, and the Great Earl was ruthless in putting down rebellious behaviour. In 1500 he suppressed an uprising in Cork and hanged that city's hapless mayor as an example to other would-be rebels. Gearóid's greatest military victory, though, came on 19 August 1504 at the Battle of Knockdoe. Once again, Kildare faced a challenge from a loose alliance of Gaelic chiefs, based principally in Ireland's western province, Connacht. Gearóid's foes included William Burke, Mac Liam Uachter and O'Brien. Burke was Gearóid's son-in-law, but Gearóid was unhappy with William's treatment of his wife (Gearóid's daughter) 'which was not so used as the Earl could be pleased with'. However, Gearóid's own connections meant that he could call on a wide array of allies, and his supporters included Mac Liam Iochtar, O'Neill, O'Donnell, O'Connor and most of the English of the Pale. Gearóid convened a council of war, which included bishops and lawyers. O'Neill was uneasy at the presence of churchmen, stating 'their profession is to pray and preach, to make fair weather and not to be privy to manslaughter or bloodshed'. O'Connor in turn had doubts regarding the inclusion of the lawyers in the council and observed that it was 'time to discuss with bow, spear, and sword rather than with pen and ink'. However, the doubters were won over and the council went ahead. Before the ensuing battle, the Great Earl's rallying speech to his soldiers was interrupted by three loud war cries from the ranks of the opposition. Gearóid's response was typical. He shouted to his men, 'What means this cry? Do they think we are crows that we'll fly with crying?' He went on to swear an oath that the opposition would face 'men indeed' in the battle that day. In the event, the inspirational Great Earl won a decisive victory, and Henry VII made Gearóid a Knight of the Garter in recognition of his success. The victory at Knockdoe marked the zenith of the Kildares' military power.

The power of the Kildares spread and in 1508 the 'Duties upon Irishmen' in their rental, listing Gaelic Irish leaders from whom they received tributes, included all the major chiefs of Leinster. In 1512 Gearóid moved against the chiefs of north-east Ulster, whose submission to his authority was, at best, questionable. He invaded the lands of O'Neill of Clandeboye and took him prisoner, before proceeding to capture Belfast.

Killea (Kilkea) Castle in 1792 by Sparrow.

He advanced northward, plundering the Bissett lands in the glens of Antrim as he went. The following year he was involved in a dispute with the O'Carrolls and set out on an expedition against them. However, on this occasion his luck ran out. The mounted earl was in a stream near Kilkea, the site of another Fitzgerald castle, when he became a prime target for a concealed musketeer, and he was shot and mortally wounded. The seriously injured Gearóid was brought back to Kildare, but he died there in early September 1513. With Gearóid Mór's passing the House of Kildare was weakened as his son and successor, Gearóid Óg, did not wield the same control as his father and his grandson, known as Silken Thomas, entered into a foolhardy and ultimately futile rebellion against King Henry VIII that quashed the power of the Kildares forever (see chapter 3).

THE PICKLED EARL

One figure who survives in the folk memory of County Kildare, particularly around the villages of Johnstown and Kill, is the 'pickled earl'. The sobriquet refers to the fact that during his final journey back to Ireland, his corpse was shipped home for burial in a cask of rum. However, there is much more to the story of the pickled earl than this, for he was a man of national and international importance. He was a member of the landed Bourke family and became the 6th Earl of Mayo. The earls of Mayo owned land in County Kildare, and were particularly significant in and around the town of Naas. In addition to being Earls of Mayo, the Bourkes, who resided at Palmerstown House, were Barons of Naas. The family played an important part in British administration in Ireland during the nineteenth century.

Richard Southwell Bourke was born on 21 February 1822 in Dublin, the son of Robert and Anne Charlotte Bourke. After the death of Robert's uncle, he became 5th Earl of Mayo. While he was at school, his son Richard did not shine in the academic field, but the young man showed a marked interest in the subjects of both history and natural science. He grew up in County Kildare and he was commissioned as captain of the Kildare militia in December 1840. The young Richard entered Trinity College, Dublin in 1841 and he graduated with a BA in 1844, going on to achieve an MA in 1851 and finally an LLD in 1852. Many wealthy young men at the time visited Europe and participated in what was known as 'the grand tour'. Following a visit to Russia in 1845, Richard published a book entitled *St Petersburg and Moscow: a visit to the court of the Czar.*

Richard Southwell Bourke's political parliamentary career began when he was elected as MP for Kildare in 1847. At that time the Great Famine was ravaging the county and the country, and Richard had his first experience of public administration while implementing famine relief schemes. He served as MP for Kildare until 1852, and was later elected as MP for Coleraine in Ulster, a position he retained until 1857. Bourke's political star was rising, and it was unsurprising that the energetic, capable and well-connected young man received a series of promotions. In 1852, at the age of just 30, he was appointed Chief Secretary for Ireland, which again reflected his family's service in British administration in Ireland. He would go on to hold this position for three separate periods. Richard married Blanche Julia Wyndham, and this union enabled him to be elected as a parliamentary representative in England; he served as MP for Cockermouth from 1857 until 1868. Richard became the 6th Earl of Mayo in 1867, and in that year he was included in the party of notables who gathered to welcome the Prince and Princess of Wales when they visited Punchestown races near Bourke's hometown of Naas. During that year also he became a Knight of Saint Patrick, which was a signal honour for any loyal Irishman, but an even more significant event in Richard's life also occurred in 1867: he was sworn in as Governor-General of India at a ceremony in Calcutta. Richard Southwell Bourke had secured a position as Queen Victoria's representative on the subcontinent.

In India, the new Earl of Mayo quickly gained a reputation as a wise administrator and a just viceroy. Although he only held the post for four years, many of his decisions and his actions were beneficial to India, while also helping to enhance Britain's status as an imperial colonial power. Bourke engaged in a protracted series of negotiations which eventually improved relations with Afghanistan. Perhaps his most significant achievement, however, was the supervision of the implementation of India's first ever census. The census was actually begun in 1865 but it met with many difficulties and ultimately stagnated before Mayo's appointment as viceroy provided new impetus for the gargantuan task to be completed. The population of the subcontinent was huge, and many rural areas were only under nominal British control, and so dangerous places in which the enumerators had to work. Many other areas were extremely remote, which posed logistical problems for the census teams. Despite this Mayo forged ahead, overcoming all obstacles while overseeing the remainder of the work and the eventual publication of the census in 1872.

Among the earl's many other significant achievements in India was the creation of a Department of Agriculture and Commerce. This new department began a programme of agrarian improvement and land reform and some of the ideas introduced at this time are still being implemented in India today. Economically, the earl's greatest success was that he managed to change the Indian budget from returning a deficit into having a surplus – a near miracle in such a huge country beset by so many economic, political, and social challenges. Though the industrious viceroy enjoyed being in India, he admitted to feeling homesick. The memorial monument that he had erected over the unnamed dead was shaped in the form of a Celtic cross, and Bourke, who at this stage was longing to return to Ireland, also requested that a similar cross be placed over his own resting place when his time came. Unfortunately for him, it was to come a lot sooner than expected.

There was an Indian prison colony located on the Andaman Islands south of the mainland, and Richard Southwell Bourke decided to visit the place. The progressive viceroy thought that a tour of inspection would help to enlighten him about conditions in Indian prisons, and it is possible that he had a view to introducing prison reforms, in line with those that were taking place in Britain during the nineteenth century.

On 8 February 1872, a convict named Shere Ali assassinated the 6th Earl of Mayo. The incident occurred at the end of a long day, when the viceroy and his party were all very tired, having been walking and continuously on their feet in the extreme heat for over six hours. Mayo was a fit man, and he was usually able to manage physical exercise, but the climate of the Andaman Islands is particularly draining, so the earl's energy levels were beginning to drop. However, some other members of the viceregal party were in a worse state, so he instructed them to rest until he returned from climbing Mount Harriet to assess its suitability as the site for a new sanatorium. With the party thus diminished, Mayo and a few others continued on their way, but when they reached the foot of the hill, the viceroy's aide-de-camp was suffering from fatigue, so Mayo ordered him to sit down for a while and rest. During the day Mayo had been uncomfortable at having the only available pony while the others had to proceed on foot but they insisted that he should have the steed in view of his status. However, halfway up the mountain, the viceroy dismounted with the words, 'My turn to walk now; one of you get on'.

At the summit of Mount Harriet he took time to sit and gaze at the sunset on the distant horizon, remarking 'how beautiful … it is the loveliest thing I think I ever saw'. With hindsight, it was as if he had a premonition of impending disaster; certainly the viceroy's eloquent aside was out of character, as he was not usually given to enthusing about the beauties of nature. The party had remained at the summit for a considerable time, so descent was made quickly as dusk was approaching. About three-quarters of the way down, torchbearers who had ascended from Hopetown to see the viceroy and his group safely home met Mayo and his companions. The light and the realisation that there was not far left to go heartened the tiring walkers.

The viceregal party headed towards the jetty and their awaiting boat. Mayo was in the lead at the top of the stairs to the launch and the prison superintendent was busy giving orders pertaining to the itinerary for the following day. Suddenly, the people at the rear of the group heard a rustling noise that, in the words of one observer, was like 'the rush of some animal' from some rocks near the staircase. Two witnesses also recalled the flash of a knife descending rapidly in the eerie torchlight. Bourke's private secretary said he heard a dull thud that caused him to turn around sharply. He also described seeing the form of a man 'fastened like a tiger' onto the viceroy's back. Twelve Indian bodyguards rushed to restrain the assassin, but all were too late. Seeing the viceroy fall, they were going to kill the assassin, Shere Ali, there and then, but an English officer used the hilt of his sword to restrain them.

The wounded Mayo had staggered over towards the pier side, where his private secretary rushed to give assistance. The bleeding and weakening Mayo told him quietly, 'Burne, they have hit me'. Some members of the party tried to stop the blood with their handkerchiefs, but an artery had been punctured and the wound was to prove fatal. They put the profusely bleeding earl on a cart with a 'great dark patch' on the back of his coat. Mayo managed to sit up for a moment, but collapsed, saying, 'lift up my head'. They were his final words. Richard Southwell Bourke was brought back to the boat while Shere Ali lay stunned and bound with ropes just a few yards away. It was believed at the time that Ali was an opponent of British rule in India wishing to strike a blow against the Raj. However, it emerged later that this was not the case. Ali was not politically minded; the vengeful convict just wished to kill a white man and an authority figure.

The trial of the assassin was not delayed for an instant, and actually took place on board the launch. British justice was swiftly meted out, and Shere Ali would pay the ultimate price for his action, but nothing would bring back the deceased viceroy. At 9.30 p.m., the partially embalmed body of the 6th Earl of Mayo was placed in its temporary coffin draped in a Union flag. On his appointment to India, Bourke had instructed that should he die on the subcontinent, his body was to be returned for burial to the village of Johnstown (close to Naas), where the family vaults were located in the local graveyard. However, the authorities in India were at a loss as to how to get the corpse back without decomposition. The novel solution was to place the remains of Richard Southwell Bourke in a barrel of rum. Mayo was duly immersed, and the pickled earl was shipped back to his home, where Palmerstown House was extended and refurbished in his honour by public subscription from a shocked local populace. The earl's funeral was a huge state occasion, with vast crowds lining the route.

However the final twist in the tale is that local folklore asserts that when the cask was opened, the corpse was there but the rum was not. Perhaps it leaked out – but it is more

'The Funeral of Lord Mayo', *The Graphic*, 4 May 1872.

likely that the ship's crew enjoyed the earl's final journey a little more than they should have! Whatever the true explanation, it is certain that the last resting place of the 6th Earl of Mayo in Johnstown, County Kildare, contains the remains of a man who, in his day, was a hugely significant figure both in his native Ireland and on the distant subcontinent of India, and who deserves to be remembered for a lot more than the fact that he was posthumously immersed in a cask of rum.

8

TROUBLED TIMES:
KILDARE 1914-24

The decade 1914-24 can be described as the Irish revolution. One hitherto untapped source pertaining to Kildare during this period is the annals of the Christian Brothers in Naas, and this chapter makes extensive use of the records kept by the community, which provide a unique insight into both the political events of the time and the everyday lives of the people. The year 1914 marked the beginning of the First World War, which was greeted with anticipation and enthusiasm throughout Europe. Many people on both sides thought that the war would be 'all over by Christmas', and John Redmond, the leader of the Irish Parliamentary Party, called on all the members of the Irish Volunteers, a pro-Home Rule organisation, to join the army when he made a speech at Woodenbridge in County Wicklow.

Naas was also caught up in the wave of patriotism. The town had an army barracks and members of many Naas families were in the forces. The third battalion of the Royal Dublin Fusiliers was stationed at Naas, and on 6 August 1914, 280 of them marched into Naas railway station. The local Irish Volunteers escorted them and a band played as the soldiers paraded through the town. Flags and banners saying *Naas Abú* and *Nás na Ríogh* were prominently displayed and everyone sang 'Auld Lang Syne' as the train left the station. This was the first of many trains to leave Naas carrying soldiers on their way to the trenches at the front line. By June 1917, the number of men who had enlisted at Naas had grown to 22,611, and many of these came from the poorest areas of the town, such as Back Lane and Rathasker Road. Naas was much smaller a hundred years ago, with a population of 3,842 people according to the 1911 census, but many men joined up from the rural Kildare-West Wicklow region around the town as well.

Predictably, there were many casualties. In total, 567 Kildare men were killed in the Great War. Many of these, such as Private Maurice Joseph Grainger, son of Mortimer and Kate Grainger of Newtown, Eadestown, were killed in northern France. Grainger is buried in the British war cemetery at Vermelles, in the Pas de Calais region of France. In all, 193 of the Royal Dublins from Naas barracks were killed and there were also many wounded, physically and mentally, who never recovered from the effects of the war.

The soldiers who did return were met with a completely different society as a result of the events of the Easter Rising of 1916, and the aftermath of the shooting of the rebel leaders. The reports of *Leinster Leader* reflected this change in attitude. In the week after the rising, the editorials lacked any sympathy for the rebels: 'Now that the rebellion has been crushed, we may in common express the hope that we may soon revert to that state of order which only peace, prosperity and mutual goodwill can give.'

A series of events soon caused the *Leader*'s editorial to change its tone. These events included the arrests of *Leinster Leader*'s editor Michael O'Kelly and two of his staff; military raids in Naas on leading Nationalist families like Pattersons, Whytes and Grehans and, most importantly, the execution of rebel leaders in Kilmainham Gaol. The sombre tone of the editorials now betrayed a shift in Nationalist opinions. On 13 May 1916, the following piece was published:

They have paid the penalties for their acts and over their graves we are silent; it will be for some historian of the future, removed from the passions and the prejudices of our day, to enquire into the motives and estimate the culpability at its true worth of these men.

The opinions of Republicans were evolving. The superior of the Naas community, Br A.A. (Austin) Kelleher, was well aware of this fact. When Kelleher arrived in Naas in 1912, the primary objective of Naas Nationalists was Home Rule. When Kelleher departed Naas in 1918, the goal of Nationalists was no longer Home Rule – it had changed to the establishment of an Irish Republic. The Easter Rising and the execution of its leaders had changed the mood of the country. One observer noted:

> The leaders who emerged in 1916 and the subsequent years were largely past pupils of the Christians Brothers' Schools ... due recognition has not yet been given to the Irish Christian Brothers for their part in the Nationalist struggle, particularly for their unqualified support of the Gaelic Revival.

The education provided in Naas, as in all Christian Brothers' schools was very nationalistic, and young men, including many past pupils, were readying themselves for another fight after the failure of the rising and the deaths of its leaders. Support for the Sinn Féin party was increasing rapidly when Br E.B. (Berchmans) O'Neill replaced Br Kelleher as superior in 1918 and the mood in the Naas area was tense as war loomed closer. A more immediate danger also loomed, however; during this time, there was an outbreak of influenza, which lasted for 'several weeks'. The annals describe this illness as taking 'plague form' in Naas. O'Neill decided to close the school two weeks into the epidemic and it remained closed for over two months and only reopened in mid-November, a week after the end of the Great War. The enforced absence of the students meant that a lot of work had to be done after Christmas to catch up with their studies. O'Neill noted:

> The power of resiliency stands very high in the character of the Irish and in none more than the sporting fraternity of Kildare ... On the resumption of classes in January 1919, the pupils in all sections manifested a very active spirit of industry in their studies,

Naas seal.

which spirit was accompanied by a diligence and devotedness to school duty, worthy of high commendation.

The hard work was worth it for some of the students. Educational achievements were given the seal of approval at local government level, and Master Jones of Naas CBS was awarded a scholarship to UCD in 1919 due to his excellent exam results. Another UCD scholarship was awarded to Master Quinlan in 1920. As well as nationalistic education, Catholic education was very strong in the Christian Brothers' schools and William Tyndall was one of many boys who opted to join the clergy during this period.

The War of Independence erupted during the years 1919-1921. The IRA randomly attacked the British forces and the RIC with the use of guerrilla warfare. Nationally, IRA figureheads such as Dan Breen, Tom Barry, and Michael Collins led the resistance against the Black and Tans and the Auxiliaries, the latter of which raided Naas and vandalised the meeting place of the local Sinn Féin organisation. They took volunteer uniforms and scrawled Loyalist slogans such as 'God Save the King' and 'Up the RIC' on the front of the town hall. According to the *Kildare Observer* of 19 March 1921, these messages were removed while the paint was still wet!

With these dangers surrounding them, the Christian Brothers couldn't express their nationalism openly in their annals, because the Auxiliaries or the Black and Tans could seize them in a raid. The annals are very muted on the War of Independence, and what is recorded seems to have been written when the conflict was over. One extract reads:

> Located as Naas is midway between the Curragh and the capital the citizens had much to fear following the advent of the Auxiliaries and the Black and Tans in the years following the First World War and the acceptance of the [Versailles] treaty. The North Kildare brigade as well as that of West Wicklow found little scope for manoeuvring their manpower in the national interests, as every call from headquarters was closely watched by the army of occupation, whose base may be said to be at their very doors. Harassed on all sides, they found themselves isolated and utterly unable to lend any substantial aid to their countrymen in Dublin, while the road to the sterner battle centres in the south was always vigilantly guarded. The daily movements of the Black and Tans on the main thoroughfare between Dublin and the South aroused a lively interest, if not a fair modicum of fear, among the inhabitants of the peaceful plains of North Kildare.

The main roads to the south and south-east met in the centre of Naas, so the town saw many troop movements on the roads to Limerick, Cork, Kerry, Carlow, Kilkenny and Waterford between 1919 and 1921. The tone and the language of the annals make it clear that the brothers supported the Nationalist cause.

The War of Independence concluded with the signing of the Anglo-Irish Treaty on 6 December 1921. This treaty was found to be unacceptable by some elements of the IRA, the Dáil, and the country in general, but the majority of people favoured the agreement. Following this treaty, Naas Nationalists were divided into pro-Treatyites and anti-Treatyites, reflecting the situation nationwide.

The British pulled out after the treaty, and the last detachment of Royal Dublin Fusiliers left Naas in early February 1922. According to the *Kildare Observer* of 11 February, they paraded through Naas singing 'The Wearing of the Green' the night before. The newspaper also stated that the final few Black and Tans left Naas the following day. The Tans marched through Main Street holding a Union Jack, singing 'Goodbye' and 'Auld Lang Syne'. The departure of British forces from Naas left a power vacuum and led to the pro- and anti-Treaty IRA confronting each other. Irish Nationalists were divided in the Civil War that followed, and many Naas families were involved in the split. In April 1922, Michael O'Kelly, Thomas Williams, and Laurence Callaghan were all arrested in Naas and were imprisoned in the Curragh camp by Free State forces. Michael Collins spoke at a Free State rally in Naas on 16 April and was an honoured guest at a banquet at the town hall later that day.

Free State forces occupied Naas in July, taking up several vantage points in the town. They were there to counter the threat from anti-Treaty forces in the Ballymore Eustace area, but Naas was not attacked and no action was taken.

The Christian Brothers were in another tricky situation; they could not show favour to one side or the other. We do not know if the brothers in Naas were divided, because the annals stay silent on the issue and instead concentrate on the boys' education. The annals are very reticent about the Civil War, and the records were again written after the end of the struggle. The very fleeting mention of both the War of Independence and the Civil War in the annals may be explained by the fact that the brothers saw danger in keeping written records, and certainly didn't want to record the names of those involved, in case the British or, later, either the pro- or anti-Treaty side raided the monastery. The Civil War is only mentioned in very general terms thus:

The civil war had thrown its dark shadows over the landscape. Very many prominent citizens were to be found identifying themselves with the policies or principles of the contending sides. The friction engendered thereby was reflected among the pupils and so it was obviously felt that a prudent attitude had to be adopted, and a firm, if impartial, line of discipline to be pursued in the best interests of all concerned. The spirit of neutrality that characterized the attitude of the Community towards these delicate and dangerous political movements in these troublesome times won the admiration of the people as a whole. Soon all North Kildare had resumed its characteristic quiet. The good name of the school grew in the popular mind and the annual collection in aid of the community and school showed a progressively upward trend.

However, both Naas and County Kildare were profoundly affected by the Civil War. Naas had a considerable number of Unionist inhabitants, and one leading Unionist family was the Bourkes, the Earls of Mayo, who resided at Palmerstown House. The principal Unionist bastion was north-east Ulster, but much of the east of the country, and many people in Dublin city in particular, were also loyal to the Crown. The Main Street of Naas was festooned with Union flags during the Punchestown races in 1904 for King Edward VII's visit to the racecourse, suggesting that there were many Unionists in County Kildare at time. According to the *Kildare Observer*, 'on the eve of the royal visit there was colour in Naas. The flags, bannerettes, festoons and arches, were of such nature as would delight the eye of the most aesthetic.' During the last royal visit to the part of Ireland that is now a republic until the arrival of Queen Elizabeth II in 2011, King George V described his reception at Dún Laoghaire, after his coronation in 1911, as 'enthusiastic as any he had previously witnessed'. Naas Unionists regarded the monarchy as a safe, paternal system, and paid it due deference, believing that the fortunes of their country, Ireland, and their people, the Irish, were best served by remaining in the Union under the monarch. This view was another sort of Irish ideology; one that has been erased from later versions of Irish history. These feelings of Irish identity and belonging were demonstrated by the 7th Earl of Mayo's refusal to emigrate to England after he and many of his fellow senators of the newly formed Free State had their houses burned down by anti-treaty forces during the Civil War; in his case, in late January 1923. Resenting the suggestion by the *Kildare Observer* reporter of the time, Mayo insisted, 'No. I will not be driven from my own country'.

By the early twentieth century, the idea of Home Rule (an Irish parliament in Dublin) scared many Protestant Unionists. In Naas, Lord Mayo's failure to be elected MP in 1898 foreshadowed even greater alienation for Irish Unionism in the following decades. Unionist ideals were rejected by Home Rule, and later by Republican organisations such as Sinn Féin. This hardening of attitudes towards Protestants and landlords led to their being targeted during the War of Independence. Following the Anglo-Irish War, more radical and left-wing Republicans refused to accept the treaty, and the inclusion of Protestant ex-Unionist senators in its government by the newly formed Free State was perceived by some as treachery, betraying traditional Nationalism and Republicanism values. Anti-Treatyites continued the campaign of arson begun during the Civil War, by burning the houses of senators of the Free State. Mayo had been offered the position of senator by William T. Cosgrave, Taoiseach of the first Cumann na nGaedhael government, for his support of the new state. Anti-treaty republicans were particularly angered by the choice of Mayo, who was reputed to be involved in the execution of seven anti-Treatyites in the Curragh Camp in December 1922. On 29 January 1923, Palmerstown House, the Naas home of Lord Mayo, was torched. The Civil War ended the Mayo residency in Naas, highlighting the sidelining of Irish Unionism in favour of a Republican Nationalism that completely rejected it.

The seven executions of the 'Rathbride Column' on the Curragh was a story that gripped the national interest, but one on which the annals in Naas are silent. On 18 October 1922, after prolonged fighting, the Public Safety Act came into effect, making the possession of arms punishable by execution. This law led to the executions of the seven anti-Treatyites. The Rathbride column operated exclusively in the Kildare area, especially around the major towns. Their aim was to disrupt pro-Treatyite communications in the region. Many of their operations targeted the railways. Cherryville junction, a vital transport hub, was blocked when the column managed to overturn an empty train on the line. They also blew up a railway bridge in Kildare. Their other operations included raiding shops and trains and ambushing a party of Free State troops on the Curragh. One soldier was killed and two wounded in this attack. The activities of the column meant that they were wanted men and, under the Public Safety Act, Republicans caught with arms could be executed.

On 13 December 1922 national army troops raided a farmhouse in Mooresbridge, about a mile and a half from the Curragh Camp. They found Annie Moore, the owner's daughter, carrying arms and she was arrested. The soldiers then discovered the men hiding in a dugout and threatened to throw grenades down. With no other option, the men surrendered. In all, ten men were captured with Annie Moore, and ten rifles, two hundred rounds of ammunition, four bombs, a detonator and two grenades were found. Of the ten arrested men, however, only nine made it back to the Curragh Camp. There were conflicting reports regarding the death of Thomas Behan at the scene. Officially he was shot while attempting to escape, but Annie Moore stated that he was struck with a rifle butt, and when he could not get into the soldiers' vehicle he was struck again on the head and died shortly afterwards.

The prisoners were tried before a military court during the week of 13-18 December. They were found guilty of possession of arms and seven were sentenced to death. Two men, Pat Moore and Jimmy White, were spared, perhaps because the government thought it would be unadvisable to execute siblings at the same time, as both men had brothers in the group of seven who were executed. Annie Moore was also spared, but she was incarcerated in the women's wing of Mountjoy Jail. However, she suffered heavily, as both her brother and fiancé were executed. The men were executed, probably by a firing squad brought in from Dublin, at 8:30 a.m. on 19 December 1922. Earlier that morning the chaplain of the Curragh Camp, Fr Donnelly, administered confession and communion. The men sang the 'Soldiers' Song' on their way to be shot. The anti-Treaty officer in command at the farmhouse, Brian Moore, (Annie's brother) offered to be shot last, as he would have to endure more anxiety and anticipation than the others. The corpses were quickly and quietly buried in the Camp, but were later reinterred in Grey Abbey Cemetery, Kildare, in 1924. Perhaps surprisingly, the initial response to the killings was muted around the Kildare area. The pro-Treaty majority in the county supported the government, but many felt that the Rathbride Column were executed simply to demonstrate to Republicans that the government was cracking down on the anti-Treatyites, and sending a clear message that the Public Safety Act would be enforced. However, it is also possible that censorship of the press contributed to the reticence and general silence on the issue in Kildare.

The seven executed men were Patrick Bagnall, Joseph Johnston, Patrick Mangan, Brian Moore, Patrick Nolan, James O'Connor and Stephen White. All of these men were from Kildare, with the exception of James O'Connor, who hailed from Tipperary. Before they died, they were granted permission to write a letter to loved ones. Stephen White wrote poignantly to his father:

> I hope you will all say a prayer for me. I never saw Jimmie since the night we were arrested, but, thank God it is me instead of him that is to go. He will be more use to you than I would, and tell him if ever he gets out, which, with the help of God, he will, to start work and give up this game as it is not worth it.

The shootings constituted the largest single recorded act of execution during the Civil War. These seven men believed in a fully independent Ireland, not one with dominion status. Though the men were ardent anti-Treatyites and faced constant danger during the Civil War, Stephen White's advice to his brother Jimmy, to 'give up this game, as it is not worth it', is telling. He evidently thought that the anti-Treaty cause was lost. Subsequent events proved him correct in this analysis, but in the eyes of the new state, their actions were inexcusable. These were violent times, and the government, having to suppress the anti-Treaty threat, felt that it needed to act firmly. Hence, the executions were carried out, ensuring that these seven men became Republican martyrs; however, one cannot but mourn the waste of young lives in County Kildare and beyond during this divisive and bitter period. Though divisive, the Civil War was short in duration. The anti-Treaty IRA commander Liam Lynch (a nephew of an ex-superior of Naas Christian Brothers' community, Br Martin Lynch) was killed in April 1923. This signalled the beginning of the end of the conflict, as a ceasefire was announced and came into operation

Grey Abbey in 1792 by Sparrow.

on 24 May. By the end of that month, the populace of Kildare and the inhabitants of Naas, including the Christian Brothers and their students, were effectively citizens of the Irish Free State.

The fledgling state and its government set to work changing many aspects of Irish life. It has been suggested that, considering they had been through a revolution, the new leaders were actually very conservative, and in many ways this is true. Changes were made, however, in the field of Irish education. Predictably, the Free State wanted to introduce a much more nationalistic education and began a series of educational reforms in 1923. In 1924, the old intermediate exam system ended in a year when eight students from the Naas school passed at junior grade, five at intermediate and five at senior. In addition to these good results, five students passed the matriculation examination and three were awarded National University scholarships. Also that year, Naas students were offered three county council scholarships, which went to Joseph Tyrell, Michael Purcell and Vincent Noone. When Professor Eoin McNeill was appointed Minister for Education, one of his first aims was to change the old curriculum. McNeill followed the Christian Brothers' lead because they had been involved in nationalistic teaching for a long time throughout Ireland.

The educational model used by the Christian Brothers was held up as an example for others to follow in the new state. In Kildare, the high educational standards of Naas Christian Brothers and the nationalistic type of education they provided meant that the nuns in the neighbouring town of Kilcullen consulted them in 1923. According to the annals, 'Within a year the Kilcullen pupils were forging ahead with an Irish-Ireland curriculum and they were very soon grappling successfully with the various subjects through the medium of Irish.'

Many of the boys in the Moat School had sisters boarding in Kilcullen School. Surnames listed in the annals include many of the leading middle-class Catholic families in and around Naas – shopkeepers, farmers, professional people and property owners – at this time. These include Purcell, Tyrell, McDermott, Broe, Dowling, Foynes, Byrne, Kinsella, Coffey, Jennings, Malone, Boyle, Tyndall and Gorry. These were the grassroots of local Nationalism; the Catholic, Nationalist, middle-class bedrock on which the new edifice of the Irish Free State was founded. The new Irish state was a place where the Christian Brothers would become religious and educational pillars of society. Unlike leading Unionists, such as the once-powerful Bourkes of Palmerstown House, which had now been burned to a shell, the Christian Brothers were among the main beneficiaries of the Irish revolution of 1914-24. During that time they had changed from a nationalistic, anti-establishment order to a respected community, leading the way in Irish education. The Naas Christian Brothers' annals reflect this change, and the County Kildare that emerged from the Irish revolution was a very different place to the one that entered it a decade previously.

9

BREEDERS AND BLOODSTOCK: KILDARE AND HORSES

When Kildare contested its most recent all-Ireland Gaelic football final against Galway in 1998 in front of 67,886 people at Croke Park in Dublin on 27 September 1998, there was a banner in the crowd that read 'Galway for races, Kildare for Sam'. However, unfortunately for Leinster champions Kildare, it was the team from the west that emerged victorious that day with a four-point winging margin on a score line of 1-14 to 1-10, thus claiming the all-Ireland trophy, the Sam Maguire Cup. However, the banner was perhaps slightly misleading, for despite the popularity of the annual seven-day Galway race meeting at Ballybrit, County Kildare is actually the centre of Ireland's equine industry. Kildare has a long and proud tradition of horse racing. According to tradition, the ancient Celts held chariot races on the plains of Kildare, and this practice continued into and throughout the Middle Ages, with the low-level Curragh being particularly popular as a racing venue. The Curragh is actually an outwash plain, formed by meltwater from the melting glacial ice at the end of Ireland's Ice Age. The undulating outwash plain extends over 5,000 acres and is still home to a racecourse, one of three in the county. For many years Eadestown was the only parish in Ireland to boast two racecourses, with both Naas and Punchestown contained within its boundaries, until the configuration of the parish borders was changed, bringing Naas racecourse into the parish of Naas itself.

The Curragh is composed of layers of carboniferous limestone, overlaid with outwash sands and gravels, providing excellent drainage and wonderful conditions for the exercising of racehorses. Any early morning visitor cannot help but notice the large number of racehorses on the Curragh Gallops. Much of the rest of the county also rests on limestone bedrock and is covered in glacial deposits of boulder clay (till), making it particularly suitable for the training of racehorses. The limestone soils also provide particularly good grazing for horses. Limestone is rich in calcium, which helps to strengthen bones, and horses need a lot of calcium and phosphorous to develop properly. Many horse-feed products are rich in phosphorus, and the limestone-produced calcium helps to balance their diet. The fact that Kildare is close to Dublin has also played a significant part in the growth of the county's equine industry and over the centuries, horses have been imported, exported and transported in and out of Dublin port and, in more recent decades, Dublin airport.

Kildare has had a tradition of horse racing since pre-Christian times, but it was during the eighteenth century that the development of the sport really mushroomed. Following the Williamite-Jacobite wars at the end of the seventeenth century, a new landed elite wielded control in Ireland. Often called the 'Protestant Ascendancy', they altered the landscape by the addition of 'big houses' surrounded by demesnes. This new gentry's sporting fraternity placed the horse at the centre of their world. They organised foxhunts, held race meetings and racecourses began to appear on their lands and in their towns and villages. The racecourses reflected the aristocratic order that they represented, and underlined social order within the regions in which they were sited. Racecourses also indicated a degree of prosperity as, in addition to village and rural dwellers, they attracted the county gentry on race days. Many Irish landlords were, rightly or wrongly, perceived as irresponsible spendthrifts engaging in conspicuous consumption, and racecourses in their villages were in keeping with their fashionable, glamorous and often ostentatious lifestyles. Villages as small as Ballymore Eustace boasted racecourses and hosted race meetings, such as the one reported in the *Universal Advertiser* of 17 July 1749.

Members of the aristocracy and gentry also underlined their position and prestige by sponsoring races. In 1791, for example, the Earl and Countess of Aldborough of Belan House, Ballitore, both donated cups for races held at Baltinglass, County Wicklow, where the family also owned land. In fact, some of the oldest 'organised' racing trophies in the world originated in Kildare. These include a silver punch bowl from 1751 for a race run at the Curragh that is currently in the Museum of Fine Arts in Boston, and a silver cup with a cover (known as the Kildare Cup) for a race run in 1757, also at the Curragh, that is now in the National Museum of Ireland. Flat racing was an old tradition, but the steeplechase was a wholly Irish invention, with the first taking place in County Cork in 1752. This was a two-horse challenge organised by Messrs O'Callaghan and Blake, and run from the steeple of St John's Church in Buttevant to the corresponding landmark of St Mary's Church in Doneraile. Predictably, Kildare was soon involved in the new type of horse racing, which was not adopted in England until 1803. One of a set of four hand-coloured 1839 aquatints by the artist Henry Alken portrays the 1803 race as the 'First Steeple Chace on Record', but the caption is erroneous, as steeplechases had been held in Ireland for about a half-century prior to their English debut.

From the eighteenth century onwards, the Curragh became one of the most significant horse-racing venues catering for the English administration in Dublin. The desire of wealthy patrons for the introduction of recognised guidelines and codes and the increasingly organised and regulated nature of the sport spawned the establishment of the Turf Club in 1784 and, in time, this organisation developed into the ruling body of Irish racing. The popularity of racing on the Curragh also prompted the erection of stables on the plain – and in adjacent parts of the county – by wealthy breeders, who were all members of the landed elite. By 1800 they had also constructed lodges on the Curragh and in its hinterland, so they and their guests could stay in the area during race meetings. Evidently, horse racing in Kildare was growing rather than diminishing in popularity at the dawn of the new century!

Horse racing and the equine industry in Kildare went from strength to strength in the nineteenth century. The British Army had established their main military barracks in Ireland on the Curragh, and there were also barracks in the nearby towns of Newbridge, Kildare and Naas. This ensured an influx of cavalry horses into the area, further strengthening the association between Kildare and horses. A new racecourse was opened at Punchestown near Naas, with the first recorded race there being held in 1824. In 1842, it was chosen as the first permanent racecourse in Ireland and later, in 1850, the Kildare Hunt Club made Punchestown the permanent venue for its annual race meeting, which attracted many of the aristocracy and gentry of the 'County Set' as patrons. Punchestown races were reorganised and rebranded as the Kildare and National Hunt Steeplechases in 1861. Moreover, the Curragh racecourse continued to go from strength to strength, and 1866 saw the first running of the Irish Derby, the greatest of all Irish flat races. Racing is traditionally known as 'the sport of kings' and in 1868 Edward, then Prince of Wales, graced the meeting at Punchestown with his

Garrison Athletic at the Curragh camp.

'The Queen's visit to Ireland', *London Illustrated News*, 7 September 1861.

presence. The royal visit attracted about 150,000 people to the course, and was a huge boost to the reputation of the meeting. Edward returned to Punchestown in 1904, this time as King Edward VII, once again ensuring that a vast multitude attended the meeting. No wonder the venue became known as 'Peerless Punchestown'! A third racecourse, Naas, was opened in Kildare in 1924, and it now forms an integral part of the Irish racing calendar. In all, there are twenty-seven racetracks in Ireland, and it is no accident that three of them are located in Kildare.

Another factor that cemented Kildare as the hub of the Irish equine industry was the coming of the railways. Throughout the nineteenth century, railway lines were laid from Dublin to the major urban centres in the south, passing through Kildare on their routes. The presence of a railway station in Kildare town linked the Curragh directly with the capital. From 1885, Punchestown was served by stations on the new Tullow branch line at Naas and Harristown, making access easier for racegoers all over the country. With the rail link in place, the building of stud farms – a logical progression from the former erection of lodges and stables – increased rapidly both in and around the Curragh and in the wider Kildare area.

78754 *Ghl 85*

ANNO TRICESIMO PRIMO & TRICESIMO SECUNDO

VICTORIÆ REGINÆ.

✱✱

C A P. LX.

An Act to make better Provision for the Management and Use of the *Curragh* of *Kildare*.

[16th *July* 1868.]

WHEREAS there is in the County of *Kildare* a Tract of Land known as the *Curragh* of *Kildare* (in this Act called the *Curragh*) :

And whereas Part of the *Curragh* is occupied by an Encampment of some of Her Majesty's Forces :

And whereas, with a view to the better Management of the *Curragh*, and the more beneficial User thereof, and the ascertaining and settling the Rights of Common of Pasture (if any) and other Rights (if any) which legally exist, either by Grant, Charter, or User, over the *Curragh*, and the ascertaining of the Claims for Compensation to those (if any) whose Rights may be interfered with by the Provisions of this Act, and for preserving the Use of the *Curragh* for the Purpose of Horse Racing and the Training of Race Horses, it is expedient that such Provisions be made as are in this Act expressed :

And whereas for the Purposes of this Act a Map has been deposited with the Clerk of the Peace for the County of *Kildare*, on

G Z   which

1868 Act to make better provision for the use of the Curragh.

Many top trainers and breeders, still mainly from the wealthy landed elite, established stud farms in the county. Kildare was tightening its grip on its position as the headquarters of Irish racing.

This position was consolidated during the twentieth century. One event at the beginning of that century was to have major significance for the equine industry in Kildare, though no one could foresee this at the time. In 1900, Colonel William Hall Walker purchased Fays' stud farm at Tully, just outside Kildare town. The colonel, who had introduced the Aga Khan to the world of horse racing, was a shrewd judge of horseflesh and certainly knew how to spot a winner. He knew how to train and breed them too, and he became probably the best known, and certainly one of the best, breeders of his time. Hall Walker's horses won many races and perhaps the best known of them was Prince Palatine, but his greatest win was when Minoru (born and bred at Tully) won the English classic, the Epsom Derby, in 1909.

During the First World War, Colonel Hall Walker gifted his stud farms and all of his bloodstock to the British Government, which had the intention of using the gift to establish a national stud. The British National Stud is now located at Newmarket, where Wavertree House is named in honour of Hall Walker (who became Lord Wavertree). The Irish National Stud at Tully, which began life under Sir Henry Greer when Ireland was still part of the United Kingdom, continued operating under the governance of the Irish Free State, with Greer staying on as director until ill health forced him to resign in 1934. The Irish Government finally acquired the stud farm at Tully, and they established the Irish National Stud Company Ltd, with the passing of the National Stud Act in 1945. The new company, which was incorporated on 11 April 1946, took over the running of the stud on 31 August that year. Success continued throughout the mid-twentieth century, with the stud producing winners of all five classic races and one horse, King George VI's Sun Chariot, made racing history in 1942 when she won the fillies' triple crown of the Thousand Guineas, Oaks and St Leger.

Meanwhile, the race meetings in Kildare continued to attract the great and the good. In 1939, for example, royalty of another kind – Hollywood royalty – visited Punchestown, when legendary dancer and actor Fred Astaire turned up at the meeting.

The Irish Derby run at the Curragh received a major boost when the Irish Hospitals Trust donated £30,000 to the prize fund, thus catapulting the race into the A-list of world races. For many years the trust ran a nationwide sweepstake on several horse races, but both the trust and the sweepstake have since been discontinued. However, the derby itself has been run in conjunction with private sponsors, retaining its prominent position on the world stage.

THE NATIONAL STUD

The twentieth century also witnessed the development of the 958-acre Irish National Stud as a major tourist attraction, run in conjunction with the adjacent Japanese Gardens. These were also the brainchild of Colonel William Hall Walker, who commissioned Japanese master horticulturist Tassa Eida and his son Minoru to create them between 1906 and 1910. The result was quite simply a masterpiece; the world-famous gardens are the best in Europe, and renowned far and wide. Japan had only recently been opened to trade with the west, so Hall Walker chartered a ship to import what he needed – including a huge collection of plants, many ancient Bonsai trees, a tea house, stone lanterns and a miniature village carved from the igneous rock found around Mount Fuji. Hall Walker's Japanese Gardens are of the Meiji period (1868-1912) but they are best appreciated in the context of the history of the overall development of Japanese gardens of three basic types – water gardens, dry gardens and tea gardens.

The theme of the Kildare gardens is 'the life of man'. The visitor walks through a beautifully planned and laid out garden, with many dramatic changes in landscape, following 'the path of life'. At places along the route the path, which brings the visitor from the cradle to the grave, offers one certain choices, and all the intervening phases of life with their happy and sad times are reflected along the journey. Birth, childhood, marriage, parenthood, old age, death and the afterlife all feature along the path of life and there is ample time and space for visitors to reflect on these and more. Eida left Kildare in 1912 and the gardens remained unsupervised for the next thirty-four years. However, Patrick Doyle was appointed in 1946 and remained in charge until 1972. Since then, the gardens have gone from strength to strength and they are now among the most loved of all Ireland's gardens, with some 150,000 visitors annually.

In 1999, another fabulous garden was opened at the National Stud site at Tully. St Fiachra's Garden is a total contrast to the Japanese Gardens, but they complement each other perfectly. Famous and award-winning landscape architect Professor Martin Hallinan designed the garden, drawing inspiration from early Irish monks and monasteries. St Fiachra was just such a monk who travelled to France. In around AD 626 he travelled east of Paris to the Diocese of Meaux, where the bishop allowed him to establish a hermitage and, over time, his love of gardening saw him become the patron saint of gardeners. Fiachra became famous throughout France for his holiness, kindness, compassion towards the poor and the infirm and for many miraculous cures. He died in approximately 670, placing him among the early Irish monks and missionaries.

St Fiachra's Garden aims to capture the essence of what inspired the monks involved in Ireland's monastic movement and the choice of 'white martyrdom' abroad during the sixth and seventh centuries. Hence, the garden seeks to work with and to show the Irish landscape in a raw state – a place where rock and water preside over a naturalised landscape of streams, waterfalls, wetlands and woods. Within this landscape, beehive huts of limestone, reconstructions of ancient monks' cells, nestle beside the water's edge, where a statue of the saint recalls the lifestyle of the monks, while a further delight – an enclosed sunken garden of Waterford Crystal flowers, ferns and rocks – awaits the visitor on entering the Spartan monastic cell.

However wonderful the gardens at the National Stud are, the principal business and the reason for its existence is the equine industry. Visitors to the stud will find the horse museum a fascinating record of past horse-racing glories. In the Sun Chariot yard, the story of Irish horse racing unfolds before the eyes of the enthralled multitude of visitors. The centrepiece of the museum, however, is the skeleton of Arkle, probably the best and most famous Irish racehorse. Though it is over forty years since he died, Arkle remains a legend in the horse-racing world: he won the greatest showpiece of English racing, the Cheltenham Gold Cup, three times. At the height of his fame, letters with the simple address 'Arkle, Ireland' reached their destination. Memorabilia from other great Irish horses such as Sea the Stars, bred by the National Stud, and Vintage Crop, winner of the Melbourne Cup, the race that stops Australia, in 1993, is also on display. The stud is also home to many of the current crop of Irish racing superstars, and visitors may be lucky enough to see legendary winners such as Moscow Flyer, Kicking King and Beef or Salmon at home. Moscow Flyer won twenty-seven races in all, Kicking King won twelve and Beef or Salmon won nineteen. All had career earnings of over €1 million. In May 2011, during Queen Elizabeth's royal visit to Ireland, she visited the National Stud, home to some of Ireland's leading stallions, to see the place that had produced winners of five classic races for her family's stables over the years. She also visited the Kildare stud farm of the current Aga Khan at Gilltown, near Kilcullen.

MODERN DEVELOPMENTS

Today, Kildare retains its place as the centre of Irish racing, as a number of innovations and developments have occurred to ensure the dominance of the area in the racing world.

A secondary equine hub in the county has grown up in the Maynooth region in recent decades, while the second half of the twentieth century saw the emergence of syndicates of horse owners. This trend was accentuated during the years of the Celtic Tiger economic boom in Ireland, with the result that many small owners (or part owners) entered the industry. In fact, despite the glamorous thoroughbred image of horse racing, over 80 per cent of all stud farmers are engaged in small-scale operations. Mega-rich owners, such as the Aga Khan and Sheikh Mohammed Al Maktoum, who owns the Kildangan Stud chain in Kildare, account for only a small part of the industry. Unlike other types of farming, stud farming does not automatically qualify for Irish government or EU grants, although additional funding may be accessed through REPS (the Rural Environmental Protection Scheme). Many equine groups see the need for this situation to change, though: they believe that grants and subsidies would help quality control within the industry, and would ensure that small stud farmers continue to breed good racehorses. They argue that the growth and development of the industry, which they see as an integral part of rural life in Kildare, would be good for the local economy, with more horses and stud farmers creating extra employment, and sustainable and environmentally friendly jobs. Further, these groups point to the economic multiplier effect of the equine industry in the county, where spin-off industries supplying everything from horse blankets to food additives for the horses have sprung up in towns such as Newbridge to service the demands of the industry.

The Irish Thoroughbred Breeders' Association has been in existence for over fifty years. It has played a leading role in the development of Kildare's equine industry, and has lobbied extensively on behalf of the sector. In 1973, the Racing Apprentice Centre for Education (RACE) was established at Tully. This body looks after the training of apprentice jockeys who are accepted into the centre not through academic qualifications, but because of an innate love of horses. At the centre they learn about all aspects of equine life and begin their riding careers on a mechanically propelled horse simulator before graduating to the real thing. This bottom-up approach to learning the industry has paid dividends and many apprentices have progressed to become stars of the racetrack. The following year, Goffs Bloodstock Sales, the principal seller of thoroughbreds in Ireland, moved its headquarters from Dublin to a purpose-built sales complex in the village of Kill, adjacent to Naas. The yearling sales at Goffs are one of the highlights of the world horse racing calendar, with individual horses often changing hands for over €1 million. The presence of Goffs in Kildare has added considerably to the county's reputation within the thoroughbred racehorse industry. This was further enhanced in 1979, when the Irish Equine Centre was founded in the neighbouring village of Johnstown. This centre provided essential services and became engaged in cutting-edge research, developing degree courses in equine studies in conjunction with Irish universities such as the University of Limerick.

The Irish Horseracing Authority, responsible for many aspects of the promotion and development of Irish racing, was established under the Irish Horseracing Industry Act in 1994. However, the organisation was superseded by Horse Racing Ireland in 2001, and the new body combined the work of the IHA with some aspects of work formerly undertaken by the Turf Club. The HRI headquarters is also located in Kill and it administers such diverse sectors of the industry as the regulation of bookmakers, the negotiation of media broadcasting rights and the provision of finance for the development of Irish racecourses.

In 1997, the Kildare Horse Development Company was founded as an inclusive umbrella organisation with the aim of acting as a voice for the many disparate equine groups in the county. One of the key ideas behind the new company was to develop Kildare Horse as a trademark brand synonymous with the county. As one participant put it: 'Horses are to Kildare what crystal is to Waterford'. The company was the driving force behind the local county council's decisions to feature the image of a racehorse in the county logo and to re-brand Kildare as 'The Thoroughbred County'. This slogan was also placed on motorway signposts at the county boundaries.

However, Kildare's equine associations extend beyond the world of thoroughbreds. Sport horses (i.e. non-racehorses, but those used for breeding, leisure and equine competitions such as show jumping and dressage) are also bred in the county. Unlike the racehorse sector, there is a lack of data concerning the sport horse industry, but the available information points to the fact that Kildare is not as heavily involved in this area as it is in the thoroughbred sector.

The sport horse industry has a much lower profile than its fashionable counterpart, but employment is created locally due to the presence of equine activity centres offering facilities such as show jumping, trail riding and trekking. There are also a number of riding schools, point-to-point races and three-day events, which generate income in Kildare. The sport horse sector took a major leap forward in 2002, when the National Centre for Equestrian and Field Sports was opened at Punchestown. In addition to a large, modern exhibition space, the new centre also includes state-of-the-art training and eventing facilities. The new centre has the potential to provide a massive boost to the sport horse sector in Kildare. However, despite these developments, Kildare lags behind western counties such as Clare and Galway in the breeding of sport horses. The image of the Thoroughbred County rests on its racehorses, and this is indeed the sector that separates Kildare from the rest of the Irish equine world.

As the Kildare bloodstock industry faces the future, it faces new challenges and new opportunities. North Kildare has become urbanised, with the area taking a large amount of overspill population from the capital: over 60 per cent of Kildare people now live in its urban spaces. If the area becomes a kind of Dublin suburb, increasing land values may threaten the stud farms, particularly the Maynooth-centred cluster in the north of the county. There is also a danger that the new Kildare dwellers will fail to understand and empathise with the county's long-standing tradition of horses and horse racing. Ireland's generous tax regime is under threat from other EU states, which view it as an unfair advantage when industries are deciding where to locate. Despite all its natural advantages, there is little doubt that any future disadvantageous changes in taxation could affect Kildare as a centre of equine excellence. It is also difficult to attract young people into the industry, as the rates of pay are low, especially for those starting from scratch. However, young horse lovers often need little enough financial incentive to become involved, and a love of horses is almost a birthright in many Kildare families. As long as that remains in place, and as long as Kildare people continue to attend race meetings at the Curragh, Naas and Peerless Punchestown, the future of the industry is assured. Whenever the next race meeting is on, if you receive a tip from a native of County Kildare, you could do a lot worse than have a flutter on the nag in question – after all, you could say that you heard it straight from the horse's mouth!

10

KILDARE'S HISTORIC TOWNS

Any tourist in Kildare is spoiled for choice when it comes to urban settlements to visit. Whether vibrant large towns or charming smaller ones, these places all have a character of their own. The land in the west of the county incorporates part of the great Bog of Allen, which stretches across the central plain of Ireland, and is very low-lying.

Here, peaty soils discourage the building of towns, so the county's more sizeable settlements are to be found in the north, centre and east, where glacial boulder clay soils predominate. There are also some smaller towns in the low bog lands of west

'Cutting turf', *Illustrated London News*, 1850.

Kildare. Whether large or small, east or west, all of them are also steeped in history and this chapter gives a brief outline of the history and heritage associated with some of Kildare's chief towns.

ATHY

Athy is the principal town of south Kildare. The town today has all the hallmarks of a planned landlord settlement, with the side streets forming a grid pattern perpendicular to the main street, which widens out into a fine market square, Emily Square (named after a Duchess of Leinster) at the centre. Athy did indeed develop as a market town, but there was settlement in the area long before the arrival of the planters, or even of the Normans. The town is situated on the River Barrow, and the name Athy means the Ford of Ae, who, according to tradition, was a chieftain from Munster that met his death here in the second century.

The Normans were responsible for the first urban settlement on the site. Richard de St Michael built a castle at nearby Woodstock, but the present castle in the town, named White Castle after a former occupier, dates from the early sixteenth century. It was originally built by Lord Furnival but passed to the Fitzgeralds, earls of Kildare, who had inherited the

Athy seal.

St Michael lands through intermarriage. In addition to housing a garrison of soldiers to guard the southern approach to the Pale, the castle also served as a jail and a police barracks. Athy was granted a charter in 1613, allowing local governance to flourish.

The Grand Canal was constructed in the eighteenth century, linking Dublin with the River Barrow, which it joined at Athy. This increased commerce in the town and the harbour developed as a trading hub. The river remains an integral part of life in the town today, and events such as dragon boating are held here. The United Irishmen were active in the area in the 1790s and blacksmiths Tom Murray and Owen Finn were 'flogged and tortured with the whole town echoing to their screams' in 1798, and just eight years later, seven men were sentenced to death for the murder of Thomas Jeffries of Narraghmore. They were marched across the bridge and hanged near the Grand Canal basin, before two were beheaded and their heads publicly displayed as a grim warning to local rebels. Thankfully, the violence had abated by 1800.

The nineteenth-century town hall encases an earlier eighteenth-century market house and the courthouse and railway station, both executed in the neo-Gothic style, also date from the nineteenth century. The town was overcrowded in the 1830s, with 1,005 families inhabiting 790 houses, so a workhouse with a capacity of 600 (360 adults and 240 children) was opened here in 1844. However, the Great Hunger struck a year later. There was an outbreak of cholera in the town during the Famine, and the opening of two auxiliary workhouses in addition to large numbers attending at soup kitchens in the town indicate high levels of distress in the late 1840s. The area certainly suffered population decline during and after the Famine.

During the late nineteenth century, the town remained predominantly a market centre serving its rich agricultural hinterland, but there were also industries such as brick-making and a small coalmine at Wolfhill, which remained operational until the 1960s. Despite this, emigration from the area continued and unemployment was high in the Athy region in the late nineteenth and early twentieth centuries. This was probably one reason why large numbers of young men enlisted in the army during the First World War. The *Kildare Observer* reported on 27 March 1915 that 'All classes in Athy have rallied to the colours and all denominations had done splendidly'.

The town was the focal point of the original Gordon Bennett motor race in 1903 and today it remains a principal venue in the annual Gordon Bennett vintage car rally. There is also a fine heritage centre in the town, which houses a real treat for visitors – an Ernest Shackleton exhibition including a sledge and other artefacts used by the great explorer. The intrepid Antarctic adventurer was born at Kilkea (also the site of a fine Fitzgerald castle) near Athy. Many other exhibits regarding the history of the town make the heritage centre – and the town of Athy – a great place to visit.

CELBRIDGE

Situated on the River Liffey, Celbridge was settled in Celtic times and its Gaelic name, '*Cill Droichid*', means the 'church of the bridge', which is taken to refer to the ancient church built by St Mochua on the bank of the river. The Normans settled in the area and established an urban centre here, with Thomas de Hereford building a mill and Celbridge first being described as a town in 1314. Despite its early urban classification however, the modern town of Celbridge really only developed after the erection of Castletown House by Speaker Conolly in the eighteenth century. Esther Van Homrigh, Jonathan Swift's 'Vanessa', lived in Celbridge Abbey, where the author often visited her. The area escaped the worst ravages of the 1798 rebellion, though nearby settlements such as Clane and Prosperous were affected. From 320 County Kildare claims for losses suffered during the rebellion, only one was from Celbridge. It was made by George and Stephen Coyle and they actually suffered their loss while travelling along a road and not in Celbridge itself.

Though the fortunes of Castletown and the Conollys declined during the nineteenth and twentieth centuries, the fortunes of Celbridge improved (excepting during the Famine years), as the town emerged from the shadow of the big house and saw growth in its industry, commerce and transport. The original Norman mill at Celbridge was succeeded by many others, and the large mill buildings along the river were used in the woollen trade during the nineteenth century. In 1837 the mills in Celbridge, when working at full capacity, employed approximately 600 people. In 1846 Celbridge was described as a small market town, and in 1856 it was noted that 'woollen and cotton manufactures are extensively carried on here and provide employment to a large number of the industrious classes'. Competition from other mills, especially those in Britain, was fierce however, and by 1912 a visitor to the town noted that 'the ruins of a large mill tell only too plainly the old story familiar to Ireland'. In spite of this, some mills continued to operate through the late nineteenth century, and during the twentieth century the Navan Carpets Company worked Celbridge mill for some years, before its eventual closure.

As one of the principal towns of north Kildare, Celbridge was also chosen as the site of one of the county's workhouses. Celbridge workhouse was opened in June 1841. Like the other Kildare workhouses, the one in Celbridge was unable to cope with the onslaught of the Great Famine and many of its inmates were buried in the Paupers' Graveyard on the Maynooth Road, where a cross inscribed with the words 'Pray for the souls of the poor and afflicted whose bodies have been laid in this cemetery since 1841' serves as a monument to these unfortunate people. During the catastrophe, in addition to the workhouse, there was also a fever hospital and an operational soup kitchen in the town, where all the soup was made from meat purchased from local Celbridge butchers. Though the Famine in Celbridge was not as severe as in other parts of the county, it is worth noting that the town's pre-Famine population in 1821 was 1,709 while the post-Famine population in 1881 was 1,219.

Another nineteenth-century development in the town was the arrival of the Great Southern and Western railway at nearby Hazelhatch. This contributed to the growth of Celbridge and in the late twentieth century the rail link was upgraded, making Celbridge an attractive commuter town for Dublin, and helping to ease the problem of traffic congestion that developed as the town expanded rapidly during the Celtic Tiger era. Visitors to Celbridge will want to view Castletown House, and they should certainly take a trip to see the nearby 'Wonderful Barn', but they will also find a vibrant town with much to offer apart from its gentry's architectural heritage.

KILDARE

The town that named the county is no longer the most important settlement in Kildare, and the functions of local governance are now located in the administrative county town of Naas, but ecclesiastical Kildare was once the primary town in the county and it remains its cathedral town. Information regarding the early ecclesiastical site is sketchy, however; it is known, though, that St Brigid settled in Kildare about AD 480 and there has been a church here since that time. The monastic site grew and in 835 a force of Vikings plundered Kildare, having sailed up the Liffey to where the present town of Newbridge now stands. Queen Flanna ordered the rebuilding of the cathedral in 868. In 1135 the site was at the centre of an ecclesiastical scandal when 'the abbess of Kildare was taken out of her cloister by Diarmaid MacMurrough, King of Leinster, and forced to marry one of Diarmaid's people'. Diarmaid MacMurrough is remembered in Irish history as the man who invited the Normans into Ireland. Following their arrival, however, they took over the ecclesiastical settlement of Kildare.

In 1223 Ralph of Bristol became the first Norman bishop of Kildare, and he began work on building a fine new cathedral. The new landowners, the de Vescis, established a house of the

Knights Hospitallers (or Knights of St John) at Tully and the remains of the Black Abbey can now be seen in the grounds of the National Stud. The de Vesci family also brought the Carmelites to Kildare in 1290, and the order has remained in the town for over seven centuries. The present Carmelite friary is west of the cathedral, behind the main street and its market square. The de Vescis also constructed a castle in Kildare, but it later became a Fitzgerald stronghold. Gearóid Mór Fitzgerald built up the power of the Geraldines, but his grandson Silken Thomas lost it all when he rebelled against the Crown in the early sixteenth century. Later that century, the castle suffered a lot of damage during the wars of Queen Elizabeth I's reign, and it was also attacked during the 1641 rebellion, finally falling into the hands of the Duke of Ormond in 1649. However, Kildare Cathedral was ruined during the rebellion. Patrick Sarsfield of Tully was one of the principal Jacobite commanders in the wars of the 1680s and '90s, but the Jacobite cause was lost and the Treaty of Limerick ended the conflict.

Ecclesiastical ruins at Kildare in 1791 by Sparrow.

The eighteenth century was generally peaceful and the market town of Kildare prospered. However, during the 1798 rebellion, there was a massacre of surrendering rebels at nearby Gibbet Rath on the Curragh. A monument in the form of a statue of St Brigid in the centre of the town commemorates the massacre. It is inscribed: 'In memory of over 350 men from Kildare and district who gave their lives at Gibbet Rath 28 May 1798. *Ar dheis Dé go raibh a n-anamacha*' (rough translation: may they rest in peace). The nineteenth century saw the remodelling of the market house (which was again restored in 1973). The Roman Catholic church of St Brigid also dates from the nineteenth century; it opened in 1833 and the tower was built in 1851.

One of the principal developments in post-Famine Kildare was the decision to renovate the ruined cathedral and in 1896 the Archbishop of Dublin, Lord Plunkett, consecrated the refurbished gem. The cathedral site now included the round tower, the top of which was replaced in the 1730s, and the High Cross of Kildare. The interior of the cathedral is indeed impressive and it contains many monuments dating from the medieval and early modern periods. These include a stone effigy of Bishop Ralph of Bristol, who held the see of Kildare from 1223 to 1232; the Wellesley altar tomb which contains the remains of Walter Wellesley, Prior of Great Connell, who died in 1539; the grave slabs of the Earls of Kildare and a baptismal font of great antiquity which, according to tradition, was reputedly used to baptise St Laurence O'Toole in 1123. There is also a heritage centre in the middle of the town, adding considerably to the visitor's experience in historic Kildare.

LEIXLIP

The commuter town of Leixlip is located where County Kildare meets County Dublin. It is a physical meeting point, being located at the confluence of the rivers Rye and Liffey, and a historic meeting point as it was here that the ancient Celtic kingdoms of South Leinster and Brega (often referred to as the Kingdom of Meath) bordered each other. It also marked the western boundary of the Viking Kingdom of Dublin in the tenth and early eleventh centuries, and the town is proud of its Viking heritage, having hosted Viking festivals in its honour. The Normans arrived in the area in the late twelfth century and Adam de Hereford erected a castle here, which was later occupied by, among others, Speaker Conolly and Viscount Townshend. The castle developed over the centuries and eventually passed into the ownership of the Guinness family. Arthur Guinness established his first brewery in Leixlip and, in recent years, the Guinness presence has been maintained in the town as the Honourable Desmond and Mrs Guinness have resided in the castle.

St Catherine's Park is the site of a priory dating from the same period as de Hereford's castle, but Thomas Alen acquired the site after the suppression of the monasteries under King Henry VIII in around 1537. The park contains a ruined church and grotto and is known for the gates designed by Francis Johnston. The parish church of St Mary is also twelfth century in origin, but it was fully rebuilt during the eighteenth century.

Also at this time, Leixlip was the location of the only iron mill in Ireland. Industry in Ireland was helped by the arrival of the canals, and the Royal Canal crosses the Rye via an aqueduct. The canal is crossed by Louisa Bridge (named after Lady Louisa Conolly) and Leixlip Spa was located adjacent to the bridge. The spa dates from 1793, at a time when it was fashionable for the great and the good to take the waters as a cure for various ailments. Examples of spa towns included Bath in England and Lisdoonvarna in Ireland, but Leixlip Spa was also very well known in its day, attracting many of Ireland's wealthier classes until a rival spa was opened at nearby Lucan, eclipsing its Leixlip counterpart. Today the waters at Leixlip serve the public in a different capacity, as a hydroelectric plant was established at Confey in 1946. A dam was constructed at

Salmon Leap to facilitate this project. Confey is the alter ego of Leixlip and is also very ancient.

The church of St Columba (also known as Colmcille), though now in ruins, is an important example of Ireland's built heritage as it may pre-date the Norman invasion of 1169. Visitors are also advised to look around the Wonderful Barn, a fascinating building near Leixlip. It dates from 1743 and was commissioned by William Conolly's widow to provide employment for poverty-stricken peasants in the area. Ninety-four external steps lead to the top of the Kildare landmark, which is 73ft high. The winters were very harsh between 1739 and 1744, reducing many smaller tenant farmers to destitution, so the employment created alleviated their plight. Moreover, the construction of the barn acted as a deterrent to peasants who were scavenging the rural area surrounding Leixlip for food and often engaged in theft during this inclement time. While Leixlip and Confey share a very ancient past, Leixlip today is known as an ultra-modern hub of computer and software industries. These have provided thousands of jobs, and pride of place must go to the huge Intel plant, but the modern visitor to Leixlip will find that the old mixes effortlessly with the new, and the town's main street, which boasts many fine eighteenth- and nineteenth-century houses, is a welcoming and vibrant place to be.

MAYNOOTH

Maynooth is Kildare's university town. It was settled in ancient times and, according to tradition, the Irish name '*Má Nuad*' means the 'Plain of Nuadha'. The original Gaelic clan who inhabited this place, the O'Byrnes, claimed to be descended from Nuadha, a legendary Celtic warrior.

In the early Christian period there were three monastic sites in the Maynooth area: Grangewilliam, Taghadoe and Laraghbryan. However, when the Normans arrived they remodelled the Irish Church and drove the O'Byrnes out of the Maynooth region into the Wicklow Mountains. The lands around Maynooth were granted to Maurice Fitzgerald in 1176 and he built Maynooth Castle. In time, the Fitzgeralds became the most powerful family in Ireland, and this became one of their principal strongholds. It eventually fell to the English during the revolt of Silken Thomas, effectively the last of the Fitzgerald dynasty of royal viceroys.

The building of Carton House altered the town out of all recognition in the eighteenth century. The main street was remodelled to constitute an extension of the avenue leading to the great house and took on a typical improving landlord appearance, with good quality houses, a uniform roofline and a tree-lined street in evidence. Carton stood at one end of the urban space and Stoyte House, the home of the Duke of Leinster's agent John Stoyte, at the other. Stoyte House was built in the 1780s but in 1795 it became the nucleus of the new Maynooth College; during penal times Catholic priests had to educated abroad. The anti-Catholic penal laws were being relaxed during the 1790s, particularly from 1793 onwards, and this led to the passing of the Act for the Better Education of Persons Professing the Popish or Roman Catholic Religion. The establishment of Maynooth College as a Catholic seminary in 1795 was a direct result of this act. The Catholic hierarchy were at pains to placate the British Government, and some students sympathetic to the United Irishmen were expelled between 1798 and 1803.

Maynooth priests soon became predominant in early nineteenth-century Ireland, and many of them were involved in Daniel O'Connell's campaign for Catholic Emancipation. The growth of the seminary was phenomenal and by 1850 it was the largest Catholic seminary in the world. In 1896 it achieved the status of a pontifical university and in 1910 it was recognised as a college of the National University of Ireland (NUI). In 1966, the decision was taken to open the college to lay students, who could now study for NUI degrees there. In 1997, the Universities Act separated the clerical and lay sections of the college. St Patrick's College retained its place as a pontifical university and the lay part of the college became known as NUI Maynooth. The historic south campus of the university is among the most charming of all university campuses in the British Isles. The brooding ruin of the Geraldine castle dominates the entrance, and just inside the gate is Silken Thomas's yew tree (where the rebel reputedly played the harp on the night before the fall of the castle). Straight ahead is the imposing façade of Stoyte House and its lateral extensions and through the arches one enters into St Joseph's Square, an imposing quad flanked by New House and Humanity House. Straight ahead is the even more imposing façade of the President's Arch, enclosed between the end of Pugin Hall and the College Chapel. Another quad, St Mary's, is located behind this building and other nineteenth-century buildings – such as Logic House, Rhetoric House and the Aula Maxima – dotted around the campus add to its charm. The John Paul II library is a modern building, while the older Russell Library houses many rare books and manuscripts used principally by researchers. The north campus is much more modern and contains the John Hume building, named after one of Maynooth's most famous graduates, the SDLP leader who jointly won the Nobel Peace Prize for his part in the Northern Ireland Peace Process. Whether one's choice of destination at Maynooth is the 'Town' or the 'Gown', one will find it a fascinating place to visit.

NAAS

The town of Naas dominated the ancient Irish region known as '*Airthear Life*' or the 'Loop of the Liffey'. Naas is at the centre of the Liffey valley, and its geographical location between the Bog of Allen and the Wicklow Mountains meant that it controlled the main routes from Dublin to the south of the island. Naas was also situated on the border between the ancient Gaelic kingdoms of North and South Leinster, and the

Irish name '*Nás ns Ríogh*' means 'the Meeting Place of the Kings', reflecting a yearly meeting between the two monarchs that occurred here. The town's coat of arms features a snake, the Celtic symbol for an annual event.

St Patrick visited Naas during the early Christian period, but the town of Naas owes its origins to the Normans, who arrived in the area in the late twelfth century. They built two motte and bailey castles here before constructing a stone fortress, St David's Castle, which still stands at the centre of the town. The Normans who settled in Naas were from the marches of Wales, and they brought a devotion to their patron saint with them, so the Welsh St David superseded St Corban as the patron saint of Naas.

The town lay just within the Pale and suffered many attacks from the Irish clans of the Wicklow Mountains and the midlands during the medieval and Tudor periods. In 1577, for

Petty's map of the Naas area in 1683.

example, Rory Óg O'More sat under a high cross at the centre of the town directing the burning and pillage of the town. By the early seventeenth century however, peace had returned and Charles I's deputy, Thomas Wentworth, Earl of Strafford, built a fine mansion at Jigginstown. The house was one of the first in Ireland to be constructed of bricks and was to be literally fit for a king, as Wentworth told Charles he wanted to erect a dwelling for His Majesty to use if he visited Ireland. However, Wentworth was indicted on charges relating to his behaviour in Scotland, and Charles did nothing to stop his deputy's execution in the Tower of London. On his way to the executioner's block, Wentworth famously uttered the phrase 'Put not your trust in princes, but in principles'. The execution of Wentworth gave rise to another saying in and around the locality of Naas: 'Wentworth's head was off before his roof was on', since Jigginstown House was unfinished. The house was abandoned and quickly became a ruin, which can still be seen today on the Newbridge Road.

The eighteenth century saw a period of peace and the County of Kildare Canal was constructed as an extension of the Grand Canal, which passed through the nearby village of Sallins. A fine new harbour was also constructed at Naas, and today the canal stores and a restored industrial crane adorn this part of the town.

Naas was the first large town to be attacked by insurgents during the Rebellion of 1798, but the rebels failed to take the town and fell back after a bloody encounter. In the nineteenth century, the Catholic priest of Naas, Fr Gerald Doyle, led Catholic resistance during the Tithe War of the 1830s. Also in that decade, the Poor Law system was introduced into Ireland and Naas was chosen as the site of one of three workhouses to be built in Kildare. Naas workhouse opened in August 1841, but the Great Famine struck soon afterwards. The number of inmates in Naas workhouse, which could officially hold 550 people, reached 700 in September 1847 and rose above 800 in December. At the height of the Famine, conditions in the overcrowded workhouse were appalling and a new paupers' cemetery had to be purchased. Today this area has been landscaped and turned into a Famine memorial park while the workhouse itself eventually gained a new lease of life as Naas hospital. In the 1880s a railway station was built in Naas as the Tullow branch line passed through the town, but the line closed in the twentieth century and the nearby mainline station at Sallins now serves Naas. The town continued to grow through the twentieth century, benefiting from the fact that the main roads to the south and the south-east met here, and it was linked to Dublin by Ireland's first dual carriageway (which was eventually upgraded to a motorway), later becoming one of the first towns in Ireland to be bypassed. During the Celtic Tiger era, Naas became the fastest growing town in Europe for a while, with many new housing estates springing up in this desirable commuter town. Kildare County Council has its offices here, and the county town remains a great place to visit.

Also from The History Press

Irish Revolutionaries

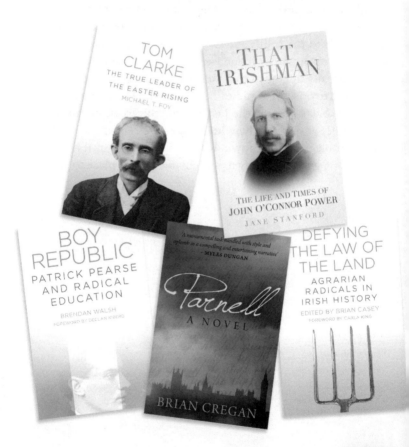

THE
SACRED
TRUST

by
Rabbi Pinchas Stolper

Published by

TRUST

Love, Dating and Marriage: The Jewish View

THE SACRED TRUST

© *Copyright 1996 by Rabbi Pinchas Stolper*

Published by the National Conference of Synagogue Youth /
Union of Orthodox Jewish Congregations of America
333 Seventh Avenue / New York, N.Y. 10001 / (212) 563-4000

FIRST EDITION
First Impression . . . April 1996

Distributed by
MESORAH PUBLICATIONS, Ltd.
4401 Second Avenue
Brooklyn, New York 11232

Distributed in Europe by
J. LEHMANN HEBREW BOOKSELLERS
20 Cambridge Terrace
Gateshead, Tyne and Wear
England NE8 1RP

Distributed in Israel by
SIFRIATI / A. GITLER — BOOKS
4 Bilu Street
P.O.B. 14075
Tel Aviv 61140

Distributed in Australia & New Zealand by
GOLDS BOOK & GIFT CO.
36 William Street
Balaclava 3183, Vic., Australia

Distributed in South Africa by
KOLLEL BOOKSHOP
22 Muller Street
Yeoville 2198, Johannesburg, South Africa

Printed In The United States Of America by
Noble Book Press Corp., New York, NY

Dedicated by
the loving children of

David and Cecile Levine
and
Fritz Lowenthal

who came to America as immigrants

Walter and Randie Lowenthal

Table of Contents

Preface to This Edition   ix

Preface   xi

Foreword *by Rabbi Aryeh Kaplan*   xvii

Chapter One: Love, Dating and Marriage:
        The Jewish View   19
Had I Only Known: An Introductory Story

Chapter Two: Defining Our Goals   23

America Has Lost its Way / Intimacy: A Private Affair / The Creative Life Force of a People / Is There an Objective "Right Way"?

Chapter Three: The Deeper Meaning of Love and Family   29
The Source of Moral Law / From Love of Man to Love of God / The Unique Role of the Family / The Human and the Animal: Basic Parenting Differences / What Makes Us Human; The Role of Speech / The Development of Giving Individuals / Why Was Woman Created? / What Is Jewish Marriage? / Intimacy in Marriage

Chapter Four: Means and Ends   49
The Jewish Approach to Intimacy / Intimacy — A Constructive Force / The True Roots of Love — Love in Marriage / Successful and Harmonious Marriage / The Significance of Family / The Right to Life / Woman as a "Person" / The Dehumanization of Women in Today's Society / Dress and

Conduct / Guidelines of Dress and Conduct for Women / Intimacy in Marriage / The Mystery of the Human Face / The Jewish Concept of Heroism / Education

Chapter Five: Understanding our Personalities:
        The Role of Desire   75
The Deeper Meaning of Human Desire / The "New" Morality / The Role of Tsniut in a Healthy Physical Relationship

Chapter Six: Youth: Launching Pad for Adulthood   79
Friendship and Physical Contact / Between Engagement and Marriage / What Is Truly Beautiful ? / Clothes and Shame / Love: Infatuation and Romance, but Much More / Choosing a Husband or Wife — The Dating Scene / The Goals of Dating / The Dangers of Intermarriage

Chapter Seven: Tsniut: An Essential Element for Holiness   93
The Behavior of Jewish Women / A Woman Sets the Tone / Woman's Nature Is Unique / The Attack on Woman and the Family / The Role of a Woman as a Mother / The Role of a Wife in Creating Man / The Equality of Women

Chapter Eight: The Surprising Biblical Record   107
Jewish Modesty Is not Prudishness

Appendix: Man and Woman: A Jewish View   115
The Unique Jewish View of Marriage / Tov = Good

Preface to This Edition

The **Sacred Trust** has proven to be more than just another book about traditional family values. This is a book whose first two editions made a deep and lasting impression on generations of young people who discovered in it compelling answers to their questions and yearnings. Many people who were already committed to living according to traditional Jewish family values remarked after reading the book, "I follow the rules, but now I understand the reasons." In these pages, thousands have found arguments, approaches and insights with which to counter the immorality of popular American culture as portrayed on television, films and the print media.

The present volume is a new and much expanded edition of the book, "Jewish Alternatives in Love, Dating and Marriage," published in 1984. In ten years much has changed in the world around us. I have taken note of these changes by thoroughly rewriting, revising and expanding the text. New chapters, sections and paragraphs have been added; words and sentences have been changed, added or deleted. If you read the book in 1984, you will discover much that is new in this edition.

A book on Jewish morality will never become a best-seller but the impact of this book *lives* in the lives of its readers, as earmarked copies of earlier editions are passed from hand to hand. Few contemporary volumes have had so strong an impact on so many lives.

This book has been a major catalyst in the return to Jewish identity and practice of many people. This is the reward of writing and rewriting, looking for and finding just the right word to convey sensitive but vital ideas.

My writing also reflects a lesson I have learned in many years of trying to help people change their perceptions and behavior. The lesson is that although book reviewers and some readers dislike repetition, it is crucial to the learning process. So don't be surprised when you run into the same ideas more than once. The repetition is deliberate. Reading the same idea with a change in wording or from a slightly different angle will surely expedite learning.

Reread the book, think through and consider the arguments — don't give up because you can't agree with or follow every single concept. By separating yourself, your conduct, your thought and your reading from America's often degenerate environment — and by entering a world of purity and spirituality — you will find your life enriched and changed.

Preface

*P*erhaps life's most difficult challenge is to adhere to traditional Torah regulations governing male-female relationships while at the same time living and breathing the air of an American culture in which the rules have been relaxed, the barriers let down, and where permissiveness has been accepted as the norm. Religious law demands restraint and permits intergender activity only within the carefully defined boundaries of marriage and private life. A young American Jew, aware of the basic conflict between what religion teaches and society allows, who struggles hard to reconcile the conflict and to resist temptation, has no greater immunity to the formidable influence of environment than his less-aware American counterparts.

That many do *succeed* in meeting the challenge of a more exacting standard of moral behavior suggests evidence of a natural inclination or deep personal need for more clearly defined standards of wholesomeness, direction and purpose in life. That so many people have changed their previous mode of behavior and have adopted traditional standards, despite the influence of America's media-created sexual revolution, attests to the existence of a basic human need for guidelines and for deeper satisfactions of spiritual experience and expression. One almost suspects that it could *be permissiveness itself* that has brought so many people back to the threshold of Torah for acceptable and convincing answers.

But how can people be expected to respond to the challenge of the Torah's ideology and practice when, for the most part, we have failed to communicate the Torah's teaching in this area of life? Even though intimacy and all that surrounds it is no longer a hush topic in today's open society, the basic attitudes, standards and laws of Torah with regard to this topic are still inaccessible to many. How can young people who assimilate and intermarry, or who fall prey to the lure of cults or missionaries, be criticized when the Jewish community has failed to adequately take seriously the yearning and need of every human being for spiritual fulfillment and the intense desire of so many contemporary Jews for initiation into a serious and authentic mode of religious observance? Clearly, compromised and diluted forms of religious experience have failed to satisfy — today there is a yearning for authenticity and substance. Youth longs to taste the authentic wine of Torah, not a wine so watered down that it no longer has the pleasing taste of wine.

If we are to "act for the Lord," we must know how to respond to the challenge of secular modernity and to compete for the respect, allegiance and dedication of the cream of contemporary American Jewry.

Thousands of searching, young Jews are still condemned to a life of assimilation, alienation or intermarriage, largely because not enough is being done to reach out to them. Even when they knock at our door we have not yet learned to respond adequately to their thirst for a life of spirituality. It is of little value to self-righteously condemn the community of secular or religiously compromising Jews for their inadequacies or failures. It is increasingly clear that all ideologies and approaches to Jewishness, with the exception of the classical Torah way of life, have lost their attractiveness, and that too many people are disinterested in a Judaism which is diluted and insipid.

In the decade since the first edition of this book appeared no one else has written a similar book. I encourage and welcome competition; the subject matter is of utmost importance.

The Torah community must continue to take seriously its responsibility to reach out and to produce literature which reveals the inner light of Jewish thought in contemporary idiom.

The Sacred Trust is an attempt to put forward a variety of approaches for understanding the authentic Jewish position on intimacy, family, and male-female relationships — the understanding of which is so crucial for successful marriage and constructive and meaningful male/female relationships. The book is largely based on insights and approaches developed in discussions with young people from every background and in nearly every city in North America during formal and informal discussions. These were held under the auspices of NCSY, the National Conference of Synagogue Youth, during the eighteen years the author served as its National Director and subsequently. The material of this book focuses on those specific areas that concern young people of the "dating age" and does not, therefore, claim to cover other related topics in detail or in depth.

It is my belief that effective discussions that concern the topic of male/female relations, in keeping with the concept of sexual modesty, are best held with small homogeneous groups of young men, or young women, separately. These study or discussion sessions are best led by men or women whose religious devotion and sense of tact are taken for granted, who are able to approach the topic with attitudes that encourage openness and sincere interest. Because give-and-take discussion sessions are almost always most valuable when they promote openness in the interests of understanding and knowledge, it is important to avoid guilt and embarrassment.

The Sacred Trust does not set forth the position or expectation of *Halachah*, Jewish law, with regard to specific situations and is not to be regarded as a "code of behavior" that would *instruct* an individual on how to respond or react in a *specific* circumstance. Indeed, people and situations vary, and each situation needs to be evaluated on its own level. What this book does suggest are methods for dealing with a series of topics whose general heading falls under the category of *tsniut*, the Jewish concept and approach to matters of family, relations, modesty and moral conduct.

For guidance *concerning* specific problems or for answers to *particular* questions, an individual is advised to approach his/her Orthodox rabbi. Explanations or rulings that pertain to personal circumstance can best be rendered through the enlightened perspective of an open, honest and ongoing relationship between the rabbi and the individual concerned.

This book does not delve into the regulations and Torah laws of "family purity" that pertain to marriage. For an excellent, modern exposition of the concept of family purity, the reader is urged to consult Rabbi Norman Lamm's *Hedge of Roses* (Feldheim Publishers), and for a unique and brilliant analysis of the ideology underlying *mikvah*, I recommend *Waters of Eden*, by Rabbi Aryeh Kaplan, published by NCSY.

I make little claim to originality. While some of the insights are mine, others were adapted from classical and contemporary sources. Many are the outgrowth of the perceptions and reactions of young people themselves. *Mikol melamdai hiskalti, mitalmidai yoter mikulam.* "I have acquired wisdom from my teachers, but even more so from my students."

Acknowledgments

The Sacred Trust, originally published under the title "The Road to Responsible Jewish Adulthood", and subsequently as *Jewish Alternatives in Love, Dating and Marriage* has been completely revised, rewritten and enlarged with the addition of a number of new chapters that reflect sensitivity to the ever-changing environment of America and to the many welcome recommendations of students and friends.

The first edition, published in 1967, was read by several individuals who offered critical comments, to whom I extend my sincere appreciation. I am especially grateful to Rabbi Norman Lamm for his many suggestions, to Rabbi and Mrs. Jack Steinhorn, the late Rabbi

Israel Klavan, to Yaakov Kornreich and Meyer Krentzman. The first edition was read in mimeographed form by more than two dozen young people. Their observations were of great value in determining the book's final form. Their frankness and friendship is deeply appreciated.

The second edition was read by Dr. Joseph Kaminetsky, Yaakov Kornreich, Marla Corush Frohlinger, Dr. Reuven Bulka and Rabbi Shmuel Himmelstein, to whom I offer my gratitude. Their critical comments are appreciated. My special thanks to Dr. Judith B. Katz for her special efforts in reviewing and rewriting sections of the second edition.

This edition benefited from the incisive observations and editorial comments of my daughter, Michal Cohen, and of Fayge Silverman. Mrs. Judi Dick made a special contribution to the book's final form. The many typings and re-typings of the manuscript benefited from the talents and care of my loyal assistant, Laura Berkowitz.

I recall with gratitude the inspiration and zealous devotion to Jewish tradition of my late father, Rabbi David Bernard Stolper, ztz"l, and my mother Mrs. Nettie Stolper.

I dedicate this volume to my wife Elaine who personifies the nobility and goodness of the Jewish wife and mother. May we be worthy to enjoy the continued growth in Torah and *yirat shamayim* of our children and grandchildren.

"For the Lord your G-d walks in the midst of your community to protect you . . . therefore your community must be holy, so that He may not see anything indecent, unseemly, and turn away from you."

Two Notes

There are sections of the book in which I speak primarily to young men, or to young women, and in these sections I address myself accordingly. In other cases, however, and especially in today's era of confused gender roles where most messages apply to both male and female, for the sake of practicality and easy flow, I employ a general or collective term, instead of the more awkward and cumbersome "boy/girl" or "man/woman" combination where such phraseology might disturb the rhythm, ease or fluidity of style.

The word *"tsniut"* is a Hebrew term that embraces the concepts of modesty, humility, decency, privacy and self-restraint — qualities of behavior and character that govern the manner in which a person should relate to his fellow man; attitudes with which to approach, fulfill and perform our responsibilities and obligations to Almighty G-d.

To "walk *humbly* with G-d" also carries the meaning of seclusion, inwardness and privacy.

Pinchas Stolper

New York,
March 1996

Foreword

by Rabbi Aryeh Kaplan

*J*udaism has always taught that physical relations are "powerful and dangerous"; not to be taken casually. For one thing, cohabitation brings the next generation into existence, and therefore, since the potential number of offspring of every liaison increases geometrically with each generation, every coupling act between two human beings has ramifications that can affect untold millions of human beings.

Judaism does not see procreation as something unclean or carnal. Rather, the Torah views it as one of the most holy human endeavors. Indeed, the Torah's strictures surrounding intimate behavior can be compared to those surrounding the permissible uses of a Torah scroll. It is precisely because a Torah scroll is so sacred that the uses to which it can be put are so severely restricted. The same holds true with regard to physical relationships.

A hint of the sacred nature of marital intimacy is found in the account of man's creation, where the Torah states, "G-d created the human in His image — in the image of G-d He created him — male and female He created him" (Genesis 1:27). The verse unambiguously states that the image of G-d is formed by man and woman in unison. This concept is echoed in numerous places in the Talmud and Midrash.

It is significant that in the Hebrew language neuter does not exist; everything is either masculine or feminine. In conceptual terms, the masculine is seen as the power to give, while the feminine is the power to receive. (This is true primarily in the abstract; it is recognized that in the real world, men and women both have masculine and feminine sides.)

When we speak of various aspects of our understanding of G-d, we use adjectives and descriptions, and one facet of these is gender related. Thus, although the creative and providential aspects of G-d are seen as masculine, there is a feminine aspect of the Divine, usually referred to as the *Shechinah*.

When a male saw a vision of the masculine aspect of the Divine, he perceived It as having his own face. However, when he visualized a vision of the female aspect of the Divine, he saw It as having the face of his wife. In the case of a prophetess, the same holds true; she viewed the feminine aspect as herself, and the masculine aspect as her husband. The rationale for this are beyond the scope of our present discussion, but on the simplest level it represents the fact that every prophet sees a vision through the spark of the Divine in himself.

When a man and a woman come together, they form the complete image of the Divine. This is a situation wrought with more holiness than even a Torah scroll. Is this not the reason that the covenant of Abraham, which is the indelible mark of the Jew, involves the male reproductive organ?

There has long been a need for a book that presents the Jewish view that the relationship between man and woman is both holy and beautiful, and, at the same time, dangerous when misused. My good friend, Rabbi Pinchas Stolper, has done an admirable job in producing such a book. It is a work that will go a long way in helping the contemporary community deal with the relaxation of moral standards and the problems it has engendered.

Chapter One

Love, Dating and Marriage: The Jewish View

Ben Zoma said:
Who is strong?
He who subdues his desires.   *Avot* 4:1

Had I Only Known:
An Introductory Story

he story is told of Rabbi Hai Gaon, the great rabbi and judge of Israel. He served as Head of the Jewish court system in Babylonia. When Rabbi Hai was old, and lying on his deathbed, thousands of students and disciples surrounded his home to honor their great teacher. His greatest student stood at his bedside. Suddenly, he noticed a tear in Rabbi Hai's eye. Turning to his teacher he said, "Rabbi, please explain why I detect

Love, Dating and Marriage: The Jewish View □ 19

sadness on your face. When you reach the highest heaven you will be carried on the shoulders of the righteous, you will be welcomed with singing and love. The heavenly gates will open to welcome you. Angels will carry you to a heavenly throne. You will sit among the most eminent of our people near the very throne of G-d.

"Why do you hesitate to leave this world of darkness when you are about to enter the world of truth, light and G-dliness?"

Rabbi Hai replied, "I am moved by your question: Allow me to explain my sadness with a story, a true story.

"Several years ago I was traveling from town to town to administer justice to our people. One day I came to a town where I was hosted at a very fine hotel. The accommodations, meals and service were superb. Duties concluded, I was about to climb aboard my carriage to depart from the town. Suddenly I saw the hotel owner running to bid me farewell. He was crying, tears pouring from his eyes. He said, "Forgive me, great rabbi and judge, forgive me for what I have done." I replied, "Forgive you for what? Everything at your hotel was absolutely wonderful." "No," said the hotel keeper, "no one informed me that you are the Chief Justice of the Jewish people. I was told that you were a great rabbi, but not that you are the Chief Justice. Had I known, I would have hosted you in the royal suite. I would have served you on golden dishes, with sterling silverware and lead crystal stemware. I would have provided you with regal meals. Had I only known," he kept crying. "Forgive me, great judge," he said as he wept. "Had I only known. Please forgive me."

Rabbi Hai continued. "I, too, am about to depart from this world. My body, the temporary residence of my soul, was my hotel. I now feel like the hotel keeper in my story. Did I not provide my soul with fine accommodations, meals and service? But it is also true that on many occasions I was not sufficiently aware of the fact that my soul is on loan from G-d. I failed to realize that it is royalty, that it can be compared to a top-ranking official being hosted at a hotel. I, too, am about to depart, I, too, realize that, 'had I known,' I would have served my soul with the equivalent of golden dishes in the royal suite. I, too, will have to answer to G-d as I stand before His great throne when He will judge me. I, too, will have to reply with the words of the hotel keeper, "Had I only known, had I only known.' "

And with these words, Rabbi Hai's soul departed.

Each of us has within us a royal guest on loan from G-d — a soul whose temporary residence is our body. Each of us will one day have to answer to G-d. "Did we treat our guest royally — or did we besmirch it?" Each of us may one day have to reply, "Had I only known, had I only known."

Hopefully the following pages will provide a guide for the superior care of your great guest. I know that with the help of the Almighty you can succeed.

Chapter Two

Defining Our Goals

America Has Lost Its Way

You will certainly agree that people, all people, cherish their privacy. There are so many things in our lives that we insist on doing in private. Yet despite this inborn craving for privacy, our society has become so vulgarized and commercialized that the *one* human activity which should be the most intimate and private is the subject of the greatest public display in world history. "Love" is bought, sold, advertised, flaunted on billboards and made the subject of novels, movies and magazines — a public exhibition unprecedented in the history of mankind. The picture this activity paints is that Western society has in so many ways lost its way. We are a society unable to preserve the essential human glue that is required to hold us together.

When we view the bill of fare presented on TV or the movies, we are constantly bombarded by the oft-unstated but nonetheless blatantly obvious message that the purpose and the goal of almost any dealings between a man and a woman is physical relations; the gratification of a biological drive, urge or need. Whatever men and women do together is in reality just a prelude, a form of game, a road that leads to but one objective, that of two people engaged in some form of intimate, private activity. In some movies, people even go through the motions of "being in love" or of getting married — but the purpose of the show is the public spectacle of a private act. This has become the essence of the "show." Any other scenarios in the story of their lives is secondary.

The traditional Jewish family relationship presents a totally different picture. In the real world, the Jewish world, a man and woman form a relationship with one objective — to create a home and build a family wherein their life's goals will be fulfilled and realized. To preserve its private and intimate nature it is guarded as a hidden, confidential matter which takes place behind closed doors. Intimate activity between them is personal and secluded. Essential though it may be, it is a means, not an end.

When you examine a Jewish family, what do you see? You see two people who are busily involved in building a home, a family. You see cooperation and harmony. You see two people who live for each other, for their children and community; people who are sensitive to each other's needs and to the needs of others, people with values and goals.

Healthy and stable man-woman relationships are building blocks in the composition of a structure, an edifice whose function stretches beyond the present — beyond instant physical gratification. The goals of the family lie in the long run, for a lifetime and for generations to come. Parents hope that their children will adopt and accept their values. Parents also desire that the families their children will build will be stronger and far superior to their own. Vital family relationships result in stability and create a framework on which a meaningful spiritual society can be erected. Without doubt the glue that helps hold a man and woman together in marriage includes love, affection, and intimacy, but these are neither discussed in public nor in any outsider's presence. They are not cheapened or made vulgar by public exposure.

Too many good people have gotten caught up in the popular attitude promoted by the media, magazines and popular novels that life, especially in its physical manifestations, is fun and games. Most people know in their heart of hearts that these attitudes are not only nonsensical but are destructive to the wholesomeness and meaning of life.

There are tens of millions of Americans, some would say a silent majority, for whom family values, the sacredness of the marriage bond and the commitment that intimacy must be reserved for marriage form the rock of their lives.

These ideas may be regarded as old fashioned and out of date by Hollywood, the media and some of your friends, but they represent the wholesomeness of ideas and attitudes accepted by countless Americans, even if in practice they are flouted by many.

This book contains a message for all people. The Jewish view of family and personal relationships based on mankind's most ancient tradition affords a glimpse into a way of life, as old as mankind itself, which offers an escape from a society which has lost its way. The traditional Jewish way opens a path into a life filled with values, harmony, purpose, warmth and truth.

Intimacy: A Private Affair

In America everyone minds everyone else's business. Interpersonal relations, intimacy and violence are the major topics of newspapers, television, literature, the movies and the stage. *Relations* are America's major obsession, and one of its most lucrative industries. Suggestive terms fill the atmosphere and the marketplace. In today's spiritual void there appears to exist a campaign on the part of the media to break down what remains of privacy, controls and restraints.

For a Jew, intimacy is nobody else's business, nobody's but his own. In Judaism, marital relations require absolute privacy, and it is this confidentiality that has permitted Jewish marriages to remain holy and that encourages the deepening and maturing of interpersonal relationships. This Jewish abhorrence of allowing the public exposure of a deeply personal activity has nothing at all to do with guilt; it reflects an ingrained respect for privacy and recognition that the protection of privacy is a basic human need and requirement.

Deluged as we are by a torrent of written and graphic materials in an obsessed society, we often wonder: What is the Jewish point of view?

The hallmark of the Jewish attitude is privacy, modesty and holiness. Whatever happens between two people does not belong in tomorrow's headlines. And it is mostly for this reason that Jews have until recently been reluctant to publish books and articles in English for the general public which discuss in public that which we believe should be discussed only in private.

The Creative Life Force of a People

The sensuous psychiatrists and playboy philosophers haven't much in common, but they are united in proclaiming the advent of a "new age of freedom" between the genders.

But people who are sensitive, thoughtful and in search of values will not allow themselves to be deceived. A counter reaction has begun, and with it a search for standards which recognize that a human being is a spiritual being, capable of reaching beyond his/her physical self and of responding to the urging of the soul, a being who takes G-d into account and who searches for a link with eternity when making life's major decisions.

Ask yourself the following questions: Are physical relations a mere biological impulse or is it the life force and creative impulse of a People? Is it simply a private matter between two "consenting adults" or does it govern the quality of life for the individual, the family and all society? Isn't life devalued and deformed when it is declared open and "free" and, consequently, isn't such an attitude destructive of the social fabric and the very essence of human society?

Do you realize that the human environment, the very landscape of life and civilization, is a precarious achievement that depends to a very great extent on our attitudes toward intimate and interpersonal relationships? According to some historians, many ancient societies, such as the Greeks and Romans, actually collapsed because the family and morality broke down first — because people became interested only in the pursuit of selfish, ego-satisfying pleasure and lost sight of anyone or anything else; their partner, the unborn, their family or the values taught by religious tradition and the aspiration to create a higher and better life.

I invite each reader to consider his or her personal stake in finding the true answers. Our momentary urges and impulses may sometimes lead us astray. Nonetheless, logic, our values, our self-respect, respect for others and our fear of consequences should motivate us to strengthen the only code of interpersonal relationships which has the potential for bringing us into harmony with both G-d and society. To the Jew, intimacy can never be a matter of fun and games. The protection of women and families is one of the few matters of life and death importance to every individual, to society and the continuity of the Jewish people. We must remember that our conduct in this area is of such significance that it always leaves its indelible impact on ourselves and/or on someone else.

Is There an Objective "Right Way"?

The purpose of this book is to help you discover that you do have a choice between the "new freedom" (which is nothing but old-fashioned immorality) so urgently promoted by the media, by our "friends" and by so much of modern society, and a standard of conduct which has stood the test of thousands of years, and offers the only proven, reliable avenue to the achievement of human happiness and fulfillment. In this book, I hope to point out the likely consequences of the choices we make. I will try to describe a way of life that has proven itself to generations of people as a potential source and sturdy foundation for the realization of successful living and self-fulfillment. The "new" standard of acceptable social conduct between the genders is a path fraught with danger, a path which far from leading to fulfillment and success in actuality leads nowhere. It has been foisted upon us, in large measure, by certain commercial and often criminal interests which have turned it into big business, a business whose only goal is the ringing of the cash registers of a contrived revolution. Unfortunately, many honest and well-meaning people have been seduced and deceived by this propaganda or by some aspects of it. Most of these have never read a book or heard anyone present the arguments for the traditional Jewish point of view.

The downhill plunge of American moral standards continues apace. Each year new magazines and movies find the audacity to go one step farther than their predecessors. The institutions of family and marriage are under constant attack. A spirit of rebellion against any objective standard of right and wrong has taken hold in some so-called intellectual and liberal circles of our society. The concept of chastity has become a relic to too many young people. We are told that there is no objective "right way," that each individual has the right to exercise the option of discovering what rules are best for him or herself.

Before we accept any of the above attitudes, we owe it to ourselves to do some in-depth investigating.

Is there an objective "right way" that has stood the test of time? Is there a "proven standard" for relationships that meets the physical, psychological and spiritual needs of people?

Is there any truth to the claim equating permissiveness with happiness? Is this modern "new morality" an original concept, or has civilization already tried similar approaches, and with what results or consequences? Does Jewish morality offer a unique alternative, not to be found in other approaches? In what way is the Jewish family the secret of Jewish survival through the ages?

Where can one find a way of life which fosters and promotes a healthy, constructive and positive relationship between men and women? And if the traditional Jewish point of view offers a meaningful and viable alternative, how can a person learn more about it?

In the pages that follow, the author will raise questions and suggest answers that he hopes will stimulate his readers to search, think, study and investigate in the hope that they will develop a deeper understanding of the Jewish religious outlook. It is his hope, too, that it will lead to a fuller appreciation of the Torah view — and ultimately to its full observance as well.

Chapter Three

The Deeper Meaning of Love and Family

The Source of Moral Law

G-d, Who created man and woman, knows what is best for us. G-d supervises the destiny of His own creation. Man (man, meaning mankind, which includes men and women) and the moral law which, according to Jewish thought, must govern man's life, have one origin, one source and one Creator. The notion that religion and life are two separate entities is foreign to Jewish thought. The idea that an unbridgeable gap separates everyday law from religious morality is a non-Jewish idea. That the secular and the holy are two separate worlds is one of the non-Jewish notions partially responsible for the social crisis that threatens the stability of contemporary life. To the classical Jewish way of thinking, all law — civil, religious or moral — flows from a common source. As a matter of fact the laws of the Torah don't govern religious matters alone — the synagogue, morality, marriage and family — they also relate to the office, the school, the factory, the government, the army — every and any area of life.

The G-d of nature, the G-d of history and the G-d of the Torah are one. There is no contradiction between the laws of the Torah and the laws of nature. On the contrary, G-d is the Master of history, nature and human destiny. The same G-d Who created man and woman commanded a single set of laws, called Torah, to govern with equal force and authority in all areas of human activity, without exception. It would stand to reason, therefore, that the G-d Who created man with a set of needs, energies, abilities, organs, urges and ambitions, would also teach him how best to meet, expend, utilize and realize them. The Torah perceives each human being as a complete world in miniature and as a miniature sanctuary. The Torah sees *all* human activity as potentially sacred, emphasizes this teaching and offers the ideal guide for human and social living and fulfillment.

Surrounded as we are by a frightening breakdown in family, social and interpersonal relationships and by a spreading crisis of identity, it is essential that we become conscious of the fact that just as G-d created the universe, with all the physical laws which govern it, He also created mankind and all the laws which govern every facet of human life and endeavor. To ignore these laws is not only to defy G-d, but to forfeit our opportunity for a mature, creative and meaningful existence.

From Love of Man to Love of God

Who is G-d? He is the Creator of the cosmos, Creator of mountains and seas, animals and birds, man and woman. He is also the Creator of love and compassion, generosity and tenderness, justice and mercy, sensitivity and holiness.

The Almighty wants us to emulate and imitate Him, to follow His example, to fulfill and perfect ourselves by aspiring to higher levels of spirituality and holiness. We can *best* imitate G-d and express our love of Him by learning to love man, G-d's greatest and most remarkable creation.

Where does human love most easily, most naturally and most frequently develop? In the various dynamic relationships that bind husband and wife, and later, parent and child. These relationships reflect the highest and most unselfish expressions of caring and concern, sacrifice, affection, regard, kindness, devotion, warmth and sharing that we classify under the umbrella definition of love, as the term "love" is understood by man. In order to better love G-d, it is necessary first to have experienced the love of man; that is, to have loved, been loved, and to have understood and experienced all the emotions, aspects and expressive avenues of the loving relationship. For this reason the Sages teach, "a man/woman without a mate is considered half a person."

If a person can deeply love, appreciate and respect those to whom he is most closely related, he may finally discover the possibility of love for his friend, or fellow man. The commandment of the Torah to "love your fellow as yourself" can best be understood to mean, "love your fellow *because* he is like yourself," which means that just as *you* were created in G-d's image, so too was *he;* that just as *you* have needs and feelings, so too has *he.*

Once a person has achieved this understanding and actually practices love for people in the physical world, he can more easily intensify his love for G-d who is more abstract and distant.

The process of learning to love G-d and of establishing a personal relationship with G-d should grow out of the experiences and habits of early childhood. As we begin to love and appreciate our parents, we develop a sense of gratitude for all the favors and guidance they bestow. We should soon recognize that all the pleasures and blessings of life have their ultimate source in G-d.

Another way to learn the love of G-d is by emulating our parents' and teachers' love of G-d, by respecting the values by which our parents and teachers live. This is especially so when they conscientiously observe the G-d-given Commandments, the *mitzvot,* which, after all, are the only way we are able to relate to G-d — *in deed.* The *mitzvot,* we soon realize, are the only tools we have for perfecting ourselves, for taming the animal and elevating the more primitive in ourselves, and for reaching toward G-d. True, our laws are ancient, but so is truth, kindness and friendship. True, we value the past, because it is only by using the wisdom of the past that we can successfully build the future. If someone will tell you that you "live in the past" tell him that "the past lives in me."

The Unique Role of the Family

In this book, our concern is with male-female relationships, and the effect of each person's behavior on the uniqueness, value, sanctity and dignity of other individuals.

Our Rabbis ask, "Why was each individual born uniquely different"? They answer, "So that he should be able to say to himself, 'For my sake was the world created.' "

If our concern is for the individual, why should this book begin with a discussion of the family? Simply put, it is because the family is the one human social institution most indispensable for creating and forming the individual.

Two people must act in unison in order to create a third. The highest act of human creativity calls for *two to act as one* in order to bring forth a new individual. If two can act as *one* (actually, this is a play on words because the *one* we refer to is G-d Who is uniquely One), they can draw a new soul down to earth and create a new human being, making G-d the third partner in a new miracle of Creation. G-d has given man the ability to duplicate His own greatest feat of Creation by creating a child. When we create a child we literally *play G-d.*

But what happens if the child we create is the product of lust or physical passion alone, what if he or she is created through adultery — through the rejection of God's laws — then what kind of child have we created? This is not to say that the child might not succeed in overcoming his or her disabilities — but such a child certainly has a few strikes going against him or her.

The adventure of man's partnership with G-d in the drama of creation does not end with the birth of a child. After birth, too, the father and mother must dwell together if a family is to be created, a family in which children can be reared and educated to develop into men or women capable of fulfilling their own human and spiritual destiny. Each person is, to a large extent, what his/her parents make him/her. If the parents are successful their children may even be better than they. Jewish parents have always hoped that they will succeed in rearing children who will be better than themselves, who will be more capable than they were in fulfilling their individual human and spiritual destinies. This explains why, as a rule, parents are not jealous of the accomplishments of their children. We find this thought in the Talmud (*Sanhedrin* 105b), "A person is jealous of everyone else, except for his child and his student."

In the historic Jewish view, it is the family and not the synagogue that is the basic institution of Jewish life. In fact, most of the crucial acts and experiences of Jewish living call for a family setting and for family observance. Judaism is family centered, not synagogue centered. The synagogue at best plays a secondary role. The Jewish home is the center of our existence, it is the place where sanctity and Torah are translated into real life. This is unfortunately no longer true of non-observant families. There the synagogue has largely replaced the home as the center of Jewish life.

The Jewish family has long been a model of harmony, love and stability; the envy of the entire civilized world. The social evils that tend to disrupt and destroy the modern home — such as divorce, domestic abuse and juvenile delinquency — were until recent times almost unknown among traditional, observant Jews. While observant Jews in America have also been affected by this generation's tendency to solve marital problems through divorce, there is a quantitative difference of very considerable measure between observant Jews and other Jews.

Marriage is not optional for a Jewish man. It is obligatory. The Talmud *(Shabbat* 31a) states that in the world to come, the first three questions asked of a man will be, "Did you buy and sell honestly, in good faith? Did you establish a set time each day for the study of Torah? Did you raise a family?" The single life is regarded as a misfortune, and a good wife the chief delight of a man's existence. It was and is relatively easy to obtain a Jewish divorce, but among observant Jews far fewer do so. Jews who observe tradition, as set forth by Jewish law, take family life very seriously and generally create stable, strong and supportive family environments. They work hard at their marriages and resort to divorce only after many and extensive attempts to keep a marriage together have definitely failed.

Every Jewish man is required to marry to fulfill the commandment of having children and raising a family. "Be fruitful and multiply" is the first *mitzvah* in the Torah. The family bond and its relationships are sanctified. Marriage and family are integral parts of the Divine plan. The love which attracts man and woman to each other is sacred in the eyes of G-d. Jews see the family as the essential force in the development of a G-d-fearing individual, and the creation of a home in which G-d dwells. If this home is dedicated to G-d, and His word reigns supreme there, it becomes the fulcrum for the entire structure of life.

The purpose of the family includes not only the satisfaction of the basic human need for comradeship, love, reproduction and raising children, but the total development of the individual, and, through the individual, the family which is the building block of all of civilization.

According to Torah laws, relations are not permitted outside of marriage. Why? Intimacy is not simply an "act" which brings *two bodies together*, but an integral part of marriage, bringing *two people together*, not for enjoyment or pleasure alone, but in order to make it possible for two people to become truly one. In Judaism, intimacy is holy because it implies much more than the uniting of two bodies for pleasure, but uniting them for always. Marriage means much more than two people who share a home. It means two people who share a home and enjoy a relationship that is so successful that by thinking and acting as one, they share their life together. When they unite, it is for the purpose of expressing their love and for bringing children into the world. Cohabitation itself is so significant and powerful that it is not only the point of origin of all of mankind, it enables a couple to bring a soul from its heavenly abode down to earth, where it will assume the shape and form of a new human being.

If the relationship between two people is based solely on physical gratification, it implies that the moment either partner finds someone else who offers something better, he/she will leave the other and take a new partner. However, if a relationship is a loving one and is made permanent through marriage, and if the family is a holy unit, then what we have are two partners who have made a lasting commitment, each to the other, to help, support and encourage one another in sickness and health, tragedy and joy, poverty and wealth, hardship and good fortune, and even death.

The relationship between a man and woman is unique because only the human being is created in the "image" or reflection of G-d. Possibly by achieving a deeper insight into the uniqueness of the human being, we might better appreciate the unique opportunity we have to create a special relationship with the opposite gender, of uniting two into one, which has the potential of achieving overtones of the unique qualities of G-d Himself. Only the human being possesses G-d-like qualities such as speech, the ability to choose between right and wrong, the ability to reach toward the spiritual and be spiritually creative. This also involves the ability to pass on traditions, skills, history and knowledge from one generation to the next.

The Human and the Animal: Basic Parenting Differences

Why is a human child so helpless and dependent at birth; why is the difference between a human baby and most animal newborns so pronounced and radical? The difference between the spiritual potential of the human and the animal can be understood by analyzing the total helplessness of the human infant.

Without the mother's constant attention, the human infant is completely lost. The infant is totally dependent for physical, psychological and emotional well-being upon the care and life support system of its mother. In fact, studies reveal that even if feeding is maintained, but emotional contacts like hugging, kissing, cuddling and talking are withdrawn, the child will deteriorate and eventually die. The human infant is all "potential," raw material awaiting the attention and care of its parents. This attention is comprised of the love, guidance, protection and support that makes growth, maturation and learning possible.

Observation of the animal world, however, reveals quite the

reverse. A fish, for example, functions as a fully independent entity from the moment it is hatched. Immediately from birth, the fish is capable of swimming, breathing and feeding itself. Some fish may never even see their parents. The simplicity of their biological design and function eliminates the need for parental support. There are no skills to teach, no emotions to convey, no knowledge to transfer. There is no civilization, history or tradition, no need for educating fish to become links in a continuing chain of history or tradition. Each generation of fish is an exact replica of the generation from which it is begotten.

The salmon, for instance, offers an excellent and easily observable example. Soon after a mature female salmon swims upstream to spawn, she deposits her eggs, turns back downstream to the sea and dies. The male salmon, drawn by instinct, deposits his sperm on the eggs already laid, then follows the same current back downstream and disappears into oblivion. Before long, tiny salmon hatch from the deposit of eggs and sperm on the banks of the stream, and begin their journey downstream toward entry into the ocean where they will live, grow and develop. As they mature and age, they too will swim upstream to repeat the pattern of their unknown parents. The infant salmon knows nothing of either parent. Why should he?

The more complex the form of life, however, the more necessary, lasting and intense is the relationship that develops between parent and child. In the animal kingdom on a scale from simple to complex, we observe that the parent-child relationship also moves from simple to complex, in both duration of time and development of family-type associations.

Because fish have nothing to teach their young, no tradition to give over, no skills or language to impart, there is no need to train or relate to their offspring. There is no need for family — there are no traditions, relationships, discipline, goals or ideals.

The human infant is *the most helpless* because it has *the most* to learn: traditions, relationships, ideals and goals. For this reason, the commitment of the mother and father to teaching, inspiring or motivating will be a major factor in determining the kind of person the infant will become. The parents will determine the degree of progress and influence and the flow of continuity, from one era to another of human civilization. The very survival of the uses and ideals of the past depend upon the ability of parents and teachers to transmit, inspire, motivate and mold. Parents teach children to use the knowledge already gained by men and women of past generations for the improvement of both their own present and future lives, for the benefit and general welfare of society as a whole, and for the intelligent responses required by the challenges of new situations and times.

The parent-child relationship requires such a great expenditure of time because time creates bonds of trust and reliance. A child who knows that his parents love him will also believe that the traditions, ideals and beliefs of his parents are reliable and accurate.

The relationship to parents must be so strong that the child feels that he/she is the bearer of human destiny: Each child must grow up believing that all that mankind has achieved since the beginning of time — and must accomplish until the end of time — is in his/her hands. Each child is a link in the chain of civilization, the bearer of human destiny and purpose, and if one link breaks, the chain will snap.

If we would only consider what will become of us if we ignore our spiritual-human potential by allowing the animal in us free reign, we would be exceedingly careful not to behave in an animal-like fashion in interpersonal relationships. If we would consider that the attraction which draws us to the opposite gender is a powerful spiritual force, we would take special care not to allow our physical impulses to overwhelm our spiritual drives. We would not allow the instinct of the moment to pervert or even destroy the potential of eternity.

What Makes Us Human; The Role of Speech

Consider the crucial nature of speech in separating the human being from the rest of creation by examining the following hypothetical model of a man-woman relationship. A young man and woman are marooned on a desert island from which there is no escape. There is no television or radio. Both find ample food and drink. Neither can speak the other's language. With no knowledge of how they have arrived or of how they might escape, with day passing day — with no end in sight — they might find themselves involved in the only activities available: eating, drinking and being intimate with one another. Even though they never met before, they may even begin to think that they are in love. Then suddenly they are rescued. They quickly discover that one is Danish and the other Greek, one is Jewish and the other a Moslem. I think you will agree that their "relationship" will most probably come to a very abrupt and emotional end. Radical differences in taste, language, religion, thought, politics, ideals, likes and dislikes would leave them with little basis for communication and very little common ground. They will most probably find it impossible to understand or appreciate each other. End of relationship.

The Torah (*Onkelus*) describes humans as "speaking beings." Speech is the major factor which separates man and animal. Speech is the human characteristic that enables men to communicate, to develop their physical and spiritual potential, to exercise choice, to establish values, to act in history, to perpetuate tradition and to live purposeful lives. Speech is the verbal articulation of thought and should guide men and women in *living responsible lives.* And since the human being is set apart and distinguished from the animal by the unique gift of speech that is *his* alone, it is only speech which can express and convey the ideals and goals of human society. Since humanity is defined through language, speech must be used *responsibly* in the creation of meaningful and dignified interpersonal relationships. Since humans are essentially speaking beings, conversation and the exploring of the other person's personality must take precedence in the creation of interpersonal relationships.

Unlike G-d, Who is unique and alone, the human being reaches his truest potential, and expresses his G-d-like qualities best, when he lives with a partner. To become a fulfilled human being, "it is not good that a person live alone," man/woman must find a partner, a mate, a helper, in order to achieve the *good* as defined by the Torah.

The Development of Giving Individuals

What is the spiritual goal of love and marriage? Man's relationship with G-d requires total surrender of self. How do we establish a meaningful relationship with G-d? By establishing relationships with our spouses based on shared ideals, goals and spirituality. Most of us have a false notion as to who we are. We have a false and over-egotistical sense of ourselves which must be stripped away. How do we learn that the purpose of life is not to live for ourselves? That we are not independent and autonomous? Through marriage. Marriage teaches us to surrender ourselves, it gives us the ability to integrate ourselves into something beyond ourselves, first by thinking in terms of a new unit — my spouse and I — and then by living for our children as well. Love and marriage are the training grounds for the sublimation of ego. Marriage teaches me to be concerned with and committed to my partner, by teaching me that my partner is as much a part of myself as I am. In marriage each of us learns to experience the world through another person. By caring for and being concerned with another person, by integrating that person into our reality, we learn to experience the world through another person. This is the first step to creating a mature and meaningful relationship with G-d.

If someone insults your wife, you will become incensed and angry. You will react as through he had insulted you. The person who insulted your wife asks, "Why are you excited? I didn't insult you, I insulted another person." You reply, "I take *that* insult personally, it is as though you insulted me." He replies, "I didn't insult your person, I insulted her person." You reply, "My wife and I are an integrated unit, we relate to each other as though we are one person. I identify with my wife and feel her insult. When my wife hurts, I hurt." When you are able to feel the world through another person you are on the way to knowing that you are linked to all mankind — and to G-d.

This is the kind of relationship we are ultimately expected to have with G-d. Marriage trains us to be capable of such a relationship. Caring produces both vulnerability and responsibility, obligations which are not easy to master but are of the utmost neccessity. If I identify and feel through you then I am no longer only me, I am also you. If I feel through you then what happens to you also affects me.

Obviously if I avoid intimate relationships I do not expose myself to being hurt, but I also turn myself into a selfish, narrow individual.

When we marry, we begin to feel responsibility for the community. Once we take upon ourselves responsibility for one another, we are expected to be responsible for the welfare of all people, this is the deeper meaning of the Torah teaching, Love your neighbor as yourself, meaning love him because he is like yourself — because he too is created in G-d's image — he, too, feels pain. He, too, is G-d's child.

In the last chapter of *Hilchot Teshuvah,* the Laws of Repentance, the Rambam describes the love of man for G-d. He says, "just as a man who is in love with a woman cannot get her out of his mind and is completely preoccupied with her, we must strive to develop the same feelings if we truly love G-d." In summary; marriage is the love of G-d in microcosm. Marriage is the training ground for the love of G-d.

Why Was Woman Created?

Almost immediately after the creation of the first person, the Lord remarked: "This is not good for man to be alone. I shall make him a helpmate (literally: someone opposite or against him)" (Genesis 2:18). Rabbi Samson Raphael Hirsch observes that the Torah's phrase did not read: "It is not good for man to be alone," but, "This is not good; man being alone," implying that when a person is alone, good cannot exist. The completion of the state of good in creation was not man, but woman. As the Talmud elaborates, "only through his wife does man *become a man."*

When it describes the creation of woman, the Torah teaches that since woman was created from a side of man, from another human being, she represents a higher level in creation than man, who was created from earth. When we examine creation as depicted in the Bible, we see that G-d created the world in progressive stages; from lower to higher beings; from simpler to more complex; from the chaos and confusion of Day One, to the order, perfection and spiritual qualities of Day Seven, the Sabbath; from the first day, when darkness covered the earth, to the sixth day when G-d created man and woman.

Creation reaches its zenith on the seventh day, the day of Sabbath rest, which is the day of messianic perfection when man emerged as a spiritual being who had overcome his dependence on materialism and the tyranny of *things.* First G-d created space, time, energy, matter and the inanimate elements and compounds; then He created plants and trees; then insects, fish and birds; still later animals; and finally man and woman on the sixth day.

Since woman was created after man, during the time between his creation and the coming of the Sabbath, woman represents the highest stage of creation. In fact, when woman was created, the Torah for the first time declared that creation was "*very* good." What was missing when man was created, what was the one last element still necessary before mankind could be established in his home in the Garden of Eden? Woman.

A specific description of the biological function of women is explicitly stated in the Biblical narrative of creation, "And Adam called his wife's name Eve for she would be the *mother* of all life" (Genesis 3:20). Marriage and family, integral to the Divine plan for the creation of mankind, are not arbitrary or artificial institutions "foisted" upon the human situation, but rather lie at the very essence of human nature. "Therefore shall man leave his father and his mother and cleave to his wife and they will become one flesh" (Genesis 2:24) follows immediately upon the creation of Eve.

The renowned Ra'avad, one of the greatest of the early commentators of the Talmud, interprets this passage beautifully:

"It is for this reason that G-d saw fit to change the order of creation when He created man. For had He created both man and woman from the earth, independent of each other, each would go his or her own way. Husband and wife would not be designated one for the other, to live together, for they would have been created separately. Instead, G-d created woman *from* man so that they would live together as one unit in marriage, each one needing the other in order to achieve the completion of themselves."

This does not imply that the Torah mandated specific roles for all women or all men, for to do so would be to lose touch with reality and the complexity of human nature. Life situations are much too intricate for simplistic definitions. But this does mean that certain roles are viewed by the Torah as being basic and natural roles for either man and woman. The fact that familial, marital and child-bearing responsibilities are the natural role for women is a concept that goes back to the Divine plan of creation, beginning with Eve and continuing through the Bible and Talmud.

What Is Jewish Marriage?

Until very recently, almost everyone took the institution of marriage for granted, never wondering at its almost universal acceptance. But in today's society, where no aspect of life escapes close and rational scrutiny, we must not abstain from investigating the institution of marriage as objectively as possible, in order to better understand and appreciate its significance for modern society.

Why are marriage and the family so basic to human society? Why should a *"single," "happy"* man or woman willingly surrender their freedom and independence to share their lives with a complete *"stranger"*? Why should a man want to feed this "stranger," house her, clothe her, support and educate her children? Why does a man assume these burdens, obligations and responsibilities? Why should a woman compromise her freedom or career to tie her star to a man? And yet even in an era when marriage and the family are under attack, with people daily exposed to propaganda promoting "alternative life styles," actual statistics indicate that as great a percentage of young people are marrying as ever before.

It appears that the impulse to create a permanent family relationship is part of our very being, involving much more than a desire for a physical relationship, which is readily available outside of marriage. Perhaps we seek to love and to be loved; perhaps we need structure and self-respect, a home in which to grow and build, a family to mold and children to raise. Perhaps, as we grow older we begin to realize that we are the bearers of the message and purpose of our parents and grandparents and that if we break the chain of history we will become the last station of a journey which began 4,000 years ago — and ended with us, ended with our failure to continue to practice and maintain our family's traditions and heritage.

For these reasons, Jewish law strongly urges that all people marry, and the earlier they marry, the better. In fact, in many observant families, it is common for young people's secular or professional education to be completed after marriage, so that the young couple can accomplish life's goals together, rather than waiting out a long period of tension and frustration before marriage.

Marriage is a mysterious force that calls man and woman to unite and become one, to build a home in which G-d will feel welcome and come to dwell. Marriage is an arena wherein the major points of life's program are enacted. In addition, the Torah regards celibacy in men as sinful, a repudiation of a religious obligation and the blessings that can only be had through marriage. The Talmud (*Yevamot* 62b) clearly states, "he who spends his days without a wife has no joy, no blessing, no good" in his life. But Torah law also contains a built-in bill of rights which gives the Jewish woman a unique status and position in the home, based on the Torah command that no matter how poor or troubled a man may be, with regard to his wife, "he may not diminish her support, her clothes or her conjugal rights" (Exodus 21:10).

Intimacy in Marriage

Marital relations are, therefore, not merely a permissible factor in Jewish marriage, but an obligation called for by Torah law. For without man and woman joining together, on a regular basis, as *one flesh*, no marriage is complete. Marital relations serve not only the purpose of creating children, but also promotes the overwhelming value that intimacy has in strengthening the family bond, in making man and woman a single unit, spiritually and physically. When the Torah says, "and they shall become one flesh," Rabbi S. R. Hirsch comments, " But that can only take place if at the same time they also become one mind, one heart, one soul — and if they subordinate all their strength and efforts to the service of a Higher will."

Unlike various Christian and non-Christian teachings, which insist that marital relations are permitted only for the sake of procreation, Jewish law has always recognized that the intimate bonds between husband and wife play a broader and more comprehensive role in the relationship between two married people. Even when conception is not feasible, marital relations are obligatory. Torah law singles out the Sabbath and holidays as special occasions during which the marital *mitzvah* should be observed, as another way of celebrating, elevating and sanctifying these special days. Similarly, the Talmud states, "It is a husband's duty to *intimately remember* his wife before he leaves on a trip" *(Yevamot* 62b). The mystical Kabbalah teaches that, "the *Shechinah,* or Divine Presence, only dwells in a home when a man is married and cohabits with his wife" *(Zohar I* 122A), for "marital relations are the highest expression of the intimate, deep, personal relationship that can exist between man and woman. On this level, marital relations are raised to holiness and purity" (Moshe Meiselman).

That marital relations are *much more* than just another marital *duty* for the purpose of having a family is obvious from numerous statements in the Bible and Talmud. To quote one source (Talmud, *Eruvin* 63b), "Rav Bruna said in the name of Rav, 'Whoever sleeps in the same room in which dwell a man and his wife, of him the Torah (Micah 2:9) says, *You have driven the wives of my people out of the home of her pleasures.*'"

This union helps strengthen one of the most intimate bonds a person can possibly establish with another person; it forges man and woman into one entity. It is a natural and spiritual force which involves our total personalities at the deepest levels of our being. Such a union is an intensely private, personal matter which, together with other personality factors, constitutes the cement which transforms two strangers into loving, intimate, lifelong companions, committed to each other and to the building of a Jewish family. Intimacy expresses love and provides intense pleasure which is very often highly spiritual in nature.

But the Torah's laws of *tsniut* (modesty and privacy) create an environment of restraint, self-respect and self-discipline that underlie the ban on these relations before marriage, so that those relations will remain a potent force for the greater good of creating an exclusive and highly meaningful, permanent relationship and bond within marriage. Intimacy in marriage is the glue that helps bind husband and wife together. To waste this opportunity outside of marriage is like irresponsibly playing with magic glue.

The Torah's laws insure that the biological impulse will be reserved for the chosen *one*, as an instrument of love, devotion and personal fulfillment within marriage. The regulations of *tsniut* teach us to master and control our appetites, rather than be controlled by them. They also train us for that time when, once married, we will again be called upon to exercise self-discipline in the observance of the laws of *the Sanctity of the Family (taharat hamishpacha).* These laws of family purity insure that for a given period each month, respect, affection, comradeship and all the *other* impulses and factors, aside from the intimate and physical, that bind two *people* be allowed to dominate the relationship of husband and wife.

While this is not the place for a detailed discussion of the laws of the *Sanctity of the Family,* we will outline a few basic concepts. Jewish law forbids physical contact, or any physical expression of affection and love between husband and wife, from the onset of her menses until seven days after the end of the flow, for a total separation of no less than twelve days, depending on the length of the individual woman's flow. At the the end of this period, the wife immerses herself in a *mikveh,* a ritualarium filled with naturally collected waters. It is only then that husband and wife may resume physical relations.

One of the most rewarding features of the Jewish laws of Family Sanctity is that they ensure a periodic renewal of the marriage relationship. There is little need to explain that the yearning and pain of missing a loved one serves to bring about a fresh awareness of how deep the relationship actually is. "Absence makes the heart grow fonder." The relationship is nurtured as much through anticipation, longing and expectation as it is through fulfillment. It is impossible to fully enjoy food without first growing hungry. A person who is constantly stuffed can hardly be expected to find enjoyment in a delicious meal. While the analogy of intimacy to food can be taken too far, it does help us understand the role of boredom and satiety in any area that relates to pleasure.

Each monthly interval of waiting again recreates the eager and joyous anticipation of the marriage day. The marriage of a couple who observe the Torah's laws of Family Sanctity has the potential, when followed properly, of becoming a series of honeymoons.

Marriage never becomes monotonous, habitual or boring. Maybe this explains why religious Jewish marriages tend to be much happier and sturdier than most. Rather then rejecting love and relations, the Torah provides opportunities for re-enacting, month after month, the drama of courtship, first without physical contact, then followed again by the loving union of husband and wife. It is this monthly reunion that makes possible deeper, more intense relationships, which transforms a biological, physical act into a deeply personal, spiritual and emotional experience.

Only a Jew who observes the laws of Family Sanctity can understand how King Solomon's Biblical book, the Song of Songs, which describes the yearnings of two lovers, could be described by Rabbi Akiva as being "the holy of holies," a description of the loving relationship between G-d and the Jewish people. Only a religious Jew can understand how the yearning of two people for each other could have been employed in the Song of Songs to describe the mystical love and yearning of the Jewish people for the ultimate Beloved, G-d, and G-d's love for the Jewish people.

While marriage demands intimate, physical relationships, it is far more than this area alone. Only the Jew has a practical formula that succeeds in preserving intimate relations as a basic and positive element of marriage, while at the same time restraining and preserving it so that intimacy does not become monotonous, boring and unappealing; an affliction that unfortunately is at the base of so many failed American marriages. Yet at the very same time, Judaism allows other vital factors in the marriage relationship to develop in a healthy and constructive fashion so that the marriage remains vibrant even when relations are not permitted, or no longer feasible.

The Jewish laws of Family Sanctity teach us that, to quote Dr. Norman Lamm, "Love does not grow stale in such an environment. A young woman's dreams remain fresh, her visions vital, her hopes radiant throughout life. All of life presents the opportunity of becoming a perpetual honeymoon. Her dreams are not defeated by success and frustrated by fulfillment." (For a unique and extensive explanation of the concept of Family Purity, the reader is referred to a beautiful book by Rabbi Aryeh Kaplan, *Waters of Eden — The*

Mystery of the Mikvah, published by the National Conference of Synagogue Youth.)

It is interesting to note that the world's highest divorce rate, highest teenage pregnancy rate and highest rate of births outside of marriage is to be found in American society, where freedom from constraints and experimentation outside of marriage are not only permitted, but are so often promoted. On the other hand, Jews, especially religious Jews who reject these ideas and believe that satisfactory physical relations and mature love will come as the result of a good marriage, enjoy the lowest divorce rate and the most stable family life.

Chapter Four

Means and Ends

The Jewish Approach to Intimacy

he Torah does not accept the view that man's body and its physical functions are base, evil or shameful in any way. In Jewish tradition, relations are not sinful, nor is the body considered evil. Such notions are strictly non-Jewish in origin, and emanate primarily from pagan sources which found their way into Christianity, and from Christianity into general Western culture.

The Torah takes a very different view by speaking of mankind and of all creation as "good" (Genesis 1: 31). The phenomenon of man and woman, with their many differences, is a wondrous manifestation of G-d's basic design. Intimacy is an instrument for the fulfillment of G-d's will. As with most instruments, it is potentially good if controlled, directed and utilized for its intended purpose;

dangerous if not. The record of the various abuses and misuse of physical relations are examples of what results when something which carries the potential for so much good is either misdirected or allowed to spin out of control.

"Man" is directed to enjoy the world. In the Torah view, all human pleasures have been established for our enjoyment, in order to motivate us to involve ourselves in the affairs of the world. But pleasure and enjoyment must be controlled by, and be subservient to, the laws, limitations and conditions set by the Torah. The G-d Who created us, Who gave us our lives and fashioned our bodies, understands the limitations that will ensure lasting happiness, along with physical, mental and spiritual health and well-being. Intimate physical relations are a positive good, a vital impulse and a basic function that is essential to the survival and well-being of humanity. It is the key to human continuity and gives mankind the opportunity for extending our life to eternity. With it, man and woman are partners with G-d in the work of creation. These relations become sinful only when misused, as when we model our personal behavior after the behavior of the animals who live by instinct rather than the dictates of the Torah. The Torah teaches mankind to rise above the animal in him and employ thought, choice and self-control.

One of the most beautiful introductions to the Jewish attitude toward marital relations is contained in the *Igeret Hakodesh* (The Holy Letter), ascribed to the Ramban (Nachmanides), the great philosopher and thinker of the Middle Ages:

> Marital relations are holy, pure and clean, when done in the correct manner, at the correct time and with the correct attitude. Whoever says that there is something disgraceful and loathsome is gravely mistaken ... All believers in the Torah believe that the Almighty created all according to His great wisdom and did not create anything which was intrinsically disgraceful. For, if we say that marital relations are intrinsically evil and disgraceful, then so are those parts of the human body, and if so, how did G-d create them? But G-d is pure of spirit and nothing comes from Him which is intrin-

sically evil. It is G-d Who created man and woman and all of their organs. But the matter is this way. Just as the hands of a human being can write a Torah and can create the highest sanctity, and at that time they are lofty and greatest, but when they steal and murder they are evil and loathsome, so too in this area of life.

Without desire and impulse, mankind could not exist. The Medrash says of man's physical desires and drives, "Were it not for *that* impulse, a man would not build a house, marry a wife, beget children or conduct business affairs" (*Genesis Rabbah* IX,7).

In describing the first human sexual encounter, the Torah employs the adjective *knowledge* to describe cohabiting, "And Adam *knew* his wife Chava (Eve) and she conceived and gave birth to Cain" (Genesis 4:1). Using the word *to know* as a euphemism for relations teaches that the image of G-d within man *(the tselem Elokim)* demands a relationship based on knowledge, spirituality and conscious purpose. To act otherwise is to mate through instinct as the animals do. Perhaps the key to the Jews' outstanding ability to create a people which is so successful in the areas of the intellect and the spirit is the extreme care with which the Jewish community strives to guide the creation of new Jewish families by not leaving matchmaking to chance.

Intimacy — A Constructive Force

The Hebrew language, the Holy tongue, possesses an inner logic and structure of its own. Thus it offers a valuable insight to the religious view of the husband-wife relationship. The Hebrew words for *man* and *woman* are so formed that if we remove from the word "*Ish,*" Man, *and "Ishah,"* Woman, the letters "*yud' and "hay,"* which together form the Name of G-d, what remains in each word are the two single letters "*alef*" and "*shin,*" which spell the word "*Esh*" or fire (Talmud, *Sotah* 17a).

This is more than a coincidence, because passion and fire share many striking similarities. Fire, necessary for the generation of light and heat, is a basic element of life and civilization, crucial to cooking, industry and manufacture. Employed correctly, fire is a constructive, essential, creative force, but when unattended and permitted to rage out of control, fire will spread and destroy all in its path. This analogy applies to humans' use of their physical impulses. When G-d is a partner in the relationship between a man and a woman, when the letters *"yud" and "hay"* remain in place, so that G-d's laws govern a man and a woman joined together as a family, *as one flesh,* intimacy is a constructive and positive force. In the absence of G-d, man and *woman* lose control, sink to the level of the beast. Their relationship then assumes the nature of "fire," with all its potentially negative, destructive, self-consuming and dangerous possibilities. For this reason, young people are cautioned not *to play with fire.* They may lose control and destroy not only their relationships, but themselves as well.

The True Roots of Love / Love in Marriage

What is the real meaning of love? What are the emotions and impulses that nourish and sustain it? There is hardly a person alive who does not harbor within himself at least a spark of the unselfish impulse to give or to share. But since giving and sharing are possible only for people who have freedom of choice, it follows that only a person who is free to choose can give of himself freely, voluntarily and unselfishly enough to enjoy the fruits of a truly loving relationship. We often discover that the more we give and the more we share, the greater the return of satisfaction and joy that serves, in turn, to nourish, deepen and sustain our love. In addition, the more we give the more we receive because the recipient of our largesse feels so appreciative that he/she wants to reciprocate. Love is a relationship dependent upon mutual activities of giving and sharing.

Love in marriage flows from the fact that both husband and wife acknowledge that without their partner they are not yet complete. Each partner becomes appreciative of the other for the complementary role they play. Mutual giving and sharing bring gratitude and a sense of oneness, twin foundations of a truly loving and successful marital relationship.

Successful and Harmonious Marriage

How can we tell if a marriage is successful? Ask a parent, "What is your greatest joy in life?" Most will answer, "My children." But if a marriage is what it should be, the answer should be, "My husband or my wife." The Talmud (*Sanhedrin* 22b) teaches this through the following comment, "when a woman dies, the person who feels the loss most is her husband." If we turn this statement around, it is clear that the Talmud teaches that when a woman is alive, the person who appreciates her the most is her husband. In successful marriages, husband and wife become best friends, they trust each other deeply and always do everything possible to meet the needs of the other person. It takes a great deal of maturity and growing up to understand that if you always go out of your way to help, please and make your spouse happy, in the end you too will be happy. It all comes back to the old paradoxical but true idea that the best way to receive is to give.

The relationship of husband and wife, built on the deep impulses of giving, sharing and loving, also reflects the selfless love of G-d for man. In fact, the human impulse to give derives from our own G-dlikeness. The more a man and woman give and share, the more they become like G-d. And the more they invest their time, effort and concern in each other, the deeper, more stable, meaningful and secure will their relationship become.

G-d's relationship to man is based on His love for man. Since G-d is complete and perfect, He has no needs. G-d needs nothing in return. His love for man is completely selfless — it is based on giving without any anticipation of receiving something in return.

The Hebrew word for love, "*Ahavah,*" is derived from the root "*hav,*" to give. To love is to give. True love is the product of continuously giving to another individual. Think of how much pleasure we have when we give someone we love a gift or do them a favor. Love in its truest form is selfless. If love is self-serving or selfish it is not love at all and will not last. This is the fundamental difference between today's notion of romance which is based on emotion and excitement which so often tarnish and wear out and the Jewish concept of love which is built on giving and commitment. Love grows stronger with time while romance can be fleeting and temporary. Hebrew has many words for love, but none for romance which is so often built on an illusion.

When you give, you feel that part of yourself is invested in the person of the recipient. An actual transference takes place. Since the recipient is no longer a self-contained entity, but contains part of the giver, each belongs to the other; each is committed to the other in a deep and lasting sense.

A person's heart lies where he or she has made his greatest investments. If a person's concern, time and efforts are "invested" in husband, wife and children, the love for them will increase and grow.

"*Chessed*," the Hebrew word for love and kindness, is one of the basic elements and qualities of Jewish life. Love is the opposite of egotism and selfishness. It is a shift in the direction of our concerns from self to family — and then to neighbors, community, the Jewish people and the world at large. Marriage creates a new world of love because one is motivated and directed to shift the focus of interest and concern from oneself to husband, wife and children. The "me generation" always asks, "What's in it for me"? The idea that a person is number one is for infants, not for mature people. A person who refuses to marry is a selfish person who denies one of the basic needs of being truly human; the need to feel for, to live for and to love another person. As the Bible clearly warns, "It is not good for a person to live alone" (Genesis 2:18). To live alone is to deny the *chessed* foundation of Jewish life, the deep human well of love — *chessed*.

A person who does not marry becomes the last link in a chain that began with the first man and woman. When we do not bear children, the many qualities that make us unique die with us; we do not live on in the next generation. For this reason, many Jewish couples who are not blessed with children of their own make special efforts to become parents, in both a spiritual and physical sense, to children who lack parents. For the same reason, Jews reject the concept of celibacy, the idea that some great spiritual good can come from a life that lacks marriage, sharing, giving and deep personal relationships.

The Significance of Family

As we mentioned above, one of man's most basic responsibilities is to insure the continuity and immortality of himself and mankind. But the act of bearing children is not a matter of physical survival alone. If a child is to fulfill the hopes of his parents, or more importantly, to satisfy the expectations of the Almighty, then man must procreate with a sense of purpose and responsibility. We are commanded, therefore, not only to bring children into the world in a biological sense, but also to rear children who will reflect the highest and best in ourselves, our families, our culture and Jewish society. Each child is a unique new personality, and should be encouraged and motivated to make his or her own mark and special contribution to the world-wide family of man.

The husband's and wife's task involves much more than bearing children. Their responsibility is to raise children who will be motivated to continue the tasks their parents began, but left unfinished. Parents dream of raising children who will promote the tasks and cherish the treasures that proceeding generations have entrusted to their safekeeping, in the hope that they will not only preserve the treasures of the past, but will pass them on in an enriched and improved form to future generations.

The family is *the* instrument of Jewish continuity; it insures the Jewish future. Each generation is a link in a chain and, as such, is responsible and accountable to the generations which preceded it, as well as to those yet unborn. The family is the basic school of Jewish life. An appreciation of the significance of the family demands a sense of history and destiny. It calls for a deep understanding that each of us bears great responsibilities as a member of the family and of the Jewish nation. No one is an island, no one can say, "I have a right to make a hole under my seat in the rowboat" — his hole might cause the entire boat to sink. No one has the right to say that his actions have no influence on the past, present or future of his family or the Jewish people.

In the Jewish view, bringing a child into the world must be the result of thoughtful, mature, responsible action, performed in sanctity, by a couple who love and respect each other — who act in accordance with the laws set forth by G-d.

The Right to Life

Even though G-d directs the world, we believe that the choices each of us make have a powerful influence on human destiny. If a person has a child with a person who is not his wife, who can predict what harm a child who grows up without family might bring to the world? In the same measure, if a married couple choose to abort their unborn child, they have destroyed a human being. They may very well have destroyed a child who was destined to have great impact on the world in his role as teacher, physician or, at the very least, the upright head of his own Jewish family.

Each of us has a destiny, but we can destroy it. Each of us has a task or mission in life — most of us have no idea what that mission might be — but our task is to live each day in such a way that we have our mission in mind. Our mission is most prominent when we are involved in the most important task any human being is able to perform — bringing a child into the world.

Each child has the right to life. Hopefully, the child will be born into a family that will not only love and protect it, and provide for its material needs, but will also guide it and mold its personality. The family must literally pour itself into the child, because, in its earliest formative years, the family is its total environment. In order to do this properly, the family itself must have goals, ideals, purpose, and discipline. Even when a child is given over to others for brief periods, such as to a baby sitter or a Day Care Center, care must be exercised to select these carefully, since early experiences can leave an indelible lifelong impression.

Woman as a "Person"

Woman is the key individual in the creation of the family. The role of the woman as wife, mother, teacher and provider, the pivot and foundation of the family — and as a result, of all of society and history — requires that each woman fully appreciate the purpose of her sexuality and attractiveness and her unique feminine being and personality.

The Jewish laws of family, sanctity and *tsniut* — modest behavior and dress — serve to protect the integrity of each individual's personality and help to restrain each one from abusing his/her natural inclinations and drives. They also help control passion, in order to prevent it from dominating our personality and conduct. Were such control absent, a person might also forget that his/her partner is also a person, created in G-d's image, deserving of respect and care; to be treated as one might expect him or herself to be treated. The Torah commands, "You shall love your fellow *'kamocha'* (as yourself)," because he or she is, like *yourself,* created in G-d's image and entitled to the same treatment and consideration you would expect for yourself. Men and women in today's society often use and then discard one another like disposable objects. Jewish morality demands that we consider the needs of our partner, and not only our needs; and that we respect him or her as a human being endowed with dignity, divinity and self-respect.

In the Jewish view women are full and equal partners, friends and companions, without whom life can never be complete or fulfilling. Most importantly, women are individuals with rights and duties which are not set arbitrarily but rather are defined by the laws of the Torah. From the joyful union of men and women comes all creation; from it there should flow all of what is best in human society. Marriage, for this reason, is never merely a social contract, but rather, and most importantly, a holy bond and religious union, sanctified and blessed by G-d. The term for marriage in Hebrew, "*Kiddushin,*" holiness, embraces an idea expressed quite effectively in the marriage service itself:

> Blessed are You ... Who has sanctified us with your commandments and commanded us concerning illicit relations: You have forbidden to us those who are merely betrothed, and permitted to us only those who are married to us through consecrated wedlock. Blessed are You, O Lord, Who

sanctifies His people Israel through the marriage canopy and the sanctification of marriage.

and later,

> Blessed are You, O Lord ... Who has created groom and bride, joy and gladness, delight and cheer, love and harmony, peace and companionship ... Blessed are You, O Lord, Who enables the groom to rejoice with his bride.

The Dehumanization of Women in Today's Society

Let us now compare this sublime Jewish view of woman with the contemporary secular approach, depicted in certain popular publications. Much of what is wrong with the "American attitude" towards women can be traced to these trend-setting magazines. But to criticize these publications on the grounds of their provocativeness and obscenity is to overlook the larger problem created by publications of this type. Their popularity and damaging influence cannot be attributed simply to their blatant unlimited and uninhibited displays of the human body.

The greatest danger of these publications is in the attitudes and distorted values they have succeeded in injecting into American social attitudes and the way they typify the inevitable result of all *"pritzut"* (breaking the rules of modesty and restraint). These magazines are anti-woman in that woman is reduced to a male accessory, diluted and dissipated because she can be kept at a safe distance. Non-involvement and non-commitment is elevated as an ideal. Women are no longer people to be respected, loved and cherished, but are converted into objects to be discarded when "playtime" is over. Pornography is anti-human because it reduces people to robots, ruled by their physical instincts, for whom life is a game that provides fun. These magazines not only deny the dignity and freedom of the human spirit, but also the true and real nature of men and women. Woman, as a person, is compromised and demeaned — all in marked opposition to the attitude of the Torah, which views intimacy as part of a majestic, healthy, permanent, workable system, in which woman is valued and protected and shares rights, duties, honors and privileges with her husband. Intimacy is far more complex, serious and significant than is self-deceptively and unrealistically projected by popular American culture, which prefers to see it as fun and games for youthful recreation.

The popular magazines appeal to alienated and spiritually deprived people, who naively accept a terribly artificial image of what it means to be a "man" or "woman." For the uprooted man or woman with time on his or her hands and money in his or her pocket, these magazines fill a twisted need. They are guidebooks to a glamorous world of false material values. They lure insecure men, searching for their male "identity" and for how to be a "man," by shrewdly feeding upon their inexperience and gullibility. Many men and women of all ages are searching for a dream, and their imaginations and frustrations work overtime.

In a world where to be "in" connotes acquisition of the latest consumer product, intimacy is treated as just another facet of leisure activity to be handled with skill and detachment, like a sports car, a CD player, a good set of golf clubs or drums. Pornography is used as a tool to merchandise consumer items. Women become desirable, even indispensable, as accessories to these objects — an "it" instead of a "she." America seems incapable of advertising any item without the picture of a pretty girl in the ad. The use and abuse of women in advertising reduces woman to a symbol on the animal level. This debasement places intimacy within the sphere of entertainment and recreation. "Don't complicate the cardinal principle of 'casualness and fun' by suggesting marriage or any permanent relationship."

Unlike real-life women, the magazine readers' fictional girlfriend stays comfortably uninvolved and distant, in her place, asking for nothing, posing no threat and demanding nothing in terms of a permanent involvement or relationship. Like any appropriate accessory, she is detachable and dispensable. She is pressured to understand the rules of the "game." No responsibilities, goals or obligations — a make-believe world of sugar-coated nonsense. It has even become a fad in some "liberal" homes to display pornographic magazines without regard for the damaging effect these pictures have on young children, without the realization that the home has been cheapened and brought low.

These magazines claim that their message is one of liberation, as they crusade for frankness and candor. Yet they, in fact, impose a new kind of tyranny, relegating life into a section of the consumer world and turning love into the worship of a materialistic world. These magazines promote a bondage to things, and to people turned into things. The higher self of man is brought low, becoming enslaved to constant thoughts of lust and desire. The mind's ability to refine human motives and to purify its spirit is crippled in the process. The mystery and magic of human personality are reduced to a visual portrayal of women who are superficial, paper-thin nonentities. The human in the person is debased, as the animal ruled by instinct takes over. American males become prisoners of their imaginations. They live their lives in a semi-fog, always chasing illusions.

That there are young people who fall for this abuse of their minds and personalities is not surprising in light of the intense media and peer-group pressure they are subjected to. Unfortunately, America's directionless and uncontrolled system of dating, including the free exposure of boys and girls to each other at parties, at the beach and with the "gang," contribute to this sad situation, as do the pressures of style and the many social pressures to conform.

Many fine individuals attend "parties" not because they want to go but because of social pressure. Many don't have the courage, self-esteem and presence of mind to team up with like-minded friends and "fight back." To be led by others and be used is to be a sheep, not a mature person.

To make a *game* of that emotion and powerful life-giving force which is the basis of the family, of holiness and which creates the next generation is an insult to the human personality and a denial of a person's divinity and dignity.

Dress and Conduct

In light of the above discussion, how are we to understand good girls who dress and act in a seductive manner? The most baffling and contradictory thing about some young women is their capacity to be forgetful of their own nature. The fine young woman who permits herself to be debased by dressing, dating, speaking or behaving seductively is practicing self-deception, and is often deceiving others as to her true character and nature. The girl who veers from the highest standards of "*tsniut*" probably has no clear idea as to what these standards are and is merely responding to her environment and the social pressures of her community, family and friends. But we would hope that she would realize that with every compromise she has made in dress, behavior or action, she has taken a few more steps in the wrong direction. It is troubling that a young woman whose physical integrity, reputation, good name and honor hangs in the balance risks her innermost dreams and hopes to submit to social pressures or to the stubborn irresponsible urgings of an impetuous, impulsive and irresponsible young man. *His* grasp of the meaning of a family, children, a home and a future is, in comparison to the average young lady of his age, very immature. Often he doesn't think — or doesn't think beyond his semi-fogged imagination. Rarely is he honorable or responsible, for otherwise he would not dishonor someone else or attempt to ruin someone else's life, by compromising any girl's future or reputation.

Human beings are much more than the illusion, or even the reality, of beauty. We are complicated, sensitive, intricate, complex and multifaceted; we are unique beings, created in G-d's image. We are personality, soul and spirit. Despite occasional appearances, or some contrary opinions, we are or should be so much more than sophisticated animals. The choice is ours.

Guidelines of Dress and Conduct for Women

The Torah teaches that a young woman who dresses or behaves in such a way that she is obviously flaunting her physical beauty is responsible, in good measure, for the advances with which some young men will respond and for the resultant compromises that may destroy her own reputation, physical integrity and self-esteem. No girl wants to be told that, "she asked for it," but how naive can she be if she dresses or behaves in such a way that she leaves little to the imagination?

Rashi describes the behavior of Ruth the Moabite girl who converted to Judaism and became the ancestress of King David, and ultimately the Messiah. When she gathered sheaves of wheat from the ground, "she kneeled, instead of bending over immodestly" (Ruth 2:5). This was one of the qualities that demonstrated her fitness to be a mother of royalty.

Immodest dress and behavior also has other consequences. When the desires of a young man are provoked, the honor of a young woman hangs precariously in the balance. He, on the one hand, may demand, "If you really love me, why not?" While she, on the other hand, should be able to respond, "If you really love me, how could you ask?"

The obvious question we might ask is, why does love enter into this at all? Shouldn't the girl simply say, "If you respect me, you'd respect my principles" — or even further, "Why don't you treat me as a person rather than as an object to satisfy your desire"?

The attraction between man and woman is not a toy. Life, love, children, family and one's own posterity are too important to be fooled around with. Their place is in a blessed and permanent partnership, in the structure we know as home and family.

The media as a whole has created a moral climate which would lead us to believe that the sole aim and goal of life is pleasure and fun, a life where morality, responsibility, God, His Torah, its goals and ideals are "dead" issues. In truth, there is nothing new about the "new" morality. It is no different than the immorality of ancient Rome, the "sacred" prostitution of the ancient pagan nations, condemned by the prophets of the Bible, or the license, debauchery or hedonistic immorality practiced by many ancient pagan "religions."

Intimacy in Marriage

Jewish tradition expects a man to do much more than simply feed, clothe and protect his wife. He is to respect her, consult with her, love her and hold her in esteem, no less than the way he in turn expects to be treated by his wife. The Torah's commandment, "And you shall love your neighbor as you would want to be loved yourself," means above all that man must treat women precisely as he himself would want to be treated. This means following strict Torah regulations that never permit the compromise of a woman's dignity, integrity, physical being and future.

Therefore, all areas related to intimacy must be kept strictly within the confines of married life. By "everything," we mean *every and any* act of physical contact between the man and woman, as well as the proper clothing or covering of the body of man and woman, in accordance with the *tsniut* standards set by Jewish law.

The human body is beautiful, but, what is more important, *it is holy*. Relations are appropriate, but only at the correct time and place and only with the person to whom you are married.

The Mystery of the Human Face

If we give the uniqueness of the human being some thought we will agree that true *uniqueness* in a man or a woman is basically to be found from the neck up. From the neck down, individuals of the same gender are rather alike. The part of our bodies that sets us apart from one another is the head — the part we generally reveal. The parts that *do not reflect the unique aspects* of the human personality are the parts we generally conceal. Jewish morality strongly urges that we cover our animal-like parts, and reveal only those features which reflect the unique aspects of our personalities; our eyes, mouth, ears, face and hands — the gates to our mind and personality. The features and functions of men and women below the neck, such as reproduction, digestion, elimination and motion, are, in appearance and in purpose, remarkably similar to those of the animals in that they are not expressions of our uniqueness.

We recognize people when we see their faces; if we cover a person's face and look at the remainder of their body we would probably not be able to distinguish anyone. Maybe this helps explain why even the most modest or pious person never suggests that animals cover their bodies. An animal is a creature of instinct, a slave to its biological urges; it reacts to stimuli and lacks freedom of choice. Animals mate when their instinct compels them to mate. Since they are incapable of free choice or creativity, their bodily functions are often performed in the open, without any sense of shame. A cow has no need to conceal her body because a cow has nothing unique to reveal. A cow is all instinct, all body from head to hoof. Now we can better understand that human beings are expected to conceal their animal-like features in order to allow their unique, G-d-like features to attract and to interact with other human beings.

Where can we see the uniqueness of the human being with our own eyes? One of the most significant ways is by looking at people's faces. When you observe the faces of any of your friends, it is quite obvious that each is uniquely different. In this obvious way, G-d has imprinted His stamp and seal on each human being. He has demonstrated that even though there are billions of men and women on earth, each person is uniquely different; each is created in the "image" or reflection of G-d.

Ask yourself the following question: Where can we actually see G-d on this earth? One interesting answer is: On the face of each human being. Just as G-d is unique, so too is each human face unique. No one has exactly your face — you are special.

Analyzed element by element, the variables of the human face would seem to be limited in number. How many different shapes of noses are there? How different are people's lips or cheeks? The eyes are an excellent example. From the pictures of people in a magazine, cut out the eyes of a hundred people. Do they look much different one from the other? Yet, when we speak of a beautiful person, we often refer to the eyes, because the eyes have that unique ability to mirror the soul and to reflect the inner self.

Despite the limited number of variables in the physical features of the human face, the number of *different* human faces in the world is infinite. No two people look exactly alike — each is uniquely different. Each human face is a reflection of G-d, Who is infinite and unique and Who endows each human being, His special creation, with a unique personality.

Unlike the English word *face*, which describes man's external physical features, the Hebrew word for face, *"panim,"* literally means, *"inside."* This indicates that the Torah views the face as a mirror of the unique qualities which make up each human personality. The human face is where we see each person's personality. The face mysteriously combines the physical, biological personality and the soul, the inner quality of each person.

The mystery of the human face is an even greater miracle when we realize that mankind originated from one father, Adam, and from one mother, Eve. Each human being is stamped from the mold of the first father and mother. Unlike a coin-manufacturing machine which will always turn out a precise replica, the human "mold" always turns out a new human being who is uniquely different. Since the human being was created in the image of G-d, and the first human being was one and unique, each human being has within him and her qualities that make it possible for him or her to be unique. Each quality of uniqueness, and the evidence that our spiritual and physical Father is one and unique, is still very much with us, no matter how many human beings there are or will be born into the world.

To quote the Talmud (*Sanhedrin* 4:5), "Flesh and blood is minted into many coins with one mold; all resemble one another, and the Holy One, Blessed is He, mints every person with the mold of the First Person. Yet no one person resembles another." This is the true source of the uniqueness and singularity of man. From this we see that the fact of "the first person having been created as one solitary person" is the source for two fundamental human principles, the unity of mankind and the uniqueness of every human being! (For a full and comprehensive understanding of the concepts of human unity and uniqueness, as well as the commandment to "love others as we love ourselves," see the lecture by Rabbi Yitzchak Hutner, zt"l, in *Pachad Yitzchak, Volume Shavuot,* Chapter 21, translated in the Fall 1975 issue of *Tradition.)*

The Bible describes Moses' face following the revelation of G-d and the giving of the Torah on Mt. Sinai by telling us that, "the people were unable to look at him because the flesh of his face was radiant." Anyone who has been in the presence of a truly saintly person knows that he has seen a unique and G-d-like face that radiates the greatness of personality and the sanctity he personifies. If you want to *"see* G-d" in this world, look into the face of a G-dly man or woman.

Because the face reflects that which is G-dly in Man, its features relate most directly to man's ability to choose between good and evil. All of the functions of the face — thinking, speaking, seeing, discerning, hearing and eating — relate to our ability to choose. The Jew even eats in a way that reflects choice and G-dliness, which is one of the many reasons for the laws of kashruth.

The reason we do not conceal our faces is because they reflect that aspect of the human being which is uniquely G-d-like. But we *do* conceal our bodies because they project our animal-like features. Unless these features are controlled, they will be governed by instinct.

We must therefore be careful to attract and be attractive to each other through those aspects of ourselves which are G-d-like and unique. *If the unique in me is attracted to that which is unique in the person of the other gender, chances are that our relationship will be unique and lasting. If the G-d-like in me attracts that which is G-d-like in the other person, chances are that our relationship will have real meaning and contain elements of holiness and eternity.*

Since the exposure of the body heightens the degree of physical self-awareness, clothing the body helps heighten spiritual self-awareness. The covering of the body does not imply that the body is sinful; on the contrary, it affirms that the body is holy. To put it slightly differently, the extent to which we cover our bodies indicates the extent to which we are human. We emphasize our humanity by emphasizing those things which are unique to human beings. Clearly then, animals have no need for clothes.

The Holy of Holies in Solomon's Temple in Jerusalem contained the Golden Holy Ark of the Covenant in which were kept the two stone tablets of the Ten Commandments. The Golden Holy Ark was an exquisite work of art, beautifully sculptured; yet it was kept concealed in the Holy of Holies behind heavy drapes. Only the High Priest was permitted to enter the Holy of Holies, and then only on the holiest day of the year, Yom Kippur. The Holy Ark was concealed because its physical beauty was but the vehicle for its spiritual essence. It was kept hidden to prevent us from being diverted from its spiritual qualities by the glitter of its art and gold. It is easy to be overwhelmed by our visual senses; the problem is that this will distract and divert us from more essential, non-visual aspects of our personality which are not easily apprehended by the senses. When a person emphasizes the physical and is overwhelmed by the senses, it becomes difficult to focus on the spiritual.

The Jewish Concept of Heroism

The Jews and Western Civilization often differ quite substantially concerning the fundamental nature of human achievement, bravery and heroism. To the Jew, our greatest and most important accomplishments are generally those which we do privately, in secret, accompanied by an attitude of humility, reserve and modesty; to the non-Jew, accomplishment and heroic behavior often call for public display, publicity and open public acclaim.

A good example are the ancient Greeks who turned physical beauty into an object of worship. Their gods were statues of stone, marble and gold. They actually worshiped their heroes and celebrated heroic achievement with public tributes, stage plays, temple monuments, hymns and songs. Their greatest accomplishments were the heroic deeds of soldiers and sportsmen on the battlefield and in the stadium. To lose in a competition was to lose self-esteem. The Greeks weren't "good sports," as we often suppose. They didn't know how to lose. The essence of the Greek heroic act was its public nature and public acclaim. There was no glorification of inner heroism — only of public display and public approval. The Greek concept of perfection was directly related to those things which could be seen by the human eye or perceived by the senses.

To the Jew, the highest accomplishment lies in the refinement of human character and the perfection of the human personality; in the educating, shaping, molding, disciplining and elevating of each person, of the inner self and, ultimately, all human society. Rabbi Ben Zoma (*Pirkei Avot* 4:1) taught, "Who is heroic? He who is in control of his passions. (He who has self-control.)" It is written, "Greater is the person who is in control of his personality and spirit than he who has conquered a city." A person who is able to control his/her impulses, rather than allowing them to control him/her, is a person who has achieved true greatness. For the Jew, moral victory is in what we do to change ourselves, elevate our personality and refine our soul. This is what G-d wants most. G-d alone is the source of all value. It is in this light that we can appreciate the classical Jewish teaching that the world is maintained in each generation by the merit of thirty-six hidden, secret *tzaddikim*, saintly persons. Since they are hidden, no one sees or even knows of their many heroic deeds. These *tzaddikim* have no titles, occupy no positions, win no awards, but it is because of *their* deeds that G-d does not destroy the world.

Maybe this explains why the Greeks, Romans and Egyptians — all the great civilizations of the ancient world — ultimately disappeared from the stage of history, while the Jew miraculously survives, thrives and marches on, despite the efforts of so many powerful empires and nations, from ancient times up to our day, to destroy the Jews.

Much remains of the physical life of the Egyptians, Assyrians, Samarians, Babylonians, Greeks and Romans. Their art and artifacts fill the world's museums, while their spiritual life is dead and forgotten. Almost nothing remains of the physical life of the ancient people of Israel — but their literature, religion and spiritual treasures fill and invigorate the lives of millions of loyal and observant people. The Torah is a living "tree of life." The Torah literature studied by the "ancients" is the foundation for the most dynamic living literature of the modern Jewish community.

Each culture and each nation in the world strives for greatness and perfection in its own way, some in art, music, architecture, drama or literature, some in the arts of war and business. At some point each society reaches its goals and arrives at a pinnacle of achievement. An inner feeling then overtakes that society; its people begin to feel that they have reached their full potential and have arrived at the heights of accomplishment. A society which is creative in music, art, architecture and literature begins at some point to feel that it has achieved "perfection" and can go no further. Once a society feels that it has exhausted its creative impulse, it loses the drive and ability to overcome its internal and external enemies. Inwardly that society behaves as though there is nothing more to accomplish; it either crumbles or its enemies destroy it.

Once a society feels that it has achieved perfection in the artistic, cultural, military or material areas of life, a process of despair and aimlessness wreaks havoc on the individual and the family, leading to increased crime and corruption. Lacking a firm code of morality, ethics and humanity, such a society collapses of its own weight or of its inability to withstand the onslaught of its enemies. It no longer has the will to fight or live, because life has lost its challenge and meaning. Soon it is overwhelmed by another, more powerful society whose armies pulverize its demoralized defenses and the cycle begins all over again as another great society rises on the world scene.

This should set us to thinking about the decadence of so much American art and culture. Our movies, television and literature have almost hit bottom, standards are dead and opposing voices are defeated by cries of "freedom."

Only the Jew has succeeded in defying this so-called law of history. Only the Jew is not subject to the cyclic process of the rise and fall of societies and civilizations. The Jew lives on, sometimes in the Land of Israel, and at times in exile, without the land. Jewish life continues whether the Temple is standing or is destroyed, as a nation of few or many, whether persecuted, tolerated or welcomed. The Jew has survived generations of destruction, exile, pogrom and holocaust to emerge again and again, generation after generation, surviving the attack of civilization after civilization, only to rebuild and again continue the long chain of creative tradition by producing new generations of great thinkers, rabbis and teachers.

This is due to the fact that Jewish creativity is concerned with the perfection of the human being, his spirit and personality. The Jew will continue the struggle until ultimately human society and human civilization will be perfected. Whatever his condition, the Jew gives priority to the inner life of spirituality, personality and family. No matter how downtrodden, the Jew continues to survive with the faith that in the *end of days* a people which does G-d's will will succeed in perfecting, refining and inheriting G-d's world. The Jew believes that one day we will see the victory of Torah and of Jewish civilization and that on that day, "the Lord will be King over all the earth." It is on that day — in the end of days when all of mankind will fully accept G-d's Kingdom — that Jewish civilization will have achieved its goal.

Mark Twain, one of America's greatest writers, had this to say about the Jewish ingredient in civilization. "If the statistics are right, the Jews constitute but *one percent* of the human race. It suggests a nebulous dim puff of stardust lost in the blaze of the Milky Way. Properly, the Jew ought hardly to be heard of, but he is heard of, has always been heard of. He is as prominent on the planet as another people, and his commercial importance is extravagantly out of proportion to the smallness of his bulk. He contributes to the world's list of great names in literature, science, art, music, finance, medicine and abstruse learning also way out of proportion to the weakness of his numbers. He has made a marvelous fight in this world, in all the ages; and has done it with his hands tied behind him. He could be vain of himself, and be excused for it. The Egyptian, the Babylonian and the Persian rose, filled the planet with sound and splendor, then faded to dream stuff and passed away. The Greek and the Roman followed, and made a vast noise, and they are gone. Other peoples have sprung up and held their torch high for a time, but it burned out, and they sit in twilight now, or have vanished. The Jew saw them all, beat them all, and is now what he always was, exhibiting no decadence, no infirmities of age, no weakening of his parts, no slowing of his energies, no dulling of his alert and aggressive mind. All things are mortal but the Jew; all other forces pass, but he remains. What is the secret of his immortality?"

To recap: In the Jewish world, the greatest accomplishments of life are most often done in private, in the home where no one sees, in the privacy of one's own heart and mind, where moral strength and determination, coupled with an ability to turn one's back on the ever-present temptation of sin and passion, are private battles to be waged and won. The ability to say "no" to sin, passion and temptation is an achievement performed in secret. Our Sages teach that above all, "G-d wants our hearts." The private heroism of the individual is most precious to G-d, Who sees and knows the secrets of our hearts, and Who rewards His true heroes in both this world and in the next.

To truly understand *tsniut* we must appreciate the idea that who-I-am is ultimately a *private* affair. Only you know deep down who you really are — and only you and G-d know what you are thinking. My relationship with G-d, the ultimate source of reality, is something which no other human being can really share. No one else but G-d knows my secret thoughts and aspirations. In Judaism, therefore, the greatest heroic acts are performed in private. A Chassidic rabbi once summed it up by saying, that a person can "be" anywhere he wants to be, because deep down a person "is" where his *thoughts* are.

Examples of great deeds performed in private include:

• Abraham is told by G-d to sacrifice his beloved, only son, Isaac, his heir. He takes him to Mt. Moriah and does as G-d commands him. But it was only a test of his faith and G-d did not actually want Abraham to sacrifice his son. This ultimate act of heroism and devotion is done in complete isolation. No one is there to observe it.

• Sarah realizes that Ishmael is a negative influence on Isaac and that his continued presence in their home can destroy her and Abraham's dreams. Her insight in convincing Abraham to send Ishmael and his mother, Hagar, back to Egypt was heroic — but was done in private.

• Jacob wrestles with the angel of G-d. This is a struggle which determines the future direction of the Jewish people. Jacob is victorious. After the battle, he is no longer *Jacob,* a name whose root means "downtrodden and heel," because the angel renames him *Israel,* which means the Prince of G-d. This spiritual battle and Jacob's ultimate victory take place in the dead of night with no one else present. Jacob is alone with no one to encourage him and no one to witness his struggle. But his victory is a turning point in the history of the Jewish people.

• Rachel reveals to her sister, Leah, the secret signs that would enable Leah to marry Jacob in the darkness of night. This was true heroism.

• When Joseph withstands the seductions of Potiphar's wife and refuses to submit, we are told that "no member of the household is there in the house." He is alone (Genesis 39:11).

• When Moses has his first encounter with G-d at the Burning Bush, he, too, is alone. Later, following the revelation of the Ten Commandments which took place in the presence of the entire Jewish people, Moses ascends Mt. Sinai to receive the remainder of the Torah. G-d warns him to ascend the mountain alone. No one else observes the greatest and most significant act of communication between G-d and man. Later, when Moses communicates with G-d on a regular basis in the *Mishkan*, the Holy Tabernacle, he also goes there alone.

- On Yom Kippur, the holiest day of the year, the High Priest would enter the Holy of Holies in the Jerusalem Temple to plead for forgiveness for the sins of the entire Jewish people. At the most crucial moment of that ceremony, he disappears behind a drapery and worships G-d alone. No one is there to observe him (Leviticus 16:17).

- Jewish history contains thousands of additional examples where great deeds and miracles take place in private — with no one else present.

Inwardness, privacy and modesty, Jewish ideals which apply to both men and women, relate in a special way to the life of the Jewish woman.

We can now understand what the Psalms (45:14) mean when they say that, *Kol Kvudah Bat-Melech Penimah — the glory and grandeur of the King's daughter is the expression of her hidden/inner qualities.* "Though the princess may appear glorious and splendid in public, she reveals her true glory in womanly virtue only in quiet, more private circles, and the splendid qualities she shows there are much greater than the exquisite beauty of the gold borders which shine at the hems of her garment" (R' Hirsch, Psalms)

It is for the above reasons that we pursue *tsniut,* privacy and modesty in behavior and dress, and believe that the opposite dehumanizes and denigrates the human being. It is for these reasons too, that we emphasize that the pursuit of *tsniut,* modesty and privacy, promotes happiness and realism in human relations, while freedom and abandon in these areas is the pursuit of an illusion at best, bringing about human misery and disillusion at its worst.

Education

In the traditional Jewish world of pre-World War II Europe, *tsniut*, inwardness and privacy was learned not only from holy books, but from the entire Jewish environment, which was a living example of a life of *tsniut*. *Tsniut* existed not only in the home, but in the Jewish street as well. A Jew could learn *tsniut* by observing and studying his mother, father, teachers and friends with the same intensity that we search for Torah truths in books. Jewish youth, in the classical Jewish society, learned even more from *source people* than from source books. Jewish youth absorbed at an early age the living example of their elders' way of life, which was the true reflection of their greatness in Torah. Jewish youth could readily see how hard they had to work, how high the stakes were and how much energy was required for every breakthrough in personality growth, for every improvement of the *neshamah*, the soul. Even in that protected environment, saturated with holiness, each individual was aware of the tension which exists between the soul and the inner force which pulls toward evil — the *yetser hara*. In molding his personality, the Jew viewed himself as though he was a lion-tamer in a cage with a wild beast. Every action, every motion, every gesture had to be measured with microscopic precision — lest the beast become bold and strike.

What is most interesting about classical-traditional Jewish societies is that education concerning private matters was not acquired from the street, from movies or smutty books. The family relationship is openly and frankly discussed in the *Chumash*, in the books of the Bible, in the *Mishnah* and in the *Talmud*. It was and is by no means unusual for a boy of thirteen or fourteen to study the Talmudic books of *Niddah* (family sanctity) and the laws that relate to *Gittin* (divorce) or *Kiddushin* (marriage). Nor do these books pull punches or hide behind subterfuge. Jewish youth learned the "facts of life" in the Jewish school, in an atmosphere of discipline and holiness, rather than from smutty jokes or obscene books secretly passed around. Intimacy was never considered vulgar — the very idea is not to be found in classical Torah literature.

In Jewish circles this education is not clinical biology, taught cynically by secular teachers who themselves lack definite moral standards. It is taught simply, frankly, with full reverence for the mysteries and sanctities of love and life, with the realization that the world of a married couple is a sacred trust that must never be taken lightly. Jewish youth were never ignorant, shocked or terrified by the "facts." They never had to turn to the streets for their initiation, because the "facts" were part of the life of a *holy people*, and were presented clearly and straightforwardly in the Bible, in the sacred texts and by parents or teachers.

Chapter Five

Understanding Our Personalities: The Role of Desire

The Deeper Meaning of Human Desire

*W*e all instinctively sense that **Sin,** with a capital S, as distinguished from crime — theft, bribery, murder, libel — and other evil, relates in some way to the area of unsanctioned physical relations. The reasons are quite simple. This is the one area of temptation that is ever present, most obvious and most common.

The point is that this area is unique; different from almost every other sin or crime — it relates to our ability to create life, to extend ourselves into eternity through our children. Because it is so very important, it can be made so very trivial; because it creates life, when abused it causes us to destroy life and/or hurt other human beings.

The overpowering urge involved also plays tricks on our sense of values. On the one hand, we say to ourselves, "What does it really matter what I do"? We might rationalize that intimacy is just a physical or biological function, much like eating. On the other hand, when an individual is all consumed with infatuation or desire, he or she may talk himself/herself into thinking that this infatuation is *the* most important thing and he/she will not rest until he/she has been successful in achieving his/her desire. The infatuation or desire can fill all of a person's thoughts, pushing everything else to the side. It is no wonder that man's greatest desire, the urge he must learn to control most, is linked to his greatest act of creativity, his most significant partnership with the Eternal and Divine — the task of creating new human life and of sharing with G-d the function of being the world's *Creator*. The greatest temptation in life is carnal desire. The greatest victory and achievement in life is being in control of our lusts, our desires, our fantasies. This passion is primarily a function of the mind and a person who can control his thoughts has achieved the greatest victory of all. But make no mistake, this is a most difficult, lifelong task.

In its purely physical aspects, these relations seems to be no less a part of our natural functions than digestion or breathing. And that is precisely *its* greatest danger — that we may be tempted not to exercise self-control, or, by using our power to rationalize, we will think of it as a natural function over which we need exercise no special restraint. So many people are tempted to act as the animals do, who copulate as freely as they eat, whenever the need takes hold of them, without "human" considerations — out in the open, without shame, modesty, ceremony or formality. Anyone who acts in this manner, though, forgets that unlike digestion or breathing, cohabiting involves two people.

If, in fact, relations could remain purely animal — instinctive and automatic, like other functions of the human body — then the *evil inclination* would have nothing to do with it. We all know that sensuality is much more than this; that it is strongly linked to love, to the spirit, to the core of our personality and self-image, to the institutions of family and procreation. Its physical aspects create deep emotional involvements and relationships. We know too how closely this area is associated with guilt, with conscience, with our sensitivity to right and wrong. Even beyond this, it is linked to our instinctive desire to live on into eternity through our children. If it were all so simple, it would not have the ability to overpower us, even to possess us.

Intimacy differs from other natural functions in that it is voluntary. Unlike air, water and food, we might feel deprived, but we can survive without it. In other words, it is a physical function which, more than any other, can be controlled by the mind and the will. It is, for example, necessary to breathe, and for the heart to beat. These are involuntary functions, in that no amount of self-control can stop or delay them. Extended abstention from food and drink will ultimately result in sickness and death from thirst or starvation, but it is possible to live for many years entirely celibate without physical harm. Thus, having relations, while a physical bodily function, is ruled by the will. We are free to use it or not to use it. Its use requires a conscientious free-will decision.

Perhaps it is so closely associated with sin precisely because we can freely choose how and when to use it. It relates most to the one area in which G-d gave man free rein — the area of "freedom of choice," the capacity to exercise our free will. Furthermore, it is essential to the highest form of human creativity. All humans have been given their share in G-d's function as the Creator through their ability to create children, to bring about future generations of men and women. Precisely because our drive for intimacy is linked to freedom of choice and to human creativity, its abuse is potentially so harmful. Uncontrolled, these drives can twist our freedom, overpower our mind, pervert our creativity, and lead us to actions not in our best interest. They become harmful only when our bodily desire takes control, leaving our mind and will out of the picture. Uncontrolled, desire can pervert the act of love, make it impersonal, or turn it into a harmful obsession.

The "New" Morality

Our generation has learned that by freeing people from repression and guilt — that is, from discipline, control and recognition of right or wrong — we are not healthier emotionally.

What are the results of removing restraint and controls, of introducing a "New Morality" of physical "freedom" and license? Modern men and women often find that without restraints relations become boring, insignificant and meaningless. This is the kind of act that dehumanizes us by turning us into robots, degrading one of the most precious of human gifts — the ability to love.

What is meant when we say that man was created in the "image" or "likeness of God"? Does it mean that we look like God? No. God has no body or physical qualities. What it does mean is that to the extent a person does that which the animal is incapable of doing, he achieves the image of God. The wearing of clothes, the practice of modesty, the restraint of passion and instinct, the elevation of mind and conscience over instinct and matter, the emphasis on the spiritual and intellectual, especially in the pursuit of Torah exellence — *that* is the image of God.

The Role of Tsniut in a Healthy Physical Relationship

The purpose of *tsniut*, with its concept of modesty in conduct and dress, is not simply to confine and restrict sexual stimulation and activity to the parameters of marriage, but also to help keep alive the normal interest in the opposite gender. Boredom, disinterest, perversion, infidelity and divorce were very seldom problem areas in Jewish communities where the laws of *tsniut* were taught, lived and genuinely respected.

Chapter Six

Youth: Launching Pad for Adulthood

Friendship and Physical Contact

*W*hy *does* Jewish Tradition demand that the relationship between men and women before marriage stop at the point of physical contact? And why is such restraint, forbidding even mere "touching" (*negiah*), so crucial a factor in the successful observance of the laws that define Jewish standards of family loyalty and sanctified existence?

Jewish law states that once a young woman matures, she assumes the status of *niddah,* and remains, from that point on, prohibited as regards physical contact with men, until the day of her marriage. Just prior to her marriage ceremony, in accordance with Torah law, she removes her *niddah* status by immersing herself in the waters of a *mikvah* (a body of water used *only for spiritual sanctification*). She then joins in union with her husband. As a married woman she becomes *niddah* once again with the onset of her period, and marital relations must then be suspended until she immerses herself, once more, in a *mikvah*, one week after the completion of her cycle.

It will be acknowledged, even by those unaware of this law, that the sense of touch in male-female relationships often constitutes a borderline where simple association begins to pass from the area of friendship into the area of intimacy. In any male-female relationship, it is easier to maintain self-control up to the point of physical contact, because, from the moment of contact, control becomes much more difficult. Also, once the principle of "no contact" has been violated, there are often no other barriers effective enough in helping two people to restrain themselves from further kinds of involvement that could lead to the ultimate act of union.

Just as a physical relationship is an essential element in binding together two people in marriage, no less, before marriage, does physical contact of any kind have the effect of forging bonds, of distorting objectivity and of introducing temptations with which most people find themselves unable to cope. Physical contact or intimacy of any kind brings people closer together and tends to bind — it is a kind of glue. But since glue should be used to *bind only* when a permanent bond is intended, physical contact should begin only after the marriage has been formalized.

As the Torah teaches: "Therefore shall a man leave his father and his mother and *cleave* (from the root word *devek,* or binding force, and hence the idea of glue) to his *wife,* and they shall become one flesh" (Genesis 2:24).

Today's youth may claim that some of the social practices which *Halachah* (Jewish law) prohibits, such as hand holding, social dancing and kissing, are simply matters of form or social grace, which young people perform without attaching to them any great significance.

It is just this point that we are attempting to make. As Jews, we take relationships between people much more seriously than does "society." Jewish society cannot tolerate a situation where a young woman or a young man lets her or himself be used, taken advantage of or hurt. Nor can we accept, for all the casualness of American youth, that kissing, or any form of expressing affection, can ever be regarded lightheartedly or as a game or social grace.

If each date begins with the understanding that before it ends there must be some kind of physical contact, then that becomes the high point of the date, and not conversation — intimacy on an intellectual level, social exchange or the excitement of sharing each other's company. If dating is limited to conversation, then each successive date can bring new and more stimulating conversation, and a greater interplay of personality. But if dating implies intimacy on a physical level, it is natural that on each date you will want to become more physical; each partner will feel impelled to give a little more, to let down a few more barriers, until there is little left to surrender. The result is a transaction in which the young woman and man all too often suffer a loss of self-respect, self-worth, self-esteem, and in many instances the breaking of the relationship.

Between Engagement and Marriage

If a young man and woman have decided to marry and have become formally engaged, do they violate any *Halachic* prohibition by beginning a physical relationship at that point? A number of matters should be discussed in response to the above question.

A man and woman, even though engaged, are prohibited from consummating their relationship. Why? Because it is prohibited by Jewish Law. That in and of itself is enough. Nonetheless, statistics bear out that many engagements are broken when partners begin to discover that intimacy without marriage creates tensions and disappointments which tend to tear people apart rather than draw them closer together. As difficult, tense and complicated as it is to break an ordinary engagement, it becomes even more difficult and emotionally devastating to dissolve a bond where physical relations have been part of the relationship.

Since marriage is not simply a permit for living together but a holy bond which requires sanctification and the blessing of G-d, a Jew who is committed to the life of *Halachah* will act only after the ceremony of sanctification has been officially performed. Jewish ritual specifies that whenever a blessing (or *brachah)* for any act is to be recited, it is recited *before* the act is performed. A couple should push up their wedding date rather than make a mockery of the wedding ceremony by performing the act first and reciting the blessing afterwards.

"Why," you might ask, "must the Torah set a *single standard* of behavior when in each case a completely different set of personalities and circumstances is involved"? It is precisely because each individual has a different threshold of stimulation and tolerance for restraint that the Torah must establish a firm and universal ruling in this area. Sensuality is too potent a force and too vital a factor in determining the success of married life to be treated casually, or to be permitted free and unrestrained expression. Outside of marriage it often leads to complications and involvements that may result in greater degrees of frustration, fear, insecurity, depression or despair than any temporary benefit, satisfaction or feeling of fulfillment can possibly justify.

The Torah seeks, as does any code of law or system of government, to establish basic uniform standards that will apply to every member of its society for the greater good of all. Therefore, when the Torah says "NO" to an individual, the law is protecting all members of society. No single moment of pleasure, according to Jewish tradition, is worth the pain of guilt, tragedy or even simple unhappiness that it might cause or inflict upon another.

We all know that no sustained physical relationship remains stationary. Intimacy contains elements of "pleasure," but to limit it to that function alone is deceptive. That approach either leads to complicated involvements and conflicts or, in the end, causes it to cease to be pleasurable. Surprisingly, it can also become a drag, a burden that brings despair, a complex of frustration, fear, insecurity and personal unhappiness as many surveys indicate it is for so many Americans.

The Torah's rules apply the brakes before the car begins to roll down the hill careening into a lifetime of misery and tragedy. A moment's thrill is hardly worth a lifetime, or an eternity, of pain or guilt.

In addition, youthful affection is not always genuine, and is sometimes the product of confusion and insecurity. As such it is often impulsive — unrelated to a sincere, personal relationship. Too often, it is based on fears, a desire to be accepted, feelings of inadequacy, misinformation, immaturity or a lack of self-control. Young people are advised not to be intimidated by the "If I don't have a Saturday-night date, I'm just no good" syndrome. Rather they should socialize in groups which respect and protect the rights of individuals who don't want to be pressured into compromising their standards, and by participating in constructive group activity. The young men or women whose security and self-esteem are based on how frequently they date are talking themselves into a good deal of unnecessary unhappiness.

What Is Truly Beautiful?

In order to master the fire of passion rather than be consumed by it, Judaism teaches the virtue and value of *tsniut* or modesty. The idea of *tsniut* differs fundamentally from the non-Jewish concept of *chastity,* which bears the connotation of prudishness and ignorance, arising from an underlying Puritanic-Christian notion of the human body as evil and "flesh as sinful."

The Torah concept of *tsniut* bears connotations of restraint, privacy, good taste and dignity, which arise from the underlying acceptance of the human body as a vessel of man's sacred soul. The body should always be properly and tastefully covered, in order to preserve a sense of dignity, worth and self-respect, rather than openly flaunted and thus debased. To the Jew, *tsniut* is a major element of true beauty. True beauty lies not in what we reveal but in that which we conceal. Only a body properly clothed is a fitting vessel for containing the true human beauty which lies beneath the surface of the physical self.

True feminine beauty has little in common with the artificial image of beauty projected by American cosmetic firms, media and the advertising industry. The notion that true beauty, allure or happiness is determined by the extent to which a girl approaches the *ideal* in a physical sense is so much deceptive nonsense. The *ideal* is an arbitrary and often cruel standard that causes needless unhappiness for those who take it too seriously, and as a result become slaves to a stereotyped notion of beauty. It is, in fact, an unmerciful hoax perpetrated by the false values of an over-commercialized, over-materialistic and physically preoccupied society.

Real feminine beauty is often a highly subjective, personal matter. It relates to the totality of the image and presence of an individual's personality. It can be much more a reflection of intelligence, poise, bearing, modesty, sensitivity, charm and values than of any specific physical feature.

This suggests two possible insights: first, that "true beauty exists in the eyes of the beholder" — that beauty is largely a subjective and highly personal phenomenon that gains true meaning in the context of marriage; second, that beauty is subjective and a truly beautiful person is one who loves and is loved by another.

In simple terms, a woman's inner feelings of desirability and beauty are to a great extent an outgrowth and reflection of her husband's love. A husband's love is sustained for many more reasons than outward appearance alone. In an enduring marital relationship, the external physical criteria of attractiveness are reduced to their rightful, secondary role, and the primary personality factors become dominant. In marriage, one soon discovers that deeds and attitudes are far more important than artificial standards of beauty. A wife's priorities and problems must become the husband's priorities and problems — and *vice versa.* There must be mutual dedication to common goals and to each other's goals, needs and well-being. Lacking these ingredients, all the physical attractions in the world will neither sustain a relationship nor provide happiness in the long run for either party.

When King Solomon said, "Charm is deceptive, and beauty is vain, but the woman who fears G-d is worthy of praise" (Proverbs 31:30), he meant, according to Rabbi Elijah the Ga'on of Vilna, that charm is deceitful and beauty false only when they are not accompanied by the Fear of Heaven, for otherwise, they are nothing but external features. But if a beautiful and charming woman possesses the Fear of Heaven, she is then worthy of praise. True beauty must radiate outward from within, and must relate to deeper qualities as well, not to external and painted-on beauty. Jewish Tradition recognizes beauty as a factor in a woman's total personality. Let us not forget that Sarah the wife of

Abraham is described by the Torah as being "very beautiful." However the woman who lacks values and reveals that which should remain concealed is considered not beautiful, but ugly and vulgar.

Clothes and Shame

The clothes we wear are closely related to the way we feel and act. The way a person dresses reveals a great deal about personality and values. A person dressed immodestly feels freer to act less modestly. The lack of restraint in dress is often a first step toward a lack of restraint in behavior and an indication of an inner lack of discipline.

The clothes we wear relate very closely to our sense of shame. When the eyes of Adam and Eve were "opened" and they became enlightened, their first awareness was of their naked state. The consciousness of being naked, rooted in the feeling of shame, and the awareness of the ability to choose, is the foundation of civilized society and represents the first step toward humanity. G-d has planted within us an inner feeling that restrains us from uncovering our nakedness, an unconscious guardian of our bodies that signals danger when we are about to falter.

This sense of shame can be destroyed, degraded or injured, just as we can pervert or suppress other natural inner feelings that G-d has planted within us. Shame protects our image of ourselves as moral people, and reinforces our sense of identification with the Torah People, a people which aspires to be a holy people.

Rabbi Dr. Joseph Breuer wrote that,

Shame is something you feel as soon as you go astray and act contrary to the will of G-d. It calls out to you: "What you just did was ugly, it was contemptible." And it warns you never to do it again. Nurture this feeling within you, do not stifle it.

A basic mark of the civilized man, which distinguishes him from the animals, is that he wears clothes. One major difference between *tsniut* (hiddenness) and its opposite, *pritzut*, which means to reveal or break forth by tearing down the walls and restraints of privacy and dignity, is in the way we relate to clothes. *Tsniut* means using clothes to conceal, thus creating sanctity, dignity and refinement, while *pritzut* uses clothes to reveal, thus degrading and dehumanizing our physical selves. Our private features, in the Torah view, must be hidden from the eyes of others in order to maintain our dignity and self-respect, and to preserve each person for his/her chosen partner alone.

To our society's discredit, its most popular fashions are all too often disgustingly provocative and brazen. Jewish Law, *Halachah*, is fully aware of how easily the instinct for modest dress and modesty can be blunted by the daily assault of the mass media and the social environment. It therefore sets forth specific dress standards for both men and women. Because so many "styles" have of late gained acceptance, it is difficult, even for a fine young woman, to avoid clothes that *Halachah*, Jewish Law, would consider borderline. But there are usually sufficient choices and options to enable a person to be in style without being a slave to style. When a choice must be made between fashion and *tsniut*, a Jew must make that choice, sacrifices and difficulties notwithstanding. In today's society, where immodest dress has become the norm, it is often an act of true heroism and courage to dress modestly, as required by Jewish Law.

Love: Infatuation and Romance, but Much More

Modern novels, movies, magazines and television programs which glorify the notion of "romantic love" are describing a type of relationship that may exist in literary form or in the poetic imagination, but which bears very little resemblance to what love is all about in the everyday world of real life. People who read romance novels or watch television soaps should realize that while courtship, chivalry, romance and passion do play their separate and respective roles in the dramatic awakening and eventual attainment of marital bliss, these are elements in a process, but they do not add up to the whole of the experience. Nor is romantic love an end in itself, so that it cannot and should not be accepted in defense of any type of behavior in a male-female relationship which is not properly controlled.

But self-control is the key, as the Sages taught, "Who is the true hero? The individual who is in control of his desires and passions."

People all too often try to convince themselves that certain forms of intimacy are less reprehensible because the two individuals concerned happen to be *truly* in love. To fool yourself through this tactic is to lose control of yourself. Romantic love is so often not related to real love, especially when it ignores the true personalities and mutual interests of those involved. To be ruled by your emotions and feelings, uncontrolled and undirected by logic, values and clear thinking, with no clear sense of goals and responsibility, is to ignore the only factors which can establish a firm foundation for a permanent and mature lifelong relationship.

The theme repeated everywhere in novels and movies is, "I am in love and my love is beyond my control"; "I *fell* in love"; it was as though someone pushed me off a cliff. It was all accidental and unintentional. The ancient Greeks invented the myth that the pagan god Cupid shoots arrows at people to force them to fall in love. But even the Greeks eventually learned not to take their mythology seriously. The Jewish approach warns us not to "love in spite of yourself," but to love "because of yourself." Find out what you're headed for. Enter into the relationship with your eyes open, not with your eyes closed. If you find that you are "falling," realize while your eyes are still open, while you can still think clearly and objectively, who this person is for whom you are falling. By whom, I refer to background, commitment, education, character, personality, family, friends, values, concern for others, goals and ideals — the things that really count — not external, superficial things, some of which may be "painted on."

Become involved with your eyes open, with the real person inside the skin and not with a certain outward curvature of the skin which may arouse your desire. Become involved deliberately, with control, not on the rebound, or because you're "in love with love." Become involved only after you have come to know yourself, not because you feel insecure and think, "No one loves me," and not because you don't get along with your parents and are anxious to leave home. Don't let your craving for acceptance or love lead you to throw yourself at the first person who on the surface fills your needs.

All this is a matter of decency, honesty and fairness to yourself, to the other person, to your family and to Jewish tradition. It is a precondition to authentic and lasting love. Beauty and charm are not evil — but a person must be mature enough not to be blinded. It's quite one thing to be charmed by beauty but don't "fall for it" until you have made a rational decision that this relationship is good for you. If you take the romantic love angle too seriously, you will lose your dignity and your role as master of your destiny.

Choosing a Husband or Wife / The Dating Scene

In making the most crucial decision of his/her life, a young person often feels alone and abandoned. He/she needs someone who can be trusted, a person who not only has experience but also has the best interest of the other person at heart. Parents who think their children may not want or need help in choosing a marriage partner are often greatly mistaken. A parent who offers a well-considered opinion (best offered in private conversation) or who helps protect a son or daughter from being pressured by friends who often use subtle, or not so subtle means of pushing each other into marriage, can contribute a great deal toward future happiness and the success of the child's marriage.

Of course, no one would suggest that a parent make the ultimate decision, but children *do*, more often than one might expect, feel grateful for a parent's help in checking on the background of a possible partner or in evaluating his or her particular suitability in the given situation.

Many young people who date for the purpose of finding a mate do not want to meet with a person who does not fulfill their basic requirements for a suitable husband or wife. It is obvious that the individual must make the ultimate decision. And this decision will come about after meeting a few, or possibly many scores of young men or women. But *before* they go out, many young people appreciate if their parents discreetly investigate the young man or woman by whom they have been asked out, or in whom they are interested, to determine whether they should be taken into consideration. Sons and daughters often have a whole list of requirements and another list of preferred qualifications. The task of parents is to see to it that dating is not left to chance, that it is not an accidental process. They and their son or daughter are entitled to know beforehand the qualities and qualifications of the young man or woman. Many young people I have spoken to refuse to go out unless their parents have inquired first about the other's plans, character, aspirations, background, ideals, goals, education, personality, accomplishments, etc. "Why waste time," they say, "or take chances with someone who does not *begin* to come into consideration"?

In an article entitled "Good Marriages, The Failure of Success," Dr. Reuven P. Bulka compares the differences in approach to marriage between Eastern and Western civilization *(RCA Newsletter,* 1978). He writes:

> One of the problems with Western civilization is that people tend to think only in logical terms. This precludes the potent impact of the mystical dimension in human behavior. As an example, Ernest Havermann once pointed out that in the East, people get married and then they fall in love, whilst in the West they fall in love and then get married.
>
> The logician, according to Havermann, would think that the Western way is more reasonable and that one must take things in their proper order. However, Havermann points out, contrary to the logician's projection, the Eastern way actually works better.
>
> In fact, by approaching marriage along logical lines, Western civilization has robbed marriage of its most vital ingredient, the element of "shared destiny." Marriage is approached too often in the West along the lines of a mathematical equation. If the times spent together add up to satisfaction, then the couple assumes that future times together will bring more satisfaction; and on this basis the marriage union is finally consummated. Where the process is reversed, however, and one obviously chooses a mate based on common background, values shared and a somewhat common view of life, marriage becomes a shared destiny, where the sharing of common values and a simultaneous affirmation of past, present and future link the couple together in deep understanding, which ultimately brings the side benefit of

real love. This is the process described in the Torah, in Genesis 24: 67, where it is related that, "Isaac took Rebecca as his wife and he loved her," indicating the Eastern sequence, that is, first they married, and then came love.

The major point, of course, is that rather than seeing marriage as an end in itself, Judaism sees it as a vehicle which helps human beings attain the higher values of life. The focus of the Jewish marriage is not on the marriage, but on the values and goals of husband and wife individually, and in their lives together. The sum total of their relationship creates Jewish destiny. This explains why in so many Jewish marriages the needs and education of children are often placed before the satisfactions of the married couple. In a true marriage, destiny and values are placed *before* pleasure and personal needs.

It is a matter of urgency that marriage be restored as a commitment that transcends the individual partners. Marriage attaches man to families. This attachment becomes the foundation of human continuity, individuality and growth. The family is the one institution of mankind that can bring about the greatest and most profound influences on its members. The family must again become *the* place to develop human personalities who have a commitment to idealism and spirituality.

The Goals of Dating

It is the general American attitude that boys and girls date for fun, for pleasure or for simple entertainment. But if the purpose of an evening out is so *completely* casual, then why don't boys simply go to the movies with boys and girls with girls?

The answer is obvious. There is a completely normal, healthy and quite universally operative attraction between the genders that begins pulling boys and girls together during adolescence, and which quickly leads to the process of courtship and eventually to marriage. Dating isn't the *completely* casual or platonic affair one might try to convince oneself it is. There is usually a physical or chemical attraction which is at play.

It is important to realize that dating must always be part of the search-for-a spouse process. The road to the marriage canopy may be long or short. You may meet the right person on the first date, after only a few dates, or you may not meet the right person for many years, so that great care must, for safety's sake, be exercised in all choices you make. A framework for restraint in behavior must be clearly defined and understood between you and each one of the people you choose to date along the way.

While you may think that the immediate goal of a date is for the simple fun of an evening out, the underlying purposes and eventual results of dating should be serious courtship and ultimate marriage. For this reason, the dating process should be considered very seriously and very deliberately. A person would be wise to take care *never* to casually date another person he or she knows from the start he or she could never marry.

Whether everyone will admit it or not the fact is that every meeting with the opposite gender is related, in some way, to mating, to the mysterious force that calls two people to join as one in marriage. So should it be. It is very rare to find a genuine platonic relationship or "just friendship" between males and females. The normal physical attraction, the pull of the opposites, is always at work.

No one would dare get into an old car to enjoy a drive without first checking as to whether or not the brakes are in proper working order. You may say to yourself, "I am not going for a ride with any particular destination in mind, just for a little ride around the corner. My intention is not serious, it is just for fun." If, however, when you reach the first corner, you apply the brakes and they fail, your joy ride could change the course of your life. In much the same way, a "casual date" could be just as fateful.

The Dangers of Intermarriage

While intermarriage in the Orthodox community is almost nil, outside of the traditional community it is a raging fire. As of this writing, the intermarriage rate is 52% — and if the Orthodox are removed from the statistic, it jumps to 70%. At this rate, in one generation almost no one will be Jewish, except for the Orthodox.

But we are all just human, and many of us attend secular schools or have jobs where we work in close proximity to gentiles. There may be a beautiful gentile girl living a few houses away from you, she may be your classmate or someone you meet at work. You may never in all your life dream of marrying her, and your relationship has probably not gone further than a polite "hello" or casual conversation. Then one day you decide to take her out, *just for the fun of it.* Your intention might be just for fun — one evening out and that's it. (This example applies just as well in the case of a gentile boy dating a Jewish girl.)

That may be *your* intention, but keep in mind that it may not be hers. During the first date, she may decide that you are exactly what she wants. The fact is, in making the first approach, you have left yourself open to an honest assumption on her part; "If I'm good enough to go out with, I'm good enough to marry." The fellow who is foolish enough to get himself into this kind of difficulty is rarely smart enough to get himself out of it. By putting a young man and woman — two *flammable* objects — together, it is only natural to anticipate the possibility of an emotional explosion. To ignore the possibility is to practice self-deception.

The conclusion is obvious. Whenever you go out, it is possible, despite the fact that your intellectual defenses are up, that your emotional defenses are down. The very nature of the dating experience sets up conditions for the formation of permanent relationships.

One criterion for maturity is the ability to give up present pleasure for future gain. It is the child who wants all pleasures immediately, without regard to consequences. To be an adult means to have acquired the ability to resist temptation; to say *no*; to live by a set of values.

Intermarriage is a tragedy the Jewish people are forbidden to tolerate. The person who marries out of the faith has turned his/her back on the Jewish people. Our tradition regards such a person as spiritually dead, and the family sits *shiva* for him or her.

Such marriages rarely last, especially when accompanied by a so-called conversion to Judaism, and certainly can never work unless the Jewish partner is seriously committed to his or her Jewishness. For the families involved, the result is heartbreak and tragedy, and for the children, a life of frustration, conflict and strain.

Chapter Seven

Tsniut: An Essential Element for Holiness

The Behavior of Jewish Women

Through her behavior, dress and conversation, a young woman has an effect upon a young man which she is sometimes unable to appreciate and evaluate. By conducting herself in a refined, reserved fashion, as commanded by the Torah, a young woman preserves her own dignity and self-respect, and does not compromise herself. If she carelessly flaunts and displays her physical self she arouses feelings which may, in the long run, prove to be her undoing.

A Jew must always be careful to refrain from any kind of public conduct or appearance that could excite another individual.

Nothing in man-woman relationships remains *innocent* for long. All too often, a young woman becomes involved in serious difficulties because she somehow has given the wrong signals by repeatedly behaving, dressing and speaking in a manner not befitting her status as a daughter of Israel.

The above applies to men as well. *Anyone* who violates the laws of society or Torah is considered culpable and is responsible for his or her actions. The whole point of the Torah is to help men and women accustom themselves to a life of discipline and self-restraint by creating a protective fence which restrains improper behavior.

Tsniut, it should be pointed out, relates not only to behavior and dress, but to language and conversation as well.

Our Sages (Talmud, *Shabbat* 33) tell us, "Everyone knows why the bride enters the bridal chamber. Yet they condemn violently anyone who speaks of this relationship in vulgar terms." Why? The introductory phrase of the Talmudic passage explains, "Everyone knows why."

For the Torah Jew, romance and the physical aspect are neither vulgar nor sinful — but talking about them in vulgar or crude terms has no place in the conduct of men or women. The very meaning of the word *"tsniut,"* translated as privacy, hiddenness or modesty, points to an attitude which abhors the modern passion for exposing to public view the hiddenness and privacy of an intensely personal relationship. And if this attitude relates to the actual relationship, it relates even more so to talking about it openly, in the company of other people.

If I have been careful to point out that young men are no less responsible than young women for behaving modestly, temperately and reservedly in male-female relationships, then why is the term *tsniut*, with all it implies, usually associated with female conduct and almost never with male? Why are women held so much more responsible than men in the realm of *tsniut* — modesty in dress and behavior?

A number of explanations might be advanced. First, a woman has much more at stake. For her, the consequences of rash, impulsive or thoughtless behavior can change the course of her entire life, overnight. In theory, a man can much more easily get up and walk away from a casual affair, with the door closed behind him. A woman, however, may carry the result of that casual affair as a physical, social or psychological blight or burden for the remainder of her life.

A second idea comes from the Midrash (Breishit Rabbah 18:2), which suggests that a unique aspect of woman's nature is the capacity to take one special facet of human personality and develop it to its highest expression. This trait, the Midrash suggests, is the capacity for tsniut. Since women have so much more to reveal, they are more refined and even heroic when they are in control and choose to conceal.

Rabbi Moshe Meiselman, in his article on "Women and Judaism" (Tradition, Fall 1975), offers a third explanation. He says,

> The root tsena is mentioned twice in the Bible, once as we have already seen in the verse, 'That he who toils in the wisdom of Torah in private will achieve wisdom' (Proverbs 11:2). And secondly, in the verse, 'He has told you man what is good and what the Lord demands from you, nothing else but to do justice, to love kindness and to walk privately with your G-d' (Micah 6:8). When we serve G-d, we must concentrate on the inner dimensions of our personality. Tsniut is the inner dimension of one's striving, which is the essence of the Jewish heroic act. It is this trait of personality that woman was commanded to develop to its highest degree. For this reason, woman was created from a part of the body which is private in two senses — first that it is generally clothed and second that it is located beneath the skin.
>
> But, hidden from public view does not imply inferiority. It is related in Genesis that when the angels visited Abraham and asked, "Where is Sarah your wife?" Abraham answered, "In the tent," (Genesis 18:9) to which Rashi cites the comment of the Sages, "Sarah was a private person." Yet, on a spiritual level, we find that Sarah achieved greater stature than Abraham, "All that Sarah tells you, heed her voice," (Genesis 21:12) to which Rashi comments, "This teaches us

that Sarah was superior to Abraham in prophecy." Although in their life together, Abraham took the public role, this implied absolutely nothing about personal importance or spiritual greatness. The Jewish hero is the hero of the inner stage, not one of the public stage.

A Woman Sets the Tone

According to the Torah view, to be a successful woman can constitute one of life's greatest, most difficult, yet most noble challenges.

The Jewish woman is the creator, molder and guardian of the Jewish home. It is the woman who provides the general atmosphere, who sets the tone which determines her family's spiritual direction for better or for worse.

If in the process of fulfilling her obligations to husband, family and Jewish life, a woman feels that she has time, energy and emotional strength sufficient to pursue additional interests as well, or if she finds that a certain amount of time devoted to the pursuit of other interests will enable her to better serve in the capacities of wife and mother, the Torah does not restrict her freedom to make such judgments, as long as the priorities of responsibility are never confused and as long as she does not, in the process, compromise her effectiveness in the scheme of Jewish life.

It is the woman who binds husband and children to herself in that magical relationship of love, devotion and loyalty that together generate the warmth and security of family life. To give unselfishly of her love, and be the recipient of so much love, must surely constitute a source of great fulfillment in a woman's life. Woman is the cement which holds together the family and all of society. Woman is the soul and inspiration of the family. Through building the family she achieves her ultimate identity and self-definition. The stamp she leaves on her family expresses her uniqueness and individuality.

To woman alone did G-d entrust the supreme role of motherhood, so important and primary a task that the Torah exempted women from most of the time-bound positive commandments, such as *tfillin, tsitsit or sukkah*. A woman's tasks are timeless — that is, above and beyond time. They are considered as too important in the scheme of things to be preempted by any other day-to-day schedule of conflicting obligations. The woman's greatest, overriding responsibility is to household, children and husband. Her home is the great school, sanctuary and laboratory of Jewish life. The task of directing this institution, where a positive, Torah-saturated environment is created and maintained, rests primarily on the woman's shoulders. The raising of children demands constant attention. A woman cannot possibly be tied down to other responsibilities that would in any way interfere with her effectiveness at home unless some other person, equally as effective and reliable, is put in charge. A woman's primary area of responsibility within the context of Jewish life is the management of family and home. While there are many other ways in which she serves G-d, nothing is higher or enjoys greater significance than family and children — nothing may be allowed to interfere with the proper execution of these vital tasks.

The work of a mother in the job of raising children and molding their personalities might be compared to the work of a great architect at the table with his blueprints, or to the work of a scientist in the laboratory with his instruments. They are all trying, with the most effective blend possible of skill, art, instinct, ingenuity, knowledge and intelligence to achieve the creation of a useful, successful and worthwhile home and family.

But even the work of the scientist or architect is insignificant and uncreative when compared to a mother at her job of molding a personality — the personality of a child. In doing so she is molding and recreating all of humanity.

Woman's Nature Is Unique

Another reason for woman's exemption from time-bound positive commandments is that she does not require them in order to achieve fulfillment as a full person. To quote from Dr. Norman Lamm in his book *Hedge of Roses* (page 75):

She is already aware of the sanctification of time in a manner far more profound, far more intimate and personal, and far more convincing than that which a man can attain by means of the extraneous observances which he is commanded. For woman, unlike man, has a built-in biological clock. The periodicity of her menses implies an inner biological rhythm that forms part and parcel of her life. If this inner rhythm is not sanctified, she never attains the sanctity of time.

The man attains this sense of sanctity of time only through "time-bound" positive commandments associated with the time of day, week and month, from which woman is exempt.

Almost all of a woman's time, every day, is involved in the observance of many other kinds of Torah commandments. As a result, her life is far more saturated with religious activity than the average man's life could possibly be. The woman's opportunity for spiritual development is almost unlimited. For instance, in the management of her household she is involved with the observance of the laws of Kashruth, in the rearing of her children with the observances of Torah study, in the relationship with her husband with the observance of the laws of Family Purity and in preparing herself, her household and all members of her family for Shabbat and the Festivals, with the observance of Shabbat and Festival laws. A woman is generally involved with welcoming guests, arranging matches between couples, helping the needy and a host of acts of kindness and generosity. A man, however, can attain the same sense of sanctity in his life only through involvement with other kinds of commandments, more associated with the time of day, week, month or year. We call these commandments time bound, from which woman is exempt.

The descriptions of the accomplished Jewish woman are ancient. While the women of most nations were treated as trivialized servants, the Bible offers us a description of women which would shock the "modern liberated" reader. I refer to King Solomon's poem at the end of the Book of Proverbs which I urge each reader to study.

The Attack on Woman and the Family

The most dangerous and fatal manifestation of the new morality comes when it denigrates the role of the family. The fact that half of all American marriages end in divorce is evidence of an instability and weakness in the commitment to make marriage work in the attitudes of present-day Americans.

Any attack on the family is a subtle form of genocide, in that it is a blow struck at the very basis of a well-ordered and smoothly functioning society. Because the family is the source and center of human love, kindness, intimacy and companionship, it is no accident that it is the pivot of society. In fact, Jewish society is defined as a collective of families, not of individuals. Rav Chama Bar Chanina of the Talmud (*Kiddushin* 10) said that, "When G-d causes His *Shechinah* (Divine Presence) to dwell among the Jewish People, He does so by causing it to dwell in the midst of the noble families *(mishpachot meyuchasot)* of Israel."

The woman, therefore, who is the foundation of the family, is particularly responsible to consider the preservation of its core, strength and integrity. She is called *akeret habayit,* foundation and mainstay of the home. In shaping the personality and in setting the tone, standards and values of the home, she guides the development of all society. And although her day-to-day accomplishments may often be measured in terms of her husband's success or her children's achievements, in a broader sense she is responsible, as a result of her determined efforts, for the success of all human endeavor. Is it any wonder that G-d told Abraham (Genesis 21:12), "Whatever Sarah tells you, heed her voice, since through Isaac will offspring be considered yours."

The above attitude is not a patronizing rationalization intended to satisfy a society challenged by the heightened consciousness of educated and thinking women. Wherever Jews have achieved greatness, whenever they have attained spiritual growth or regeneration, there have been women at the center; idealistic, selfless, highly motivated, willing to sacrifice. Throughout Jewish history it was the wives who were prepared to raise their families, sometimes with only the bare necessities, so that their husbands could devote themselves to Torah scholarship.

The revival of Torah scholarship in America, for instance, has been largely due to the idealism and commitment of women who have either worked hard to translate an inspired concept into reality through yeshivah day schools for their children or who have enabled their husbands to devote themselves to Torah scholarship. That there are thousands of households in America where the full-time occupation of the husband is Torah scholarship is a tribute to the idealism, self-sacrifice and Torah devotion of Jewish women. Without these idealistic Kollel families the great renaissance of Torah learning in America just would never have happened.

The Torah ideal adequately demonstrates that the wives of successful men are seldom passive and self-effacing. On the contrary, they are often forceful, insistent, influential and directive.

The Bible and Talmud are filled with numerous stories of outstanding women who led their people and serve as examples to Jewish women throughout history. Sarah, Rebecca, Rachel, Leah, Miriam, Esther and Deborah are just a few. Similar heroines fill the annals of modern Jewish history as well.

The Role of a Woman as Mother

In bearing and raising children, the woman participates in the most creative and unique miracle on G-d's earth. She has given birth and is in charge of the creation and formation of human beings — the unique creation of her love, devotion, her very body, for which her skills, instincts and temperament are specifically designed.

Are the chores of mother and homemaker beneath a woman's dignity? When a woman is cooking or cleaning, sewing for or bathing her children, is she reducing herself to a lowly or servile level? Or is the time she spends teaching her children to be honest, fair, sensitive and self-confident better spent in a more lucrative manner? Why should it seem more prestigious to "fire" a clay pot than to "bake" an apple pie? Why should it be considered more creative to cook for a restaurant than for a family? Why do some people think that a woman gains greater status by working as a child psychologist, in the counseling of other people's children, than she would by staying home to supervise her own? Or finally, is there any good reason why the woman who holds a formal teaching position teaching other people's children should be held in higher regard than the woman who stays home to teach her own children?

If its only paid accomplishments that society respects, then what will be the future of such terms that were used for ages to characterize the more meaningful activities of men and women for which they were not paid, such as "love," "kindness," "generosity," "nobility," "dedication" or the like? Shall these terms, with all they convey, be simply stricken from the dictionary and from the thinking and behavioral habits of men and women?

The Hebrew word for "womb" *(rechem)* and the Hebrew word for "mercy" *(rachamim)* derive from the same root. This indicates that in the very roots of its language, Jewish tradition considered the attributes of mercy and compassion as both natural and essential to the function of a woman in carrying, giving birth to and in rearing her children. If a woman will not set an example, where will her husband or children learn the attitudes of caring, and where, if not from the lesson of the family, will the human community at large learn the lessons of accountability and responsibility? Where will we learn to regard every man, woman and child as our neighbor to be loved and respected?

The Role of the Wife in Creating Man

The role of the wife in maintaining the centrality of the family relates not only to the raising of children, but to the creating of the context of family and home so that men too can function effectively in society. As our Sages (Talmud, *Shabbat* 118) have said, "A man's wife is his home." If the wife does not feel her role keenly and deeply, then the husband will find great difficulty in forming his own deep relationship to the family. It is the wife who cements the family through physical and emotional ties created by her personality, her attractiveness, her ideals and her ability to integrate her husband into the family by promoting and deepening the shared relationships of love and responsibility — which express themselves in the creation and education of children.

Essentially, the family is the mother's sphere of influence. The father must create and mold his function and role within the family by *becoming* a responsible breadwinner, by *becoming* involved in the decision-making process or by *helping* his wife in her tasks, while the role of the mother is more obvious and natural.

In general, woman's role and self-definition are much more obvious than man's. Man must make something of himself to *become* a man. Without study, accomplishment and skills — without proving himself — he forever remains a child. A man must constantly demonstrate and prove his male role, to himself, to his parents and to his wife, before he believes in himself as a man. From the very beginning, a boy's self-identity as a male is dependent upon acts of creativity and initiative.

In a biological sense, a woman is born a woman. She is created whole and complete, while a man is born incomplete. A man must be circumcised in order to *become* a man; something must be *done* to him to make him a man. The act of circumcision sets a pattern which follows all through a man's life. He must constantly "*circumcise*" himself, meaning, prove himself and make something of himself. Man must always be outwardly creative in order to become and remain a man.

The above can also be demonstrated by observing the physical development of both men and women. Outwardly, a boy appears essentially the same even as he passes from boyhood to adolescence to maturity. Compared to the changes that take place in an adolescent girl, the physical changes in the boy are minor as he matures into manhood. Outwardly, physically, a man's appearance is essentially the same at six, at ten, at fourteen and at eighteen. A girl, however, might have the build of a boy before adolescence, but when she matures, the internal and external transformation is so striking and so significant that it is quite evident that she has *become* a woman.

Woman's personality is a reflection of her biology. In this sense a woman is much more a *woman* than a man is a *man*. A woman *need* not be creative in an external sense in order to *become* a woman. No matter what else she may do outside of the home, no matter what areas of creativity she may be involved in, her highest creation is internal — within herself. A woman does not need to be circumcised because she is born complete; her femininity dominates her being, appearance and personality. The only external event that causes a fundamental change in a woman is her relationship with a man. Only then does something external enter her being and transform her into a wife and mother.

Woman's self-identity is clear, obvious and stable. Her role as a wife and mother is an expression of her biology and appearance. Her internal and external biology define and describe her. In addition, the woman's gender is demonstrated and affirmed monthly by her menses. Even if she does not bear a child, she is constantly reminded of that possibility — that only *she* can perpetuate her family and mankind. No matter what anxieties or crises society is undergoing with regard to defining the role of men and women, the woman *knows* that she has a role. This knowledge is stamped on her very being.

The family is the one social structure that can most effectively bring about changes in the ideals, character and commitment of individuals and society. But most importantly, the family is the primary instrument which transforms men into participants in the development of a healthy society.

Why did God prefer Isaac's son, Jacob, to Esau? Esau is described by the Torah as a "man of the field." Rabbi Samson Raphael Hirsch says that Esau believed that the essence of human creativity takes place in the "field," in the "market place" of man's world, in the great world of commerce and industry; in the "field of art," in the "field of medicine," in the "field of business," etc. But Jacob was the "perfect man who lived in the tent." He centered his life around the "tent," the home. To Jacob, the family and the home were *the* focal point of life. "Jacob recognized and taught that the highest mission of life lies in achieving the knowledge and practice to be obtained in the sphere of the homes of mankind." It is for this reason that he merited to receive his father's blessing and to become the father of the Twelve Tribes of Israel.

The Equality of Women

Is the Jewish woman man's equal? Our answer is a resounding yes, as long as we understand what is meant by that statement. Equality in value does not imply equality in function. Man and woman are equal in the eyes of God, and in the eyes of His Torah, but man and woman do not have the same functions in life. The fact is, that in *her* areas of expertise, in her special realms, woman is far superior. Most of the earlier fighters for woman's equality falsely equated equality with forcing woman into man's mold. They wished woman to be masculine and envisioned her as imitating man and living in man's world on equal terms with man.

It is our hope that in spite of the propaganda of the women's liberation "movement," propaganda which has had to refocus the means to its goals, Jewish women will continue to view the unique tasks of motherhood and family as *the* most rewarding, and will choose these roles above others. Even among women who pursue an outside career in addition to their families, most continue to insist that they are happiest and most productive when they can function and fulfill themselves as wives and mothers, not when they seek to emulate and imitate the man's role.

The differences between the genders are far more than physical. They relate to woman's innate and unique special nature, perceptions, talents, priorities, mentality, behavior and temperament which are so different from man's. Woman is psychologically, emotionally and behaviorally different in a thousand and one ways ranging from biology and appearance to sensitivity, relationships, cooperation and intuition.

The place where a woman generally achieves the most and derives her most meaningful fulfillment is in her home. Here she is queen, and her rank of nobility must always be protected. While many Jewish women find a sense of contentment and accomplishment in performing constructive tasks outside of the home, serving as educators, youth leaders, social workers, nurses, physicians, business people, judges, lawyers and in many other valuable occupations, these tasks are valid and rewarding only when the home and family have first claim on her time, love, interest and loyalty, while the career or job is supplementary.

My wife, who is in charge of an outstanding school, always insists that she is a "working woman," not a "career woman." Her career, she always insists, is her home and family. More than anything else, we are talking about priorities. What is the woman's source of personal identification, satisfaction and achievement? What takes precedence when there are conflicts between the home or the job?

A woman's career is her family; her job or profession result in positive achievements when they function as additional commitments, second in importance to home and family. Jewish women have, throughout the ages, been especially prominent in private and communal efforts on behalf of the sick, the poor, the wayfarer, the new bride and the student. Philanthropy and helping those in need, *tsedakah and chesed*, are the special areas in which the Jewish woman excels. Where the Jewish woman entered the business world or pursued a career, as often has been the case in Jewish history throughout the world, it has often been hand-in-hand with the common goals of her husband and children in pursuit of a life of *mitzvot* and Torah study.

Chapter Eight

The Surprising Biblical Record

*I*t is paradoxical that the Jews and our Bible are often blamed for the negative attitudes towards women which exist in our society.

Let's examine the Bible. 98% of the first book of the Bible, Genesis, is devoted to narratives describing the creation of the world, the beginnings of mankind, and the lives of Abraham, Sarah, Isaac, Rebecca, Jacob, Rachel, Leah and the Tribes of Israel. The reason Genesis dwells on biography, personalities, events and not laws is to instruct us to pattern our own lives on their struggles, their challenges and the solutions which they employed. Of course, were the Bible to have recorded the full biographies of Abraham, Isaac, Jacob, their wives and their children, many heavy volumes would have been required. Rather, the Bible selects a very few crucial incidents, because these specific events represent the special life situations which the Bible expects us to learn from and emulate.

Let's study a few examples relating to the "place" of women in Jewish history.

- Abraham and Sarah are childless. Sarah devises a plan for offspring by giving her handmaid to Abraham. She says, if my handmaid gives birth, I will "be built up through her." The handmaid gives birth to a child, Ishmael. Eventually Sarah conceives and bears a son. As Ishmael matures, Sarah comes to the painful conclusion that he will have a negative influence on her son, Isaac. As a result, she urges Abraham, "Banish your son, your firstborn son and his mother from this house." The Torah tells us that this request was "evil in the eyes of Abraham." Nonetheless, G-d comes to Abraham and tells him, "Whatever Sarah tells you, heed her voice," because, "since through Isaac will offspring be considered yours" (Genesis 21:12). The Sages teach that, "Sarah was superior in prophecy to Abraham." Otherwise, why would G-d insist that Abraham follow Sarah's instructions? Abraham banishes Ishmael and accedes to Sarah's demand. Thus begins the saga of the Jewish people. Were it not for Sarah's insight there would not have been a Jewish people.

- In the next generation we read a similar story. Isaac, now a father, wants to give his blessing to his eldest son, Esau, and not to Jacob. Rebecca, his wife (their mother), disagrees. After failing to convince Isaac that her impressions are valid, she devises an elaborate plan of deception. She dresses Jacob in Esau's clothes and instructs him to impersonate Esau and take his blessing. Neither Rebecca nor Jacob are criticized for this deception. On the contrary, Jacob receives his father's blessing and becomes the progenitor of the Jewish people.

    The important conclusion to be derived from this incident is that Rebecca acted on her own judgment, took the situation into her own hands and deluded her husband in order to preserve the Jewish people. It was her courage, her judgment, her wisdom and her action which created the Jewish people.

- Later, the Jewish people are enslaved and oppressed in Egypt. The Talmud tells us that Amram, father of Moses, was the leader of that generation. When the Egyptians decreed that every Jewish male child was to be drowned at birth, Amram reasoned that since he could no longer risk bringing children into the world, he would separate from his wife. All the Jewish men followed his lead. At that point his daughter, Miriam, demanded, "Father, your decree is more cruel than Pharaoh's. His decree applies to the male children alone. But yours applies to all Jewish children equally. Pharaoh's decree may or may not succeed — but because you are a righteous man, your decree will succeed." Miriam's insight convinces her father, he returns to his wife, and all the other Jewish men return to their wives. As a result, Moses is born and thus begins the chain of events which results in the liberation and birth of the Jewish people. Were it not for Miriam's insight, initiative and argument there would not have been a Jewish people.

- The Talmud (*Sotah* 11) clearly states that it was the superior moral stature of the Jewish women in Egypt in whose merit the Jews were liberated from slavery and that the final redemption will also be accomplished in the merit of Israel's righteous women.

- In the desert, the Jews worship a golden calf. The Talmud relates that only the men were involved in this felonious act while the women refused to participate. When Aaron the High Priest solicited gold to construct the golden calf, the Torah informs us that the wives refused to contribute their jewelry, but not out of a love for jewelry. Subsequently when the time came to build the Holy Tabernacle, we are told that the women gave generously with their contributions of gold.

- Later on, while the Jewish people were still wandering in the desert, they decided to send twelve spies to the Land of Israel prior to attempting to invade it. Ten spies returned with a frightening and negative report, "There is no way we can conquer the land," they reported. "Giants live there, the cities are walled to the heavens, their armies are much too powerful."

As a result, the Jews rebelled. They complained to Moses, "Why did you bring us out of Egypt to be slaughtered by our enemies?" As punishment, the Jews were forced to wander in the Sinai desert for an additional 38 years. Rashi, the most famous Biblical commentator, teaches that only the men rebelled — the women were prepared for whatever sacrifices were required in order to conquer the Land of Israel. Since the men rebelled, only they were condemned to die in the desert while the women merited to enter the Land of Israel.

The bottom line in all of these incidents, and many more which I didn't cite, is that when faced with crisis, not only did the men and the women differ in their judgment and ideals, but the judgment of the women proved to be consistently correct. In each and every instance described above, the women exercised independent judgment and freely disagreed with their husbands. Not only did the women possess independence of judgment, they possessed independence of action as well. Rebecca did not simply say, "I disagree." She acted on her convictions as well.

This picture of the Jewish woman is consistent. It depicts a person of moral strength and stature who overcomes crises and provides the stability and determination on which the future can be built. Women were leaders, prophetesses and scholars in Jewish society at a time when the nations of the world demeaned women and viewed them at best as chattel.

This is a far cry from the stereotyped "traditional Jewish woman" we read about in so many of the articles and books written by so-called experts.

We often think of the Torah primarily as a book of laws, while in truth the Torah places its *greatest* emphasis on the life stories of people. The reason for this emphasis on people is that the Torah wants us to relate to our ancestors not as remote, ancient historical personages, but as parents and grandparents. The *fathers* are more than the founders of the Jewish nation; the *fathers* are just that — fathers, founders of the families of Abraham, Isaac and Jacob and by extension, the fathers of each Jew. It is the aim of the Torah to inspire us to learn from their example, emulate them and see them as role models after whom we will pattern our lives. Most of all, the Torah expects us to see ourselves as members of their immediate family, so that we will continue to live their dreams and fulfill their aspirations.

Jewish Modesty Is not Prudishness

Jewish modesty is not prudishness or fear of intimate relations. The Torah speaks openly and frankly about physical relations and the human body. The Biblical book, "The Song of Songs," regarded by Rabbi Akiva as "holy of holies," even uses the imagery of physical love, where "caresses are better than wine," to highlight the courtship of G-d and His beloved Jewish people. This sacred book is replete with Hebrew terms equivalent to such English words as, "delight," "love," "beauty," "beloved," "pleasant," "lovesick," "sweet" and "comely." So much is the Jew at home with the normal functioning of the human body that the very concept of "dirty word" is unknown in the Hebrew language. Hebrew is possibly the only language that doesn't have two sets of words, "proper" and "vulgar," to depict the body and its physical functions. The body and its functions were created by G-d and are sanctified through the love and mutual esteem of the family that observes the Torah principles of the "sanctity of the family."

The Torah is concerned with human dignity and with preserving the rights of our fellow man. In man himself, in his very body, resides the Divine spark breathed into him by his Creator. This body is not an instrument designed merely for pleasure, but rather for creating and molding a world built on G-d's pattern.

The laws and customs of *tsniut,* or modesty, are designed to help, not hinder Jewish men and women in the fulfillment of their own physical and emotional needs. The laws of *tsniut* are designed to engender respect for, not fear of relations. They are designed to encourage a healthy attitude of decency and propriety in physical relations and do not seek to encourage repressive, prudish or guilt-ridden attitudes. They attempt to define what is fitting, suitable and appropriate to given times, places and circumstances. Founded in the firm belief that there is much more to the bond of love than physical or sensual pleasure, they distinguish between what is holy or vulgar, sacred or profane, noble or base, honorable or corrupt, refined or crude, civilized or barbarous, dignified or demeaned.

Intimacy is a private, personal matter. It relates to the most privileged bonds we can possibly establish with another person. It is a primary natural force which, together with other personality factors, comprises the cement which transforms two strangers into intimate, loving, lifelong companions, committed to each other and to the building of a Jewish family. The laws of *tsniut* make possible a constructive and harmonious life by creating an atmosphere of restraint and dignity. The Torah by no means opposes intimacy, but it does condemn making a *cult of it,* and its false worship. The abuse and misuse of this by immature and irresponsible people can turn this instrument for man's good into an instrument turned against man, used for the most evil and destructive ends.

One of the greatest Torah commands is, "Choose life." The only beings on earth who possess the unique ability to make free-will choices are men and women.

Life is filled with constant opportunities to make choices. The most important choices we regularly face are between those thoughts and actions which bring us closer to G-d and those which alienate and distance us from Him. Even though G-d is to be found everywhere, He designed the world in such a way that He is most intensively found and felt under very special circumstances and conditions. Why is this so? Because if the path leading to G-d was easy, if there was no challenge, if it required little effort, how would we achieve personal growth and improvement? If we are not regularly challenged, how would we mature, grow and better ourselves? We all know that every journey requires planning, imagination and effort, and that it is only by overcoming the obstacles along the way that we succeed in reaching our goals. To challenge us and force us to exert the effort which is required to grow spiritually and intellectually, G-d conceals Himself so that we will search for Him. This search compels us to use our talents, our intellect and our resolve in order to find Him. Life is not a level playing field; it can be likened more to learning to climb a high mountain.

The things which separate us from G-d and make our journey challenging and difficult are usually the temptations which entice and attract us. Unfortunately, so many of the things our eyes and heart lust after are either unethical or immoral. Why is this so? In order for impropriety to be a plausible choice for good people it was necessary to make it very attractive. And because evil is often enticing and attractive, we are constantly forced to make difficult choices. This explains why we are pulled by the magnetism of these forces even when these are forbidden, even when they threaten to sink us in mire and sin.

The temptations and distractions of this world are to be found all over — and no one is immune. They surround us, especially in this age. The temptations of life are often overpowering. They come in many forms and disguises, they present themselves in colorful and attractive ways. They entice us and "tell" us to deceive ourselves. The greatest deception is self-deception, and often we allow ourselves to be deceived. When we want something badly enough, our mind plays tricks on us. Our mind rationalizes and tries to tell us that evil is good. The Sages taught that when we sin once and sin a second time, the third time we sin, we deceive ourselves into thinking that our sin has become something permissible. Think of the thousands of homosexuals who have allowed themselves to be convinced that their perversion is an "alternate lifestyle," equivalent to a normal family life. Rabbi Israel Salanter, a great rabbi of the last century, taught that when we sin a fourth time, we often even deceive ourselves into actually thinking that our sin is a *mitzvah*, a positive divine commandment. There are even homosexuals who go to "ministers" and "rabbis" convinced that their "marriage ceremony" actually represents a legitimate marriage, equivalent to a normal marriage between a man and a woman.

In a world filled with difficult choices, the only way to grow spiritually is to constantly remind ourselves of our values, convictions and goals. How? By creating an environment which will make it possible for us to win the battle against temptation and self-deception. The inner struggle between good and evil continues throughout our lives. No one, even the greatest among us, is free from this struggle. This is because the struggle between the beast and the angel within us is the essence of human existence.

Like everything else we *want* and are attracted to, such as money, success and beauty, physical beauty constantly attracts us. But beauty can be both good as well as evil. It depends on what we do with beauty and how we react to it. Like money, it can be "the root of all evil," as well as the source of much good. This all depends on whether we use it for good or allow it to control and hypnotize us, so that we forget our values and allow ourselves to be pulled away from our principles, convictions and beliefs.

Rabbi Joseph B. Soloveitchik said that, "the experience of

beauty is not redemptive." What he meant is that beauty often hypnotizes us and takes away our freedom to choose. Striking beauty has to a degree the ability to deny us the dignity that the human being achieves when he is free to make free-will choices, choices that are not subjected to external pressure. In other words, beauty can be hypnotic; it has the ability to overpower and overwhelm our rational thinking. Beauty intimidates and suppresses our freedom of choice by making it more difficult for us to choose between options. This is not to say that beauty is not essential, for otherwise G-d would not have created beauty in nature and in humans and would not have built into mankind a deep appreciation for beauty.

Maturity means not eating a gallon of chocolate ice cream in one sitting. If something attracts you, your mind, your heart and inner discipline should have the strength to allow you to say "no." Only a child risks playing with fire and getting burned. Obviously, fire has great value — without it, we would freeze to death — but fire must be controlled, and its use must be governed by strict safeguards and rules. Physical attraction is similar to fire; it is alluring and enticing. Controlled, channeled and directed, this attraction is among the most important, constructive and necessary forces in the world — but if we become hypnotized by it, if it robs us of our freedom of choice, if it overpowers our mind, it can consume us like fire.

The greater the potential of something for good, the worse it is when it is used for evil. Bad wine is far worse than bad water. The disintegrated corpse of a human being is far more obnoxious than the dead petals of a withered rose. Intimacy, when it is linked to mature and lasting love, and when used in accordance with the tested guidelines set forth by the Torah, can be the greatest and most beautiful life-giving force. When perverted and misused, it becomes an instrument for human misery. The Torah puts the responsibility squarely in our hands, "See, I have given you this day life and death, the good and the bad. Choose life."

For further study see the Appendix, Man and Woman: A Jewish View.

Man and Woman:
A Jewish View

The Unique Jewish View of Marriage

The Biblical view of marriage is unique among all the other competing religious, philosophical and sociological views. The Bible sees a married couple not only as two people who have made a legal agreement to live together, not only as two individuals who have entered into a lifelong loving partnership, but as two halves of a whole. Dating is a process of man or woman looking for and finding his or her missing half; when they marry, they become a whole "person." The Bible's married couple is higher than the most harmonious, romantic, united-in-eternal-love, "we" of the greatest love story. It represents the creation of a new "I." The Bible sees G-d's creation of man and woman not only as two halves of a unit called the family, but as two halves of a new "person"; a "person" whose two halves were designated, even before birth, to become one personality. In marriage the couple overcomes their temporary, post-birth separation. Dating means that each side is looking for and finds its other half. When man and woman marry they recreate an ideal, reconstituted personality who has previously existed.

This single being, while made up of two people, can be compared to the human being. Each human being is composed of many organs — hands, heart, brain, ears, fingers — all of which operate some-what independently but have no real significance unless we view them as the organs of one person. A person might say her ears hurt, but actually *she* hurts. A tooth might be infected but the pain disables the entire person. In the same way, the new "I" which is created through the marriage of two people assumes an independent identity. Much as a king employs the royal "we" to indicate that he is speaking for his kingdom, when a married person says "I," it really should mean that he or she is speaking for the elevated, united "we." This united per-son is *ha'adam*, the first man/woman, whom the Torah describes as having been created as one person. The family is *the* place where a man and a woman have the opportunity to return to the united state *ha'adam* enjoyed prior to his/her sin and separation.

Let us first investigate how the Sages understand the man-woman relationship, how the Bible describes the creation of the first man and woman, the reason for the creation of the sexes, and the relationship that should ideally exist between them. The center of our investiga-tion is Genesis 2:18, *"And the Lord G-d said, it is not good for the man (ha'adam) to be alone; I will make a fitting helper for him."*

The entire history of mankind is packed into this one sentence. The key to understanding this basic sentence is the word *ha'adam*, usually but wrongly translated as man.

But who is *ha'adam*? He is neither a man (*ish*) nor the first man (*adam*), otherwise the Torah would not have used a special word, *ha'adam*, "the adam." In order to identify *ha'adam*, we must turn to Genesis 1:27. "And G-d created *ha'adam* in His image, in the image of G-d He created *him* (*oto*). Male and female, He created *them* (*otam*)." The first part of the verse seems to indicate that *ha'adam* is a single being. The second half goes on to say that this single being is both male and female. Strangely, at the end of the verse this single being, at the conclusion of the creation process, is described in the plural — *"otam* (them)," two individuals.

The key to decoding this mystery is to be found in Rashi, the outstanding Biblical commentator, who generally elucidates the obvious meaning of the text. Rashi explains, "They (*ha'adam*) were created *shenai partzufim* ["of two faces," *androgynous*] in their original creation; it was only later that G-d divided them." In other words, *ha'adam*, the first human being, is a unique creation; both male and female, simultaneously, a single being made up of two "faces," who is also two people.[1]

According to this ancient tradition the first man and woman were created at the very same moment; not, as is generally assumed, that Adam was created first and Eve second, from Adam's "rib." Precisely how *ha'adam*, the first human, would be described in human or bio- logical terms is beyond our ability to understand. But, the Midrash, a book where the Sages look for deeper meanings in the Bible, teach- es us that *ha'adam* was an individual who possessed a combination of both male and female characteristics — a single, G-d-like being, who was both male and female at the same time.

How did *ha'adam* split? How were man and woman created as one being and then separated? The Torah tells us, "*the Lord G-d put ha'adam* into a very deep sleep and He took one of his *tzela'ot* (ribs?) *and closed the flesh under it.*" Rashi says that "*tzela'ot*" does not mean "one of his ribs"; it really means "one of his sides." Rashi presents a number of proofs from the Torah which demonstrate that the word *tzela'ot* means sides.[2] These proofs support the teach- ing of the Talmud that the first human being was "created with two faces." *Ha'adam* was originally a unified individual with "two faces," personalities and sexes — who was then divided into two people, a man and a woman.

---

1. *Ketuvot* 8a serves as Rashi's source. "Rabbi Judah questions: In one instance it says, 'in the image of G-d He created him'; later it says, "male and female, He created them.' How are both possible? In the first instance G-d's concept was to create them as two, but in the end he created them as one."

2. Rabbi Samson Raphael Hirsch notes (Genesis 2:21) that "*tzela* does not occur else- where in the Bible as a 'rib,' but always as a 'side,' which is also why *tzalua* means to be inclined towards one side, to limp."

This explains the mystery of marriage. No matter how carefully a man and a woman employ rational means to determine if they are suited for each other, ultimately G-d puts them into a deep sleep, a kind of hypnosis in which their critical, logical, rational capacity is overcome by the deep "sleep" of love. The function of love and marriage is to rejoin that which G-d had separated; to restore the unity of *ha'adam*. In seeking a mate, each person is looking for his or her missing half. Marriage is a search for someone each human being once lost; each partner is in search of their other "half." Each of us lacks fulfillment until we are rejoined into a new personality — a human entity which is both new and ancient. The powerful impulse which all of mankind shares in uniting in marriage is to recreate *ha'adam*, the unique, united being who once combined both sexes.

Built into each person's heart and mind from the moment of birth is a hidden search — a search for a deep relationship with a future partner who is the missing half of him or her. Marriage represents the urge to become "one" again. In a deeper sense, it is a yearning to become like G-d, Who alone is "one" — Who combines in one being the creative energies of both male and female and Who rules His creation by employing both male and female qualities.

Each human being is created in the image of G-d. The true image or reflection of G-d is *ha'adam*. In a human sense, the Image of G-d is created when husband and wife marry and live together creatively. Married, they have the unique ability of creating, or better still recreating, humankind's original "image of G-d." In essence, every man is a potential Adam and every woman is a potential Eve — their story is the story of all mankind, their origin is at the root of the origin of each married couple. The Talmud (*Sanhedrin* 58a) says, "a domesticated animal and beast are exceptions, [they do not reach a state of spiritual unity] since, when they mate, they do not become *one flesh*." They lack the ability to become a unified spiritual being, as do a man and woman when they marry. The Torah's instruction that "a man will leave his father and mother and cling (literally, glue himself) to his wife, so that they become one flesh" (*Genesis* 2:24) does not apply to animals.

From this we see that marriage is not only a contractual, biological or physical unity, it is even more than a family where we unite and create children. Marriage represents the ideal unity of mankind. We marry in order to accomplish the highest ideals and goals that were planted into our personalities by the Creator. Part of this goal is the desire to become, again, united, as is G-d. Like G-d, the family requires both male and female qualities. In marriage there is an emotional discovery and fulfillment that no other kind of human relationship provides. Together, man and woman can create a temple in which G-d's presence will be found.

In the *Midrash Rabbah*, Rabbi Chiya Bar Gamla says, "He is not called a complete person [for his second half is missing], as the Torah says (Genesis 5:2), 'And G-d blessed them and called their name Adam.' Only when they are both married can they be called Adam. There are those who say that he who does not marry lessens the image of G-d, for it says [*Genesis* 9:6], 'for in G-d's image He created *ha'adam*.'"

Tov = Good

Let's examine the remainder of the key verse; "*G-d said, "It is not good (lo tov) for ha'adam to be alone (levado). I will make a compatible helper for him."* What is the definition of the Hebrew word *levado*? Does it mean alone or does it have a special higher meaning? Why doesn't G-d entrust the first person, *ha'adam*, with the task of accomplishing the ultimate goal of creation, of reaching a level of perfection the Torah describes as *levado*, thereby accomplishing the ultimate good (*tov*)? As we will soon see, *levado* does not mean alone; it describes the special goal of perfection to which all humans must aspire.

Also, why does the Torah use the phrase *lo tov*, "it is not good"? If the intention of the Torah was to describe evil it would have used the word, *ra*, "bad." *Lo tov* does not mean bad, it means *not good* or *not yet good*, a state of existence that is *not yet* the highest level of good (*tov*).

What is *tov*?

The Torah employs the word *tov* to conclude each step in the drama of creation. *Tov* is repeated six times in the first chapter of Genesis. Finally, when the first human is created on the sixth day, the

Torah exclaims, as though in a finale, "And G-d saw that this was *tov me'od*, very good." *Tov me'od* is therefore the high point of creation, it describes the ultimate good. *Lo tov* (not yet good) is the opposite of *tov* (good). It now becomes clear that it was not G-d's intention to bestow upon mankind the status of *tov me'od* / *levado* at the very beginning of creation without his working very hard to achieve it. Arriving at *tov me'od* / *levado* is not a gift which comes to man and woman without effort and hard work. On the contrary, we were placed on this earth to struggle and discipline ourselves, to choose good over evil, to elevate and refine our mind, personality and society. This struggle represents the task for which mankind was created.

What was G-d's purpose in saying, *Tov Me'od* (very good), when *ha'adam* was created, and why did He create man/woman as *levado*, the moment he/she was created? G-d's intention in initially creating the first human being as *levado* is to teach all men and women that since the very first man and woman were created in the perfect state of *levado*, *this* represents the goal of mankind. G-d is telling us that it is possible to achieve the perfect state of being mankind had, prior to the sin of Adam and Eve. In those few moments following creation, when they were united as one person, Adam and Eve were on the high level of *levado*. During those moments they had only spiritual desires and inclinations.

The above point is best understood when we understand how the word *levado* is used throughout the Bible. Here are a few examples:

1. The Torah describes the struggle between Jacob and Esau as a struggle which resulted in Jacob being elevated from his status as the defeated, persecuted, exiled Jacob (the root of the word Jacob is *akev*, meaning heel). The angel gave him a new name; *Israel*, "prince of G-d."

   When Jacob struggled with the angel (Genesis 32:25) the Torah tells us that, "Jacob was left alone (*levado*) and a 'man' wrestled with him until the break of dawn. When the man, who was an angel, saw that he could not defeat Jacob, he wrenched Jacob's hip at its socket so that the socket of his hip was strained, and the angel wrestled with Jacob. Then the angel/man said, 'Let me go, for dawn is breaking,' but Jacob answered, 'I will not let you go, unless you bless me.' Said the angel, 'What is your name?' He replied, 'Jacob.' Said the angel, 'Your name shall no longer be (only) Jacob, but Israel, for you have struggled with divine beings and human beings and have been victorious.' " "And Jacob was left alone — *levado*."

Rabbi Shlomo Wolbe comments:[1]

"Just as it is written concerning G-d, '*ve-nisgav Hashem levado*, in the End of Days G-d will be triumphant, *levado*' (Isaiah 2:11), *levado* also refers to Jacob, concerning whom it states, 'And Jacob was left alone, *levado*.' *Levado* also refers to G-d Himself Who, when the Messiah comes, will reveal His singularity and uniqueness in the presence of all humankind. This is the high spiritual level that was attained by our father Jacob, and it is because he reached this high spiritual level that he was able to fight and defeat Esau's angel."

2. Isaiah (2:11) says, "Man's arrogant looks will be brought low, and the pride of mortals will be humbled; no one but the Lord will be exalted on that day (*ve-nisgav Hashem levado ba-yom ha-hu*). With the coming of the Messiah, when all mankind will accept G-d as King and will accept His rule, G-d will be seen by man as being in this very highest state: *levado*.

3. When Moses approached G-d, he was *levado* (Exodus 24:2). To be able to approach G-d in order to receive the Torah, Moses too had to achieve the G-dly level of *levado*. "Moses, alone, shall come near the Lord; but all the others will not come near, nor will the people go up (to Mt. Sinai) with him."

4. Deuteronomy 4:35 says, "It has been clearly demonstrated to you that the Lord alone (*levado*) is G-d; there is none beside Him." No one other than G-d is on the level of *levado*.

From the above quotes we see what Genesis 2:18 in effect says: "Ultimate good cannot be achieved if the unified *ha'adam* (man and woman in one body) begins his/her journey on earth by starting out on the level called *levado*."

Rashi confirms this interpretation.

"Man and woman united in *ha'adam* should not be allowed to claim that there are two realms, one in the upper sphere in which

---

1. Aleh Schur, Volume II Page 414, 1982.

G-d alone rules, because G-d is One and does not have a mate; and one in the lower realm in which I, *ha'adam*, am the ruler because I am also one and do not have a mate."

The classic translator of the Torah into Aramaic, Onkelus, translates *lo tov* as *lo takin*, not perfected. This means that *tikkun olam*, universal perfection, cannot come about as long as *ha'adam* begins his earthly journey by starting out on the level of *levado*. It turns out that starting out as *levado* is *lo tov*, the opposite of good.

When a man and woman marry, they become one again and acquire the potential to recreate the state of *levado* — their point of origin. Since each person was *there* once before, each is capable of reaching *levado* again. How? By toiling in Torah and *mitzvot*, by refining and perfecting their personalities, each from the unique vantage point of his or her gifts and potential. By creating a home and a family which is dedicated to becoming *echad* — One — they can again become *levado*.

Rabbi Yochanan Zweig offers a further insight into *levado*.[1] When the non-Jewish prophet, Bilaam, at the bequest of King Balak, attempted to curse the Jewish people, he blessed them instead. What did he say? "*Hein am levadad yishkon u'vagoyim lo yitchashav* (they are a nation living *levadad*, not taking into consideration the opinions of the nations)" (Numbers 23:9). In this context, *levadad* cannot mean alone or lonely. What it does mean is that Bilaam's powers of prophecy tell him that Israel is autonomous, independent and self-sufficient. Israel requires the alliance of no one but G-d in determining its path on earth. Israel is dependent on G-d alone. By extension, we understand that the purpose of marriage (i.e. reaching the state of *levado*) does not imply forming a partnership. Why? Because partners often quarrel and break up. Marriage, on the other hand, unites two people as "one" by creating an autonomous *unit* whose two parts together achieve the unity represented by *levado/levadad*. In marriage, a man and a woman dare not behave as though each is autonomous, independent and self-sufficient, because each needs the other and is dependent on the other for the realization of their collective dreams. Each contributes his and her maximum effort and resources without

---

1. Oral Lecture, Orthodox Union Yarchei Kallah July 1989, Homowack Lodge, New York.

regard as to whether the other is capable of making a similar contribution. And each requires the qualities, talents, wisdom and contributions of the other to achieve true independence and self-sufficiency.

Genesis 2:18 continues, "I will divide *ha'adam* and make *lo* [*of* him, not *for* him] a helper who will be opposite him" (another way to translate: "a helping counterpart in juxtaposition to him.") Man and woman are of equal value; neither was created prior to the other. Each helper in marriage is opposite and equal to the other. Each contains an opposite pole of a unity; and each exists in tension with the other. The purpose of this tension is to work out a unity of goals and purposes by tempering and negotiating different points of view and by resolving conflicts. Man and woman *are* different. They need not think alike, but they must think together. By creating a unity of purpose, man and woman have the ability to rise to the state of *levado*.[1]

Where do we see the origin of man and woman reflected in our prayers?

The true significance and meaning of the blessing recited at Jewish weddings, "Blessed are You, Lord our G-d, King of the Universe, the Creator of *ha'adam*," is often misunderstood because in most prayer books the words are translated in the past tense. "Blessed are You, Lord our G-d, King of the Universe, *Who created man*." To be accurate, the blessing should be translated as either the Creator of *ha'adam* or, I believe, more accurately as "Who is creating man." However translated, it must be translated in the

---

1. Note Rabbi Samson Raphael Hirsch's comment to Genesis 2:18, "It does not say: that it was not good for man to be alone, but 'this is not good, Man being alone.' As long as Man stands alone it is altogether not yet good. The goal of perfection will never be reached as long as he stands alone. The completion of the 'good' was not Man but Woman, and it was only brought to mankind and the world by Woman. And this fact has been so deeply appreciated by the 'Rabbis,' that they teach in the Talmud: only through his wife does a man become a 'Man,' only husband and wife together are 'Adam.' A task which is too great for one person must be divided, and just for the accomplishment of the whole of Man's mission, G-d created Woman for Man. This Woman is to be *ezer kenegdo*. Even looked at superficially, this designation expresses the dignity of Woman. It contains not the slightest reference to any physical relationship, she is placed purely in the realm of Man's work, it was there that she was missing, she is to be *ezer kenegdo*. *Ezer kenegdo* expresses no idea of subordination, but rather complete equality, on a footing of equal independence. Woman stands to Man *kenegdo*, parallel, on one line, at his side."

"That is why it is *Isha*, a 'feminine man,' who stands, not with him, but *next* to him, *negdo*, works at another point in the same line, so that each one of them fills a separate position, and they mutually complement each other."

present tense. The blessing refers not to the creation of "man" in the past, but to G-d's creating man and woman (*ha'adam*) in the present. The blessing becomes most meaningful and relevant when we realize that its subject is the couple standing under the marriage canopy, an event taking place before our very eyes — the recreation of *ha'adam*. The rejoining of a male and female who united have the potential of becoming *tzelem elokim*, the image of G-d Himself.

To Recap:

The goal of the marriage ceremony is to "recreate" *ha'adam*. The first human was not a "man" but a united bisexual being. The Torah describes *ha'adam* as *"levado,"* a word describing the Messianic perfected state of human existence when G-d will be worshiped and obeyed by all people. This state of *levado*, which describes mankind's goal, is not a gift; it represents life's challenge.[1] G-d separated the primeval being — *ha'adam* — into two personalities, two halves, male and female. Their task in marriage is to bring about *tov me'od*, the ultimate[2] good, by working toward and reaching the state of *levado*.[3] This is accomplished by struggling against the forces of evil, filth, sin and materialism, by living a life of purpose and sanctity. Interestingly, much of the challenge of marriage is to constructively channel and direct the very manner in which man

---

1. Note Rabbi Samson Raphael Hirsch's comment to Genesis: 2:24, "As long as the man was alone it was not yet 'good.' Once the division had been made, it was no longer possible for the man to fulfill his calling by himself, because his wife was to be his *ezer kenegdo*. Without her he was only half a man, only with her he became a whole man. Therefore a man leaves his father and his mother, attaches himself to a wife, and they become one single body. Just as before the division, originally, the man's body subordinated itself under one spirit and under one Divine Will, so after marriage, man and woman again become one single body. This can take place only if they also become one mind, one heart, and one soul. This is possible only if they subordinate all their strength, efforts, thoughts and desires to the service of the Higher Will."

2. Breishit (5:1,2) concludes the chronicle of man's creation by stating: "This is the book of the Chronicles of Adam: On the day that G-d created Adam, He made him in the likeness of G-d. He created them male and female. He blessed them and named them Man (Adam) on the day that they were created." Says Rabbi Elazar (*Yevamot* 61:2), Any man who does not have a wife is not a man — for it says, "Male and female He created them and He called their name Adam."

Here the Torah clearly states its position — the "likeness of G-d" is "him" — the united individual who in marriage is man and woman. He called their name Adam (singular) on the day he created them (plural). The mixture of the singular and plural in the "*pshat*," the plain meaning of the verse, bears out the interpretation of the Sages.

3. Additional *levado* references: Psalms 72:18, Psalms 148:13, Job 9:8, Deuteronomy 4:35, Micah 7:14, Psalms 4:9.

and woman control and direct the very magnetic forces which draw the genders to each other, to resolve their differences and live a life of *shalom bayit*, tranquility, peace and harmony.

Shalom bayit — the harmony and peace of the Jewish family — is one of the great ideals of Jewish life. When a husband and wife live as though they are one person, when they achieve true unity and harmony in their family life, they come as close as a human being possibly can to duplicating the state of perfection which humanity achieved in the early moments of *ha'adam's* creation.

Every wedding restores the bride and groom to the united state of Adam and Eve, enabling two halves to find their missing half and become whole again. Every wedding reminds us of the theme of the first marriage ceremony blessing, "Gladden the beloved companions (the bride and groom) just as You gladdened Your creations (Adam and Eve) in the primeval Garden of Eden." In marriage, the two sides of humanity are reconstituted and reunited. Man and woman become one — a single entity who support and restrain each other in such a way that they work opposite each other, by helping and complementing each other — by creating a unity of creative tension. Marriage is a dynamic state of highs and lows, joy and sadness. Most of all it is a structure through which man and woman combine forces to create a permanent, everlasting structure (*"binyan adei ad"*) through which they pursue the goal of creating a purposeful, sanctified, harmonious home built on love, compassion and resolve.

The magnetic force which pulls husband and wife together is the creative energy which motivates them to create the *echad*, the *One* on this earth. The *Sefer haSharashim*, the Book of Word Roots, written by the great sage Radak, says that the root of *echad* (one) is *ach* (brother); that is to say, in marriage two human beings combine to become one. Two people become so appropriately matched (marriages *are* made in Heaven) that they create a home which evolves into a miniature sanctuary in which compromise and the blending of individual's likes and interests create the unity of *echad* — *ach*. To achieve this goal they must become so devoted to each other, be so in love, so much in sync with their goals that they function as though they are one entity: *ha'adam*.